Rastafari in the New Millennium

2005 acrylic on canvas painting of Rastafari patriarch Bongo Wato, by Clinton Hutton. Courtesy of Dr. Clinton Hutton.

Rastafari in the New Millennium

A Rastafari Reader

Edited by
Michael Barnett

Foreword by
Rex Nettleford

SYRACUSE UNIVERSITY PRESS

Front jacket and frontispiece illustration: 2005 acrylic on canvas paining of Rastafari patriarch Bongo Wato, by Clinton Hutton. Courtesy of Dr. Clinton Hutton, original copyright holder.

Dr. Hutton lectures in political philosophy and Caribbean and African diasporic culture and aesthetics at the University of the West Indies, Jamaica. He is the author of the book *The Logic and Historical Significance of the Haitian Revolution and the Cosmological Roots of Haitian Freedom*. He is also a noted painter and photographer.

First Edition 2012
First Paperback Edition 2014
14 15 16 17 4 3 2 1

For a listing of books published and distributed by Syracuse University Press, visit https://press.syr.edu.

ISBN: 978-0-8156-3283-2 (hardcover)
978-0-8156-3360-0 (paperback)
978-0-8156-5079-9 (e-book)

Library of Congress Cataloging-in-Publication Data

Rastafari in the new millennium : a Rastafari reader / edited by Michael Barnett ; foreword by Rex Nettleford. — First edition.

pages cm

Includes bibliographical references and index.

ISBN 978-0-8156-3283-2 (cloth : alk. paper) 1. Rastafari movement.

I. Barnett, Michael (Michael A.), editor of compilation.

BL2532.R37R388 2012

299.6'76—dc23 2012006903

The authorized representative in the EU for product safety and compliance is Mare Nostrum Group B.V, Doelen 72, 4831 GR Breda, The Netherlands.
gpsr@mare-nostrum.co.uk

Of fair peace.

subvention by
FIGURE FOUNDATION

Contents

Tables

Foreword

REX NETTLEFORD

The advent of this volume assembled by Michael Barnett is a welcome addition to the still growing literature on the Rastafarian movement, which has achieved an immense global reach since its early beginnings in colonial Jamaica in the 1930s. It is particularly welcome in these times misguidedly and inappropriately designated "postracial," no doubt in the wake of the admittedly historic presence of an African American president in the U.S. White House. The chapters that follow will confirm the stubborn persistence of the issues that have shaped the agenda of concerns of arguably one of the most innovative, impressive, and impactful responses to the obscenities of half a millennium that resulted in the enduring afflictions of deracination, dehumanization, intolerance, social injustice, colonial subjugation, and Eurocentric bias.

We can add to these the lack of recognition and status for non-Caucasian peoples but especially for ones who carry the stain of Africa in their veins. The consequences of the trans-Atlantic slave trade, plantation slavery, and colonial conditioning, which prompted the Rastafarian response, are undoubtedly actively still in place, whatever the indications to the contrary, including the congenital denial by many compatriots that that horrific past is of little or no importance to the present or the future.

It is to the credit of the editorial vision of the volume that the complexity of the movement in praxis is addressed, clearly in recognition not only of the dialectical sophistication of the movement itself but of the demands of the diverse, multifaceted, multilayered third millennium. The volume exposes the reader to the progressive development of the movement in resisting, confronting, and above all, engaging the realities of a world that has seen to the severance of millions of forebears from ancestral hearths, the suffering in the by no means endearing "Babylon system" (plantation America), and the advocacy (in theory and practice) for a return to a Promised Land, whether it be the material comfort of Shashamane in Ethiopia or the spiritual release from psychic disarray, anomie, self-contempt, and self-denigration that are the bane of all who have suffered man's inhumanity to man, but remain determined to settle for survival and beyond.

The attraction of the Rasta creed to some New Zealanders therefore makes sense, as it indeed did in the case of German youths who sang a Bob Marley song while tearing down the Berlin Wall. The Rastafarian beat also provided a source of energy for the fight against apartheid in Southern Africa. It did no less among Jamaicans and the wider Caribbean youth population whose parents had to come to terms with the movement from the late 1960s. The movement has likewise come to terms with the wider society, winning a place of serious accommodation in a society that once saw it as a blasphemous and an even treasonous escapist indulgence.

Here the appropriation of the movement's vision, ideology, and religion by talented popular musical artists and dub poets, who found in the movement ontological and epistemological refuge, has in turn helped the movement in its global reach to all corners of Planet Earth. It has also served to trump the rampant racism that has been the inheritance of an ex-slave colonial history and existence. But at the core of the Rastafarian movement there has been this significant phenomenon among its devotees: Rastafarians are not that unsophisticated to be racist but they are by no means foolish enough not to be race conscious. And that delicate balancing of sensibility has long marked the movement off from many others fighting for African liberation.

The movement has not, however, entrapped itself in such race consciousness, and Barnett wisely chooses to expose the reader to such no less important issues as gender, the Rasta experience in Africa, the challenge of participation in the partisan political system of "Babylon," and the movement's iconic place in the shaping and development of Jamaican popular music.

The volume therefore serves to raise questions about the future of a movement that, despite its core tenets of the divinity of Haile Selassie I and mandatory repatriation to Africa in general and Ethiopia in particular, also advances the plot in the ongoing discourse about respect and understanding among human beings and the quest for the restoration of decency, social justice, freedom, and humane considerations to all of humankind.

Vice Chancellor Emeritus
University of the West Indies
2009

Acknowledgments

Many relatives and friends have provided me with support and encouragement as I have embarked on this project, too many to mention, in fact. But I want to take the opportunity to thank my parents, Easton Chamberlain Barnett and Madge Hyacinth Barnett, both of whom were born on Jamaican soil and who always took the time to provide me with guidance in my boyhood days and my early adulthood. They also took pains to remind me of my African ancestry, for which I am grateful and of which I am truly proud. They have now (sadly for me) transitioned to the land of the ancestors, but are fondly remembered. I also want to take time out to thank my brothers Paul and David for their support and encouragement.

In terms of academic inspiration, I would like to make mention of Professor Rex Nettleford and Professor Barry Chevannes of the University of the West Indies, who although now having departed to the land of the ancestors, provided me with encouragement and support in this endeavor. I must also say thanks to my former graduate assistants, Anna Branday and Deborah Fletcher, who assisted me in the assembling of the manuscript for this book.

I would also like to acknowledge the indomitable workers of the Rastafari movement, both past and present, who have helped to maintain the movement's vibrancy and relevance in the twentieth and twenty-first centuries. Again, there are too many names to mention, but their works speak for themselves; if not at present, they certainly will in the future.

Last but definitely not least, I must say thank you to all the contributors of this volume, both in terms of the written work they provided as well as the cover artwork. Without their contributions this book would not have been possible.

Contributors

LAWRENCE O. BAMIKOLE is presently a senior lecturer in the Department of Language, Linguistics and Philosophy, University of the West Indies, Mona, Jamaica. He holds a PhD in philosophy from the Obafemi Awolowo University, Ile-Ife, Nigeria.

Bamikole lectured at the University of Ado-Ekiti, Nigeria, between 1985 and 2010. He has published extensively in the areas of social and political philosophy, Africana philosophy, and comparative philosophy. He has recently contributed articles to *Caribbean Quarterly, Journal of Philosophy and Related Disciplines,* and *Journal of Caribbean Philosophy.* Bamikole is currently working on a book project entitled "Violence and Democratic Politics."

MICHAEL BARNETT is presently a lecturer and academician in the Department of Sociology, Psychology, and Social Work, University of the West Indies, Mona Campus. He holds a PhD in sociology from Florida International University in Miami. Since obtaining his PhD he has lectured as an assistant professor both at Florida International University and at Temple University prior to lecturing at UWI. He has written numerous articles in the field of Rastafari studies, some of which have been published in *Caribbean Quarterly, Journal of Caribbean Studies,* and *Journal of Black Studies.* Barnett is also interested in Black social movements in general, and Black liberation theology movements in particular, especially in regards to their emergence in the Caribbean and the United States, as outcomes of the emergent perspectives of Pan-Africanism, Black Nationalism, Ethiopianism, and Black Power.

ALLAN BERNARD is presently a researcher in the field of violence prevention and human development, focusing on youth social participation, political culture, and popular culture in Jamaica. His latest project is called "Saving Lives through Enterprise" and is an important part of his current work with the Youth Crime Watch of Jamaica and the Office of Social Entrepreneurship at the University of the West Indies, Mona Campus. Bernard's other research interests include African politics and Africa/African Diaspora relations.

KENNETH BILBY is director of research at the Center for Black Music Research, Columbia College Chicago, and research associate in the Department of Anthropology at the Smithsonian Institution. He is the author of *True-Born Maroons* (2005); co-author of *Caribbean Currents: Caribbean Music from Rumba to Reggae,* second edition (2006); and author of numerous articles on Caribbean music, folklore, and language. He has also produced, recorded, or compiled fifteen albums featuring Caribbean and African musical genres. His most recent publication is *Music from Aluku: Maroon Sounds of Struggle, Solace, and Survival* (2010).

IAN BOXILL holds the Carton Alexander Chair in Management and is the Director of the Centre for Tourism and Policy Research at the University of the West Indies, Mona Campus. He has researched and written on culture, ethnicity, and development in the Pacific region, Latin America, and the Caribbean. He obtained his PhD in sociology from Colorado State University, and his masters in philosophy from the University of the West Indies, Mona Campus. He was the editor of a special Rastafari edition of the Caribbean journal *Ideaz,* entitled "The Globalization of Rastafari" in 2008.

BARRY CHEVANNES (now deceased) was known more commonly as Professor Barry Chevannes. He was a graduate in philosophy and classics from Boston College. He obtained an MSc in sociology from the University of the West Indies and a PhD in anthropology from Columbia University. He was a professor of social anthropology, former head of the Department of Sociology, Social Work, and Psychology, and the former dean for the Faculty of Social Sciences at UWI, Mona Campus. Having written *Rastafari:*

Roots and Ideology (1994) and edited *Rastafari and Other African-Caribbean Worldviews* (1995), Chevannes had long established himself as an authoritative voice on the Rastafari movement.

A notable innovative initiative of Professor Chevannes was his founding of Fathers Incorporated (an organization dedicated to men, especially fathers). Additionally, he made an enormous contribution to the Jamaican Peace Management Initiative. At the time of his passing, Professor Chevannes was the chair of the Council of the Institute of Jamaica, the vice chairman of the Jamaican Peace Management Initiative, and head of the UWI Township project (which engaged August Town, in St. Andrew). This distinguished Jamaican received many awards nationally and internationally. He received the Vice Chancellor's Award (UWI) for outstanding achievements in research, teaching, and public service; was recognized for his original contribution to Jamaican folk and religious song heritage; and received the honorary Lifetime Award from the *Jamaica Gleaner* newspaper just days before his death in 2010.

JANET L. DECOSMO is professor of humanities at Florida Agricultural and Mechanical University in Tallahassee, where she currently teaches courses on Caribbean religion and culture and African film.

DeCosmo has published numerous articles on Bob Marley and Rastafari in Jamaica as well as on Rastafari in Bahia, Brazil. Her research interests also include Bahamian Junkanoo, Caribbean Carnival, New Orleans's Black Indians, and the Creole cultures of southwest Louisiana, a place she visits frequently. She also travels to many of the islands of the Caribbean as well as to countries in Central and South America to continue her research on cultures of the African Diaspora.

EDWARD TE KOHU DOUGLAS is a New Zealand Maori (Kaitahu/Kati Mamoe). As a Jamaican Commonwealth Scholar he studied demography and sociology at the University of the West Indies, Mona, and later worked for the Jamaican Ministry of Education. When the fieldwork for this study was undertaken, he was a senior lecturer in sociology and social anthropology and director of Maori development at the University of Waikato. He is currently a senior lecturer in the Department of Property,

University of Auckland Business School, where he focuses on Maori land tenure and development issues.

OBIAGELE LAKE is an independent scholar in Kansas City, Missouri. She is the author of the books *Rastafari Women: Subordination in the Midst of Liberation Theology* and *Blue Veins and Kinky Hair: Naming and Colour Consciousness in African America,* among other publications.

ELLIOT LEIB received his BA from Haverford College in 1974. He received his MA in African studies from UCLA in 1979 and then his MPhil in anthropology from Yale University. Leib and Renee Romano produced and directed *Rastafari Voices* (1979) and *Rastafari: Conversations Concerning Woman* (1983). While doing ethnographic fieldwork in Jamaica on a Fulbright Fellowship, Leib coordinated the production of *Churchical Chants of the Nyabingi* for Heartbeat Records, which also issued *From Kongo to Zion* (with Ken Bilby).

Leib and Romano owned and operated Trade Roots Reggae in San Diego for more than twenty years. In 2009, Leib received a preservation planning grant from the Grammy Foundation. Ongoing work to preserve the Trade Roots Reggae Collection is linked to the development of a research center for the Jamaican Music Museum (JAMM).

ERIN C. MACLEOD has a PhD in communications from McGill University and is also a teacher at Vanier College in Montreal, Canada. Her research interests lie in the relationship between Jamaica and Ethiopia, Rastafari and Jamaican music in Africa, and the connections between Africa and the African Diaspora. Erin's research into these areas has been supported by both doctoral and postdoctoral fellowships from the Social Sciences and Humanities Research Council of Canada. She has written about music and popular culture for the *Montreal Mirror, Toronto Star, LargeUp,* and *Pitchfork,* among others.

JAHLANI NIAAH is a lecturer in cultural and Rastafari studies at the Institute of Caribbean Studies, University of the West Indies, Mona Campus, where he also coordinates the Rastafari Studies Unit and Archive.

He has published several articles on Rastafari in scholarly journals, including *Cultural Studies, Caribbean Quarterly,* and *Jenda: A Journal of Culture and African Women Studies.* Additionally, Niaah has visited Europe, Africa, and the Americas lecturing and presenting papers on Rastafari. Recently, Niaah has turned his attention to examining Rastafari in Africa.

ADWOA NTOZAKE ONUORA is a doctoral candidate in the Department of Sociology and Equity Studies in Education (OISE) at the University of Toronto. Her areas of interest and specialization are African and Black feminist theories, feminist pedagogy, cultural studies, Afro-indigenous knowledge production and dissemination, and arts-informed research methodologies. Her doctoral dissertation employs a narrative inquiry approach to examine the relationship between mothering and teaching among African Canadian women.

ANNA KASAFI PERKINS is the senior program Officer in the Quality Assurance Unit at the University of the West Indies, Mona, and adjunct faculty at St. Michael's Theological College. Her most recent publication is a book entitled *Justice as Equality: Michael Manley's Caribbean Vision of Justice* (2010). Perkins holds degrees from UWI, Mona/St. Michael's Seminary, Cambridge University, and Boston College. Her research interests include faith and political life, sex and sexuality, religion and popular culture, gender and the scriptures, and business and professional ethics.

MAUREEN ROWE (now deceased) was affectionately known to her friends and colleagues as Sister P. She was an environmentalist, a consultant, a community liaison officer, and a Rastafari woman. Her articles on Rastafari women appeared in *Caribbean Quarterly* and in the book *Chanting Down Babylon: A Rastafari Reader.*

IMANI M. TAFARI-AMA is a specialist in gender and development studies, urban violence, Rastafari studies, child and youth development, and audio-visual documentation. Her work experiences include social development management, baseline and monitoring, and evaluation studies. She is also an insightful leader and manager, a creative and accomplished academic/activist and a development consultant who specializes in using multimedia communication methods for development initiatives.

She holds a PhD in development studies (2002) from the Institute of Social Studies, the Hague. Her research was a case study of Southside, an inner-city community in Central Kingston, Jamaica. The project provided a prism through which to analyze the political economy of power, gender, and the body as expressed in this Northern Caribbean context. She holds an MA in women and development (1989) from the Institute of Social Studies and a BA (1982) in communication with language and literature from the Caribbean Institute of Media and Communication, University of the West Indies, Mona.

ANITA M. WATERS received her PhD from Columbia University. She is the author of *Race, Class and Political Symbols: Rastafari and Reggae in Jamaican Politics* (1985), *Planning the Past: Heritage Tourism and Post-colonial Politics at Port Royal* (2006), and other studies of political symbols in the Caribbean. Her most recent project is an exploration of Cuban public history over the past fifty years. She also works with the Somali refugee community in Central Ohio. Waters teaches Black studies and chairs the Sociology/Anthropology Department at Denison University in Granville, Ohio.

CADENCE WYNTER is an associate professor of history and African Diaspora studies at Columbia College, Chicago. A Jamaican, Wynter taught in the compulsory education sector and further education sector and worked as a college education counselor in Manchester, England, before moving to the United States. She joined the Columbia College faculty in 1996 and teaches courses in Caribbean, African American, and Latin American history. Her work and research interests span the African Diaspora and focus on migration, labor history, oral history, and women's studies. Her forthcoming book, *Jamaican Migration to Cuba, 1885–1930*, reveals the ways in which during the early post-emancipation period, Jamaica remained in the orbit of British colonialism as an important pool of labor that was to be quickly expendable and undesirable once a project was finished as in the annual sugar harvest in Cuba. She is currently the acting chair of the Department of Humanities, History, and Social Sciences.

Rastafari in the New Millennium

Rastafari in the New Millennium

Rastafari at the Dawn of the Fifth Epoch

MICHAEL BARNETT

The Rastafari movement in this dawn of the new African millennium (which I believe may be considered the dawn of its fifth epoch) has achieved an unheralded amount of growth and visibility in its more than eighty years of existence. The movement has touched much of Caribbean and world culture: it does not encompass just the domain of spirituality but also that of music and lifestyle. In addition to an aesthetic, cultural, and spiritual component, an epistemological perspective has done much to affect Caribbean and world sensibilities.

For the sake of reconceptualizing the historical and present trajectory of the Rastafari movement, I have formulated various timelines corresponding to various epochs. These are detailed in Table 1.1.

I firmly believe that, having just entered a new millennium (according to the Ethiopian calendar), the Rastafari movement is now at a literal and figurative crossroads. As such this is an appropriate time for strong consideration to be given to the likely path or paths that the movement will chart in this the new millennium (fifth epoch).

The First Epoch

I posit that the first epoch of Rastafari history stretches from November 2, 1930 (the coronation date of His Imperial Majesty Haile Selassie I), to the late 1940s. During the early period of this epoch, the founders of the Rastafari

Table 1.1.
Timeline of the Rastafari Movement

Epoch	*Start*	*Finish*
First	November 1930	1948
Second	1948	April 1966
Third	July 1966	1981
Fourth	1981	September 2007
Fifth	September 2007	Present

movement (in Jamaica), Leonard Howell, Robert Hinds, Joseph Hibbert, and Archibald Dunkley, professed the divinity of Haile Selassie I to small congregations of Black Jamaicans (Jamaicans of African origin) in the Kingston and St. Thomas regions of the island. Notably, Trinityville in St. Thomas, which had been a strong site for revivalism, became a strong site for the early preaching of Rastafari. Although Robert Hinds and Leonard Howell collaborated to a large extent during the early thirties, Dunkley and Hibbert preached to a large extent independently (Smith, Nettleford, and Augier, 1960) so that even during the formative years of the movement there were multiple mansions of Rastafari. The movement has always been characterized by its heterogeneity and has never ever really been a homogenous entity, even in the very early days of its existence in Jamaica. (This is contrary to many assumptions and pronouncements that are made about the movement today, wherein a romantic past is configured in which the movement is conceived to have evolved from one Rastafari mansion, with one Rastafari theology.)

In 1934 Hinds and Howell were sentenced to prison for sedition, largely because of the effectiveness and the propensity (prolificacy) of Howell's preaching. Notably, Howell was sentenced for two years whereas Hinds was sentenced for just one year. In fact, during the course of the sentencing, the judge (Chief Justice Sir Robert William Lyall-Grant) encouraged Hinds to distance himself from Howell, if he knew what was good for him (*Daily Gleaner*, March 17, 1934). Of interesting note is that whether as a direct or indirect outcome of the term of imprisonment, the degree of collaboration between Hinds and Howell (as well as with the other Rastafari leaders) noticeably declined during the late thirties.

In 1940, Howell firmly established himself as the main Rastafari leader on the island[1] when he secured a vast plot of land known as Pinnacle. Pinnacle became the first Rastafari commune and formed the blueprint for future Rastafari communal communities (such as the one that presently exists on Bobo Hill in Bull Bay in St. Andrew). The Pinnacle community epitomized perfectly the collective sensibilities of the Rastafari movement (which arguably are in opposition to the individualistic sensibilities of the wider community).

The Pinnacle community suffered much harassment from the state and was raided several times by the colonial police; Howell was imprisoned once again for another two years after the first raid in 1941. As soon as he was released in 1943, Howell, undeterred, went back to Pinnacle to continue to lead the community there. In 1954, however, Pinnacle was raided once more, but this time with a vengeance, and the camp and its crops were almost completely destroyed. Many occupants were hounded and forced off the land, which resulted in the scattering of thousands of Rastafari adherents, many of whom went to Kingston to reside.

The Second Epoch

The second epoch of Rastafari history, I posit, starts in the late forties, with the emergence of the dreadlocked Rastafari and the establishment of the Youth Black Faith (YBF) Mansion of Rastafari, the precursor of the Nyahbinghi Mansion (McPherson 1996). In addition to the emergence of the dreadlocked Rastafari, the second epoch was characterized by a second generation of Rastafari leaders, notably Bongo Wato (Ras Boangeres); Arthur and Pan-Handle, the founders of the Youth Black Faith Mansion; and Prince Emmanuel, who went on to found the Ethiopia Africa Black International Congress (EABIC). The Youth Black Faith leaders despised

1. The renowned Rastafari studies scholar Barry Chevannes considered Robert Hinds to be the most successful and influential of the first generation of Rastafari leaders (Chevannes 1994, 2010), though many other Rastafari scholars think of Howell as the most influential. One scholar even dubbed him "the first Rasta" (Lee 2003).

the revivalist and relatively mild-mannered ways of the original Rastafari leaders, and they sought to inject a more intense rebellious spirit into the movement (Chevannes 1994). The dreadlocks that were proudly worn by the Youth Black Faith House were arguably inspired by the Mau Mau of Kenya, who were fighting a revolutionary war at that time for independence from England (Campbell 2007). The Mau Mau, with their hair matted into thick locks, had a distinctive countenance that clearly displayed a fierce rebel spirit. Their images were effectively carried worldwide by British and British colonial newspapers that reported them as an impediment to peace and stability in perhaps their most treasured African colony at that time, Kenya.

The other significant second-generation Rastafari leader, Prince (King) Emmanuel, became visible and active in Kingston during the fifties, notably founding the EABIC at Jamaica's first Groundation on March 1, 1958. In 1959, Claudius Henry, who called himself the repairer of the breach and who was another second-generation Rastafari leader, came to Jamaica and formed his own mansion, which was named the Africa Reform Church. With his false repatriation initiative[2] in October 1959, however, he effectively brought the Rastafari movement into disrepute. This was compounded in early 1960, when the police found a stockpile of arms in his residence. After Henry was sentenced to prison, his son and a few other armed renegades came to Jamaica to spring him from jail. They ended up creating mayhem when they ambushed and killed two British soldiers. As a consequence of this the Rastafari movement became even more unpopular in Jamaica than it already was. In an attempt to improve the movement's public image, notable second-generation Rastafari leaders such as Ras Sam Brown and Mortimo Planno approached the University of the West Indies with a proposal that the university carry out a study on Rastafari in order to dispel the widely held negative misconceptions of the movement. By the

2. Claudius Henry, the self-styled "God's Anointed Prophet and Repairer of the Breach," had issued to thousands of the faithful (Rastafari followers and admirers of his church) membership cards for his church, at one shilling per head. He promised that the membership cards would facilitate repatriation to Africa on October 5, 1959. All the faithful needed to do was turn up at his church. Thousands did turn up at Henry's Africa Reform church in Kingston only to be disappointed, as no ships came.

middle of 1960, the famous university Rastafari report was written, and ten recommendations were made.

The first recommendation was for a fact-finding mission to be sent to Africa. Premier Norman Washington Manley agreed to this mission, though perhaps only to placate those in the movement, according to conversations I had with Sir Roy Augier (one of the authors of the university report) in 2008 and 2010. The Rastafari members of the fact–finding Jamaican delegation to Africa were Douglas Mack, Fillmore Alvaranga, and Mortimo Planno. In 1961, they, along with other Jamaicans, traveled to various African countries, the most notable nation perhaps being Ethiopia. The fact-finding mission facilitated the first-ever meeting between Rastafari adherents and His Imperial Majesty Haile Selassie I. The university report, serving as a social lens on the Jamaican Rastafari community, was able (albeit to a limited extent) to quell some of the negative sentiments that the wider Jamaican community had toward the movement.

This was short-lived, however, as in 1963 on Good Friday (referred to as Bad Friday by Rastafari), a series of events led to the now-famous Coral Gardens Rastafari massacre. There are conflicting estimates regarding how many Rastas were killed by Jamaica's security forces during this brutal period in Jamaica's independent history, but various accounts estimate that at least one hundred fifty were brutalized by the security forces. According to personal Rastafari testimonies at the Coral Gardens remembrance event, which was held at Dump-up Beach in Montego Bay, April 2007, it is certain that many Rasta were brutalized, but not so certain how many were killed. According to the event organizer Junior Manning, hundreds were brutalized by the police.[3] Andrea Williams-Green, Jamaican Irie FM radio host for the renowned talk show *Running African,* stated that:

> During the Coral Gardens massacre, under government orders, hundreds of Rastafarians were rounded up, murdered, brutally beaten, shaven, tortured, and imprisoned following an incident on Holy Thursday, in St.

3. Interview with Junior Manning in March 2007, Rastafari elder and organizer of the annual Coral Gardens remembrance event in Montego Bay, Jamaica. He transitioned in March 2010.

> James, in which two policemen were killed by persons thought to be Rastafarians. Ironically, this took place during the Easter week, one of the holiest weeks in the predominantly Christian island.[4]

Alexander Bustamante, who was the leader of the Jamaica Labour Party (JLP) and the prime minister of Jamaica at that time, is reported to have said in his call for the capture of Rastafari, "Bring in all Rasta dead or alive—if the prisons can't hold them, then Bogue-hill Cemetery or the Mad-house can" (interview with Junior Manning, 2007).[5] This undoubtedly was one of the darkest chapters of Rastafari history, and a clear example of a gross atrocity committed against the movement in Jamaica.

Things began to improve for the Rastafari movement during the latter part of the sixties, specifically April 1966, when His Imperial Majesty Haile Selassie I visited Jamaica. The emperor was well received by both the Rastafari community and the wider Jamaican community. Never had a head of state been given such an overwhelming reception in the history of this Caribbean island before. As a result of His Imperial Majesty's visit, the Rastafari movement experienced a notable rise in popularity and started to be embraced by a wider body of the Jamaican community. Its relative size started to swell, and many musicians (notably Rita Marley, Bob Marley, Peter Tosh, and Bunny Wailer) started to think seriously about embracing Rastafarianism.

In 1962, Ras Sam Brown (a prominent Rastafari leader at the time) made history when he became the first Rastaman to run for political office in any national election in Jamaica (and in fact worldwide). His initiative, though controversial within the Rastafari movement at the time, proved to be a defining moment in Rastafari history.

The Third Epoch

The third epoch (1966–81) started in July 1966 with the bulldozing of the popular Rastafari enclave in Kingston, Back-a-Wall, to make way for

4. Andrea Williams, http://iriefm.net/running_africa/runningafrican. Last accessed on April 3, 2009.

5. More material provided by Junior Manning in my March 2007 interview with him.

Tivoli Gardens. One cannot help but wonder whether this was a governmental response to the popularity gained by the Rastafari movement as a result of Haile Selassie's visit to Jamaica three months earlier.

In 1968, Walter Rodney grounded with the Rastafari community and was able to bring the university community closer to the Rastafari movement as a result. Because of his efforts, Black power fused with the Pan-African sentiments of the Rastafari movement, and the movement gained in terms of its popularity in Jamaica. The movement became more appealing to middle-class Jamaicans, and its membership swelled significantly. However, the government barred Walter Rodney from reentering Jamaica on October 15, 1968, when he attempted to return from a Black writer's conference in Montreal; he was deemed to be a serious threat to the island's national security by the JLP administration, which was led by Hugh Shearer. The famous Rodney Riots resulted in Kingston on October 16, the day after Rodney was prevented from reentering the island. As news of Rodney's expulsion spread across the Caribbean region, so too did the riots, largely fueled by dejected and angered youth who were appalled at the decision taken by the Jamaican government.

The year 1968 also heralded the founding of the Twelve Tribes of Israel Mansion of the Rastafari movement. This mansion epitomized the gravitation of members of the uptown (non-grassroots) community to the movement.

Also during the third epoch, the Rastafari movement firmly established a symbiotic relationship with Reggae music. Rastafari dominated this genre during the seventies; popular Rastafari artists include Bob Marley, Peter Tosh, Bunny Wailer, Dennis Brown, Burning Spear, Third World, and Inner Circle.

The Fourth Epoch

In the fourth epoch (1981–2007), the Rastafari movement started to lose its influence in the reggae music industry, and its undeniable domination of the genre during the 1970s began to wane. A major contributor to this was arguably the death of Bob Marley in 1981; however, the increasing popularity of slackness-oriented lyrics by such artists as General Echo and Yellowman undoubtedly played a large role.

With the onset of the eighties, roots reggae music, which had once enjoyed wide-scale popularity, was eclipsed by DJ and dancehall music, dominated with recordings by such artists as Yellowman, Admiral Bailey, Shabba-Ranks, Flourgan, Colonel Josey Whales, Ninja-man, and the first incarnation of Capleton (with songs like "Bumba Red"). Additionally, with the onset of the eighties, the Twelve Tribes of Israel Mansion went on rest status (by the order of Gad-man) and, as a result, started to lose its impact on the rest of the movement (Tafari 1996).

It may be argued that during the fourth epoch, the movement started to lose its revolutionary impact, whether by design or by default. Additionally, some of the key leaders and movers and shakers of the movement transitioned (died). In 1987 Peter Tosh was assassinated by gunmen in a hail of bullets at his home.[6] In 1994, Prince (King) Emmanuel transitioned, which led to a power vacuum in the Bobo Shanti Mansion and a notable degree of fragmentation. (There were once three different camps at Bobo Hill instead of the one central original camp that originally existed.) In August 1998, Ras Sam Brown transitioned in Barbados at an international Rastafari conference (I was present at this conference).

In October 2000, Ras Boanerges (also known as Bongo Watto) transitioned. He was the main founder of the Youth Black Faith movement, considered by many to be the founding house for the Nyahbinghi Mansion, and therefore by default the leading patriarch of the Nyahbinghi Mansion.

In March 2005, Gad-man (Prophet Gad) of the Twelve Tribes of Israel Mansion transitioned, causing a significant and serious power vacuum in this branch of the movement (just as in the Bobo Shanti Mansion). Additionally, in March 2006, Mortimo Planno, considered to be the last of the living second-generation Rastafari patriarchs by some Rastafari, transitioned. Planno (who in his later years resided at the Mona Campus of the University of the West Indies) had been ill for several months, so his passing did not come as a great shock, but I believe his death effectively marked the end of an era.

6. I believe that Peter Tosh was assassinated, based on a personal interview in 2003 with Joy (Free-I) Dixon, one of the survivors of the bloody massacre at Tosh's Kingston home on September 11, 1987.

The Fifth Epoch

I believe the dawn of the fifth epoch began on September 11–12, 2007, which marked the new Ethiopian (African) millennium. During this time of great anticipation for the Rastafari movement as a whole, a bold initiative has taken place within the Jamaican Rastafari movement, namely the formation of the Ethio-Africa Diaspora Union Millennium Council. This Rastafari multimansional organization was formulated to first facilitate unity within the Rastafari movement in Jamaica and then across the wider reaches of the globe. However at the time of this writing much ground still needs to be covered in terms of the effective coalescing of the talent and human resources of the membership of the millennium council if the potential of the movement is to be realized.

I am sad to report that the founding chairman of the council, Ras Junior Manning, who was a stellar example of strong and effective leadership, transitioned in early 2010, leaving temporarily a power vacuum of sorts, causing the then embryonic council to stall for a few months, but thankfully for not too long. However, in its enthusiasm to regulate and coordinate the activities of the movement both in Jamaica and globally, the council must be wary that it does not duplicate the role of the Vatican in the Catholic church (a religious institution that ironically has drawn much criticism from many in the Rastafari movement) in its administering of Rastafari affairs.

Also in early 2010 the internationally renowned and popular Nyahbinghi elder, Bongo Tawney, who was then the chairperson of the Nyahbinghi order and the Ancient Council in Jamaica, transitioned. Although this was a sad loss to the Rastafari community of Jamaica and abroad, it sparked a historic first: an authentically Rastafari funeral, conducted and presided over by Nyahbinghi priests and attended by a mainly Rastafari congregation in early April 2010. Never before had this happened in the Nyahbinghi Mansion (who have traditionally been the mansion most radically opposed to death rituals), and it would certainly have been unthinkable prior to the dawn of this new African millennium. The Nyahbinghi mansion has long been famous for reciting the biblical quote, "Let the dead bury their dead," thus implying that Rastafari should have nothing to do with the dead in any capacity whatsoever.

Barry Chevannes mentions in his conclusion to the chapter he contributed to this volume that the internal adjustment that the Rastafari movement as a whole has had to make to their belief concerning the natural phenomenon of death is the most convincing evidence that routinization of the movement is underway, and in this regard, I must say that I agree.

In this fifth epoch, the Rastafari movement is at a figurative and literal crossroads, at which it can either move toward further fragmentation and dilution of its potential potency or toward greater unification, in which case it will be able to achieve many of its goals and objectives. As to which path the movement will take, or in which trajectory it will move, only time will tell.

Part I An Assessment of Rastafari in the New Millennium

1

Rastafari and the Coming of Age

The Routinization of the Rastafari Movement in Jamaica

BARRY CHEVANNES

All religions of known origin, following the death of their charismatic founders, either wither away or enter a period known in the literature as routinization, which is marked by two processes: the creation of an administration of roles and functions to replace the effectiveness of the personality of the founder, and internal adjustments aimed at finding a modus vivendi with the rest of the society. The Rastafari movement, at more than eighty years old, and more than fifty since the passing or effectiveness of the men who founded it, not only stands as a robust and influential religion in Jamaica itself, but also has been attracting members from diverse nationalities and ethnic groups across the world. In this chapter I discuss the routinization process that is making this accommodation and growth possible.

The first to write about this process among the Rastafari was Leonard Barrett, who based his analysis on Anthony F. C. Wallace (Barrett 1988). In what became a celebrated article, Wallace presented a view of a religious movement in its original state as a revitalization movement, "a deliberate, organized, conscious effort by members of a society to construct a more satisfying culture" (1956, 265). The need arises from a disjuncture between people's "mazeway" and the social reality they confront, the "mazeway" being the mental image that everyone has of the society, the culture and the self. When an individual's mazeway is not providing the solutions he or she may adopt to reduce chronic stress, an individual may decide either to live with the stress or to change the mazeway. Changing the mazeway entails "changing the total *Gestalt* of his image of self, society and culture, of nature and body, and of ways of action" (267). If the individual goes further and seeks to change social reality in order to achieve greater congruence with the mazeway, and if others join in this effort, together they constitute a revitalization movement.

A revitalization movement is therefore a movement seeking change. Wallace identifies six "tasks" or phases that the movement has to accomplish or undergo: the reformulation of the mazeway; communicating the new mazeway to others; organizing the group; making adaptations in the face of resistance, for example "doctrinal modification; political and diplomatic manoeuvre; and force" (276); transforming the culture; and routinization. For Wallace, routinization involves making such desired impact on the society that social transformation occurs and the society can resettle into a new steady state in which the movement, having accomplished its goal, can now restrict its action to the ritual sphere. "It becomes a church" (278). In stressing the social impact of the revitalization movement Wallace extends Weber's (1947) meaning of routinization, which focuses on the problems of the internal changes that are necessary and possible in order to maintain the community of believers following the loss or departure of the charismatic authority of the founder.

Leonard Barrett studied the Rastafari from 1963 to the mid-1970s. His timing could not have been better—three years after the university report and one year after Sam Brown had run as a Rastafari candidate in the general elections (Smith, Nettleford, and Augier 1960). Barrett missed the April 1966 visit to Jamaica of Emperor Haile Selassie, but he was an eyewitness to the bulldozing of the Back-a-Wall slum in July of the same year. By the 1970s he found sufficient evidence of a cultural and social impact to describe what he called "an ambivalent routinization"—ambivalent because of the movement's dissonance with the society coexisting with its increasing consonance with it. It is useful to summarize his findings.

The first sign of routinization was the increasing accommodation of the Rastafari by the state, beginning with the university report, whose recommendations, including exploring migration to Africa, housing, and the cessation of police harassment, were accepted and in part implemented. Second, Barrett was struck by the recognition the Rastafari were beginning to receive for their artistic creations in the national festival competitions, in the drawings of Ras Daniel Heartman and other artists and in the music of Count Ossie, who was at the head of a long list that by the final years of his fieldwork included the likes of Bob Marley and the Wailers. Barrett's third sign of routinization was the mass support for the movement as "the avant garde who are carrying the fight for freedom, justice and a better Jamaica" (1988, 162). In summary:

> The Rastafarian movement in Jamaica has demonstrated all the classical techniques of a real revitalization movement. It emerged from a period of stress . . . , and moved through a period of heightened tension in search of a reformulation of the mazeway . . . ; the movement then undertook the task of communicating this ideology. . . . By astutely maneuvering against the opposition, the movement attained some acceptance. . . . It further sought to adapt itself to the social and cultural realities of Jamaica by using a variety of strategies. (165–66)

Despite this summary, Barrett's main emphasis was on the diminution of hostility on the part of the state and the middle and upper social classes, in which regard the power of Rastafari creativity, especially in the realm of music, proved decisive. But with respect to the internal changes the movement had to make, the only notable change he found was in the views of those with whom he spoke that political engagement in local affairs was a necessary prerequisite to repatriation. In what follows I seek to extend Barrett's analysis past the 1970s and give an outline of two critical changes underway in the belief system.

Any assessment of routinization among the Rastafari will of necessity be hampered by the acephalous nature of the movement as a whole. Groups there are, groups there have always been, headed by charismatic personalities, all sharing a common belief in the divinity of Emperor Haile Selassie and in the necessity of repatriation, but as to having a single head over and above these groups, the movement has been quite resistant. Thus, it is a somewhat complicated task to speak of routinization of the movement as a whole, though the process is clear enough in any one group. For example, although Leonard Howell is credited with being the first to announce the divinity of Haile Selassie, almost simultaneously there were several other preachers: Joseph Hibbert, Archibald Dunkley, and a man known as Brother Napier, as well as Robert Hinds, who had broken away from the charismatic Howell to found an independent organization. None of these groups survived their leader's demise, with the exception of Howell's, which continues but as a small and insignificant remnant of a once large and viable organization. By the time Hinds died, his King of Kings Mission had completely disintegrated, but the message was taken up by some of his own lieutenants, each setting up his own group under his own authority, without any claim to succession.

In the case of the Ethiopian African National Congress, popularly known as the Bobo, founded and led by Prince Emmanuel Edwards, a council of priests presided over the group following the leader's death in 1994. However, it was not long before two priests broke away to form two separate groups further along the mountain range, one of them claiming to have inherited the spirit of Prince Emmanuel, whom every Bobo revered as a member of the triune Godhead.[1] Meanwhile, the Twelve Tribes of Israel, which remains impervious to study by outsiders, seems to have had a managing council set up by its charismatic founder Prophet Gad, and representing each tribe, which has continued after his death in 2005. As the third of the three main groups of Rastafari, the Nyahbinghi House has never recognized a founder as such, having morphed from a loosely organized group called the Youth Black Faith, based in Trench Town, and influenced by the asceticism of another trend called the Higes Knots, originating in the east end of the city (Homiak 1995). Largely responsible for the defining characteristics of the Rastafari, such as the dreadlocks, the nyahbinghi drumming, and the reasoning under the sacramental effects of ganja, the Nyahbinghi appoint from among its most venerable elders a patriarch and high priest, whose roles are sanctioned by the assembly.

1. Data on the council and breakaway factions were collected during a field visit in July 1998.

Thus, from the beginning, the Rastafari movement has never been subject to the authority of a single charismatic figure, but has thrown up in the course of its history charismatic leaders who more often than not found their own groups, to which they give particular accents while still adhering to the two central tenets of Selassie's divinity and repatriation. The latest is the School of Vision founded in 1997 by Dermot Fagan, who with his followers has set up camp in the Blue Mountains overlooking Kingston, awaiting the return of the King of Kings in spacecrafts to repatriate them, thus signaling the end of the world. In this tendency toward decentralized engagement with the society, the Rastafari movement very closely resembles the movement from which it could be said to have emerged, Revivalism. The Revival movement took shape as an 1860 development of Myalism, a Pan-African religion that had emerged a hundred years before to forge a united multiethnic front against slavery (Schuler 1979). As such, Revivalism has known no single founder or leader, but as many charismatic leaders as there were bands, or churches, as they are now called. Alexander Bedward flourished as its greatest charismatic leader, a prophet and healer, from 1895 to 1921, yet at the height of his popularity membership in his church included Mother Rita, an independent healer from St. Elizabeth (Beckwith 1929, 29). Thus, everywhere Revival's belief system, rituals, and organizational structure are unmistakably uniform if not identical, giving it the character of a folk religion. Rastafari grew out of Revival in the sense that it had nothing on which to peg the new vision, other than the ritual processes of Revival, including even baptism. Until the revolt of the Youth Black Faith radicals beginning in the late 1940s, the doctrinal innovation was the principal distinguishing mark of the Rastafari. Even as late as the mid-1970s, the Revival influence in Nyahbinghi celebrations was still evident, including its choruses sung to the slower, more somber nyahbinghi kete drum beat instead of the quick-tempo rattler, and with critical word changes, such as "Zion" for "heaven."[2]

Routinization is the response of a group bereft of the charismatic authority of its founder in its search for continuity. It must become rou-

2. See Chevannes 1995 for a discussion of the Revival influence in Rastafari.

tine or die. Notwithstanding its decentralizing character, taken as a whole Rastafari has already entered a routinization phase. In no other area of its belief system than its position on death is this more manifested.

Death

To better appreciate the profundity of the changes underway in Rastafari theology of death, it is useful to summarize the Revival-based folk beliefs about it. The human being is a composite of spirit, body, shadow, and soul. The soul is the life principle, and the shadow the personality, which is subject to the malign influence of obeah. The spirit is the eternal part of the human that cannot die, that is capable of extracorporeal existence, and that lives on after death as an ancestor. Immediately after the departure of life, the spirit exists as an uncontrolled and dangerous entity, until the transition to ancestor status is properly enacted and complete. It involves rituals of mourning and community participation centered on the wake or set-up, and involving feasting, singing, games, story-telling, precautionary measures against the spiritual influence of the deceased, such as the presence or ingestion of salt, and the "turning out" on the ninth night or on the eve of the interment, a private ceremony in which the spirit is appeased with libations, led to the nearest crossroads, and entreated not to return. The bedroom in which he or she lived is swept and rearranged. Then follow the rituals of respect, involving the bathing and dressing of the body, its display in as expensive a coffin as can be afforded, a funeral service in a church attended by expensively dressed mourners, friends, and other well-wishers of the family, a eulogy, a procession after the church service and interment in the family's burial plot or a cemetery. The transition complete, the dead becomes an ancestral spirit that guards the living, communicating with them in dreams.

The Rastafari movement's attitude to death, so obviously an inescapable condition of life, seemed to have been determined by the fact that the God it worshipped was a living person, this in turn finding support in Christian teaching that the true believer would never die but live forever. It is not clear what, if anything, the leaders and first generation of converts believed about death and dying, given their need to imprint on the minds of an incredulous public the fact that God was a living Black man. And if God was living in the flesh, come to redeem Africa's scattered children, of what import would a theology of death be to these groups of believers? Thus for the first two decades and a half the Rastafari movement was to remain silent on the issue. When Robert Hinds died in 1950, according to informants, none of his followers attended his funeral (Chevannes 1994, 142), an extraordinary omission, given the cultural expectation of paying respect to the deceased. Regardless of the fact that by then his King of Kings Mission had disintegrated, as one by one his lieutenants went their separate ways, for no one to have attended his funeral, considering his fame as one of the original preachers of the doctrine, and the most successful, makes no cultural sense, unless it was to make a point, namely that the new religion differed fundamentally from the old in having no truck with death and funerals, and that those who died had no part with the living God.

That this may have been the general attitude of the Rastafari at the time becomes clearer with the rise of the Dreadlocks, who were not prepared to remain silent on the issue, coming as they were out of the Youth Black Faith, an organization of young rebels who denounced the ways of the elders as being too Revivalist and introduced into the movement a way of engaging one another in intense debate and exposition they called reasoning. It was in these encounters that the dreadlocks identity found its justification, the concept of nyahbinghi introduced, Rasta talk emerged, and with the philosophy of the self, "the I." Here the appropriation and sacralization of ganja took place and the theology of it elaborated. The Dreadlocks gave to the Rastafari movement many if not most of its principal characteristics. It is, thus, most unlikely that Hinds's death would have escaped their reasoning circles, what with their savvy for interpreting current events. It is also hard to imagine them not seeing in his obscure passing his just desserts for corrupting the faith with his revivalisms. According to Wato, one of the key members of the Youth Black Faith, whose yard, or camp, became an important site of reasoning, they were unrelenting in their criticisms of the earlier preachers for the latter's too many retentions of the Revival tradition (Chevannes 1994, 154).

At first the Dreadlocks were a trend, and even up to the time of Barrett's fieldwork shared membership of the movement with the "Combsomes,"

Rastafari who chose not to cut their head or facial hair but to groom it with comb or brush. Indeed, of the three Rastafari members on the government-appointed mission to Africa, Mortimo Planno was the only Dreadlocks. But by the end of the 1960s Rastafari had become synonymous with Dreadlocks, and talk of death explicitly anathema. "Let the dead bury their dead," Jesus is said to have advised his followers. The Rastafari now began to take this quite literally. When a Rastafari died, his relatives had to see to his burial; to his own Rastafari brethren it was a sign that his heart had been corrupt, and his death the reward by a just God. The truly faithful would never see death. That was what Jesus himself assured those who believed.

The first sign of a change from this rigid interpretation came with the death of the emperor himself in 1975. The news threw the Rastafari community into some confusion. The first reaction of members was a stout denial, explaining that the media, no friends of the Rastafari, were somehow complicit in sowing falsehoods about Haile Selassie. The unexplained reluctance on the part of the revolutionary government that had taken command of Ethiopia to say where he was buried convinced many Rastafari brethren that Selassie was not dead. If he were dead, they argued, how come nobody had seen his grave or could say where he was buried? Soon, then, the standard response was that His Majesty had disappeared, that is, he had used his own mystic power to spirit himself away. Bob Marley's "Jah Live," a song rich in pathos, conveys the feelings of a flock whose shepherd cannot die but that is mocked by unbelieving fools. It was a heroic gesture at a time when the movement was demoralized and its faith tested by the inevitability of death.

Marley's own death in 1981 was another marker. Before him, the only other Rastafari of renown whose death had been widely noticed was the popular artist, Jacob Miller, who had perished in a motor vehicle accident, and whose funeral service had been conducted within the Ethiopian Orthodox Church (EOC). In the church Rastafari of whatever "denomination" found a formula for handling the conundrum that presented itself when a public figure dies. Believing death to be a sure sign of loss of faith or of having strayed from the chosen path, they nevertheless were forced by the sheer weight of public outpouring to acknowledge the national significance of the life of the deceased and to allow the rituals of mourning and respect to take place without decrying them. The EOC was in fact offering a sort of middle-ground, half-way solution, which benefited the movement through the gains in respectability made by the publicly acknowledged achievement of one of its members, without itself having to compromise its theological stance on death. Thus it was that nearly every major Rastafari personality has been buried by the EOC. Marley's was without doubt the largest and most significant. But there were also Peter Tosh and Garnett Silk, both of them dying tragically, and Dennis Brown. Whatever ambivalence Rastafari themselves might have had about the personal lives of these artists, regardless of the houses or groups to which they belonged, none could deny their roles in spreading the Rastafari vision and way of life across the world. Death presented the Rastafari with a dilemma: if they denounced these superstars as false for having been exposed by death, they could not with a clean conscience glory in the internationalization of the movement brought about by these men; on the other hand, if they accepted their roles in spreading Rastafari, they could not with any credibility denounce them as false Rastas. The result was a softening of the Rastafari stance on death, led particularly by younger brethren. By the late 1980s a split in attitude was evident (Chevannes 1994), and when in 1999 a participant died during the Nyahbinghi celebrations at Scots Pass in Clarendon, Patriarch Wato, despite his role and personal weight, was defeated in his bid to impose a nine-year ban on the use of the site because of the contamination. Ironically, when he died a year later, his death was marked by a ninth night celebration.

Mortimo Planno was perhaps the most celebrated Rastafari prior to Bob Marley. He was reputed to have taught Marley the rudiments of the faith when they both lived in Trench Town during the 1960s, Planno at his famous yard on Fifth Street, Marley at his on First. Planno met the emperor three times, first as a member of the 1961 mission to Africa, then in an audience at the palace on his return to Ethiopia two years later, and in 1966 when he saved the day by helping the emperor to deplane at the start of his state visit to Jamaica.[3] Despite a chronic thyroid problem that forced

3. As soon as the emperor's plane landed, the Rastafari broke through the police cordon and swarmed the aircraft, preventing the emperor from disembarking. When repeated efforts

him into semiretirement, he was still well-known enough to a younger generation of Rastafari to have created a big impact among them when the University of the West Indies made him its first Folk Philosophy Fellow in 1998. Planno was still a member of the university community when he died. His death was widely acknowledged in the local press. On the eve of his funeral, a long EOC ceremony, made even longer by the twenty tributes that the priests allowed, a nine-night ceremony was arranged for him on the university campus. It had nothing in common with the traditional ninth night, except the large gathering of Rastafari men and women and other well-wishers—no table with a bowl of salt, white rum, water, and Bible, around which stand those who would lead and track the songs, no games or story telling. Instead, there were the unmistakable marks of a Rastafari gathering: a sacred fire fed with dry logs, an ensemble of drummers accompanying well-known Rastafari songs, and Rastafari elders and queens bedecked in formal garb. After several hours the drumming and singing ceased and various persons were called upon to speak in tribute to Planno. Instead of the words "death" or "died," euphemisms such as "passing," "passed," and "transition" were used. The sole exception was by the well-known poet and broadcaster Mutabaruka, who in his tribute boldly criticized the older generation for trying to deny the inevitability of death. He did so without any of the usual verbal signals of disapproval—shouts of "Blood!" or "Fire!" condemnation. The brethren listened.

The nine night (and it was referred to as such) was a remarkable manifestation of the fact that the Rastafari movement had reconciled itself to the inevitability of death and was striving for appropriate ritual forms to incorporate it. To further deepen the routinization process underway, following a procession of cars and buses led by a motorized chariot carrying his body decked out in an expensive white casket, Planno was given a "family plot" burial in Scots Pass on the same site as the Tabernacle, with the kind and

on the part of the authorities failed, according to Planno himself, as he told me, the emperor recognized him in the crowd and sent for him. Planno bowed, shook his hand, and directed the brethren to open the way. The official ceremony was abandoned, and the emperor was whisked away in a motorcade through the city.

understanding permission of Bob Marley's widow, Rita Marley, the owner of the land. His grave was the first.

Repatriation

The second belief undergoing change is repatriation. The hope of return seemed to have always been present among the Africans who were forced into slavery, not all of them, but a significant section. Schuler (1979) found among the descendants from the Kongo who settled in St. Thomas belief in the possibility of spiritual return through abstention from salt.[4] The late eighteenth century conversion to Christianity, principally through the efforts of the Baptist and Methodist missionaries, put the slaves in touch with the "children of Israel" trope, which they immediately appropriated as their own, with results that bore close parallels to what was taking place in the American south, where it was woven into the folk religion to provide the slaves there with a rich source of hope. The story of the children of Israel's captivity, Egypt, Babylon, Pharaoh, Moses the Leader, the promise of liberation, a Promised Land, the crossing of the Red Sea, Zion, Jerusalem, home—all these were the subject of a hermeneutics that found contemporary meaning in historical events. Through the Revival cosmology, therefore, the sense that Jamaica, and all the suffering and sadness it represented, was not associated with home was the possible sentiment. Home was somewhere else.

> I want to go home to that land
> I want to go home to that land
> I want to go home to that land
> where I am from.
> For there is joy in my soul,

4. The salt taboo could have found its way into the Rastafari movement through Leonard Howell, who had spent several years proselytizing in St. Thomas during the 1930s (Chevannes 2006, 57), although there is also a more generalized belief in the power of salt found in Jamaican culture, as evidenced by its presence at nine night ceremonies and the special meaning it is given when used to describe a person who has undergone a series of misfortune.

peace and happiness in my mind
I want to go home to that land where I am from.

Revival choruses like that one served to direct the hopes and aspirations of the people outward. By the second decade of the twentieth century, the followers of Alexander Bedward were linking their leader to Marcus Garvey by way of the children of Israel trope: Aaron, the high priest to Moses, the prophet-leader, both in pursuit of the Promised Land.

Before proceeding further, it should be pointed out that repatriation was not the ideal of everyone. As far back as the eighteenth century, the struggle against slavery was not aimed at returning to the homeland, but at freedom. This was what the Maroon War, which ended with the peace treaty of 1739, was all about, and the siblings Kojo and Nanny set up separate autonomous regions, Accompong and Moore Town, respectively. Then following the suppression of the Taki rebellion of 1760, it was revealed that the intention of the rebels was to set up small kingdoms in the island, and one of them even tried bribing his captive with the promise of making him the overseer of the estate to which he belonged and hoped to return a free man (Hall 1988, 102). It is reasonable to conclude, therefore, that both sentiments of repatriation and freedom coexisted throughout the history of slavery, with the latter being the more dominant, however.

Repatriation was from the beginning of the Rastafari one of the cornerstones of their beliefs and their agitation. It should not be forgotten that Marcus Garvey's Back-to-Africa movement would have created in the popular imagination a sense that Africa and its development were central to the destinies of all the descendants of the once enslaved. Returning to build Africa into a powerful empire capable of commanding the respect of the rest of the world was Garvey's vision, but framed in Rastafari lenses it became the *right to physical return*. Tied closely to the belief in the living God, the Emperor Haile Selassie, whose identity at first was that of the returned Messiah, Jesus Christ, redemption through repatriation was seen by the early believers as imminent—that, after all, was why he was crowned King of Kings, "our King." In imitation of him, they began to grow beards, which, according to a report made by one of the delegates to Garvey's Universal Negro Improvement Association's conference in 1934, was to serve as markers of identification for the repatriation on August 1, the centenary of the Declaration of Emancipation (Post 1978, 189). But no public manifestation of any sort took place on that day, as it would certainly have been carried in the press, which only a few months before had given extensive coverage to Howell's trial and imprisonment for seditious speech in St. Thomas. Instead, repatriation, though not abandoned, took second place to the more important imperative of convincing an incredulous populace that a Black man, recently crowned King of Kings in a ceremony attended by a representative of the British crown, was the Messiah, the Son of God, and therefore one of the persons of the Holy Trinity.

But what did repatriation mean in practical terms? How was it to be effected? There have been two coexisting trends, one that takes repatriation as a divine act, the other as a human act. The first, of which there are three instances, emphasizes the interpretation of signs to determine its timing; the latter emphasizes human action, whether personal or political, and of this there are several. Neither is exclusive of the other, as when the inevitable failure of the first leads to the second, or when frustration with the second leads to the first. Of late, however, a third trend is discernible—Repatriation as essentially a spiritual act.

Miraculous Transformation

To most members of the Rastafari movement, repatriation was to be a divine act, a return home organized by God himself through the agency of his prophet. But as no one knows when, the faithful simply wait until God sends one of his prophets to declare the fullness of time. The first in the history of the movement to make such a declaration was Claudius Henry, who announced "Decision Day," October 5, 1959, when the "miraculous repatriation" of God's chosen people would take place. Exactly how the miracle would come about, no one knew, and Henry never said. But curiously, the blue cards that he sold for a shilling were to be used in lieu of passports. No one asked why a card or passport would be necessary for a miraculous event, but hundreds came, and, of course, were disappointed.

But there was another aspect to repatriation, which once it became clear, enabled an explanation of the timing of Henry's Decision Day.

Although his "miraculous repatriation" had failed, and he had become a laughingstock to other members of the movement, Henry was undaunted, and in the following year embarked on another repatriation scheme with his most faithful members. They amassed a large number of conch shells, dynamite, and "swords" (expertly sharpened machetes) and prepared a letter to dispatch to Fidel Castro, who had taken Cuba on January 1, 1959. The letter invited him to come take control of Jamaica, as they were about to leave for Africa. The state intervened and arrested Henry for treason on the basis of the letter and the arms cache. The truth, however, was that the Rastafari in their hermeneutics of contemporary events had interpreted the Cuban revolution as the native peoples of the Americas, represented by Fidel Castro, taking back the land that had been theirs before it was stolen by the Whites. What Henry was saying was that Jamaica, too, belonged to the Amerindians and he was returning it to its rightful owner before leaving for Africa for good. Repatriation therefore also implied restorative justice—Africa for the Africans, the Americas for the Amerindians, and Europe for the Europeans. It becomes clear, then, that Decision Day was inspired by what had taken place in Havana nine months earlier, and that Henry had interpreted it as a sign of the imminence of repatriation. How he decided on October 5 is not clear. Repatriation meant more than the return of the children of Africa to "the land where they were from"; it meant as well the correcting of the injustice in the rape of the Americas, and only a miracle, indeed, could make that happen.

The second instance of miraculous repatriation was in 1975 in the actions of a small group led by the late Jah Lloyd and Bongo Black Heart Man that split with the Nyahbinghi House. Interpreting the formation of a third political party and the staging in Jamaica of a Commonwealth Heads of Government Meeting, at which a number of African nations were to be present, as favorable omens, they boldly declared that the meeting of the heads would rule on repatriation, and that if that failed blood would flow. Their prophecy having failed, they came up with a plan to engage in local politics as a way of getting the political power to bring about repatriation. Needless to say they never got very far with this endeavor.

Repatriation as miraculous transformation surfaced again for the third time in 1997, in the founding of the School of Vision by Dermot Fagan, who preached that repatriation would take place in September 2007, which marked the end of the millennium according to the Ethiopian calendar. He arrived at that conclusion by interpreting the signs of the return of the apocalyptic beast, whose number is 666. The rise of Ronald Wilson Reagan to the presidency of the United States was the first sign, with six letters in each of his names; the introduction of Jamaica's tax registration system on June 6, the sixth month, 1996, the second sign; and the calculation that the end of the millennium marked 6,000 years from the first man, Adam. Then, Emperor Haile Selassie would send a fleet of flying saucers to repatriate the faithful and consume with fire those that chose to remain. Fagan and his group have set up camp in the Blue Mountains, where they continue to await the miraculous transformation to take place any time now.

Human Action

The first example of an attempt at personal repatriation was that of one John Ricketts, who as early as 1934, the same year Howell was tried and sentenced for seditious speech, made his own way to Ethiopia, but had to turn to the British consul for assistance to get back to Jamaica, after being robbed of all his money.[5] But the story that captured the imagination was that of Noel Dyer, who in 1964 hitchhiked his way from London, where he had migrated and had discovered Rastafari, all the way to the African continent, across the Mediterranean to North Africa and finally through Egypt to the Promised Land, Ethiopia. When news of this extraordinary man reached the emperor, he sent for him. Dyer's story was so much like a fairy tale—the hunger, deprivations, imprisonment, illiterate, penniless, without passport or visa, that his friend Kathleen Eaton has put it together into a book for children, *The Adventures of Ali Thunda* (Eaton 2008).

In 1948 the *Empire Windrush* sailed with the first West Indian migrants to Britain, setting off in its wake a trek of scores of thousands. There sprang up virtually overnight a plethora of travel agencies offering cheap fares. Britain was the place to go, and thousands of Jamaicans took

5. *Jamaica Times*, Oct. 24, 1934, 14–15.

advantage of the opportunity to find work. This was the context in which stout-hearted members of the Rastafari movement stepped up their agitation for repatriation. They staged marches and confronted political leaders. Then in 1955 an emissary of the Ethiopian World Federation (EWF) came to Jamaica to set up local chapters and to inform of the emperor's 500-acre land grant in Sheshamane. Many joined the federation, or set up charters of their own. One who was later to make the greatest use of the EWF was Vernon Carrington, the founder of the Twelve Tribes of Israel, who became better known as Prophet Gad. Twelve Tribes developed into a highly organized and tightly knit group that in the 1970s set about in earnest to settle its members in Sheshamane, with funds earned from the music events it regularly promoted at its headquarters on Hope Road in Kingston.

Prince Emmanuel Edwards's Back-a-Wall Convention of March 1958 was another example of human action to realize repatriation. Smith, Nettleford, and Augier (1960, 14–15) report that many Rastafari came from as far away as Montego Bay in the west of the island in the expectation that after the three weeks of celebration the convention would end in repatriation. Although there is no evidence that Emmanuel himself had so preached, one is left to speculate that his motive could have been to force the government to act. For, in the early morning of the final day, he led hundreds of those in attendance to the municipal park, which they symbolically captured by planting their red, green, and gold flags and taking possession of it. When the authorities came to evict them they demanded that they be repatriated.

Perhaps the most celebrated case of human action for repatriation came with the implementation of the recommendations of the university report. Following the Claudius Henry affair, which had brought about a terrible backlash on the members of the movement from both the state and the general public, a group of Rastafari, including Mortimo Planno, appealed to the principal of the University College of the West Indies to undertake a study in order to allay public fears about the movement. Led by M. G. Smith, Roy Augier, and Rex Nettleford, the study, a rapid appraisal lasting two intense weeks, recommended, among other things, that the government "send a mission to African countries to arrange for immigration of

Jamaicans" (Smith, Nettleford, and Augier 1960, 38). The mission visited Nigeria, Sierra Leone, Liberia, Ghana, and Ethiopia, where they were given audience with the emperor. Based on their favorable report on return, a technical mission was set up to work out arrangements and was already in Africa when a referendum to decide whether or not Jamaica should remain in the West Indies Federation caused it to be aborted. That there were three Rastafari brethren on the nine-man mission implied that many members were looking to it for a fulfillment of their repatriation dreams.

Over the past forty years the population of Shashamane has been growing. In chapter 3, Niaah gives a recent estimate of between four and five hundred, their origins divided evenly between Jamaica and the rest of the Caribbean, with a smattering from Germany, New Zealand, Japan, and Ireland. The estimate of those living throughout all of Ethiopia is in the region of a thousand, drawn from over twenty nationalities. Among the challenges faced by these Rastafari who have repatriated themselves is the denial of citizenship even to those born to them in the country.

Mention must also be made of a settlement in Ghana by the Bobo, as the members of Prince Emmanuel's Ethiopia Black African International Congress are known. Little is written about its size and composition, the activities of the settlers, or their relationship with the parent body in Jamaica.

Finally, a word about engagement in the political process to effect repatriation. The first to take this path was Sam Brown, who created quite a stir in the 1962 elections but ended up losing his deposit.[6] Brown campaigned on a platform of vying for political power in order to respond to the needs of all Black people in Jamaica and in so doing to realize Rastafari dreams of repatriation. He was one of the main informants of Leonard Barrett (1988), who saw in his political ambition an example of the kind of maneuvers revitalization movements undergo in their process of routinization. The exact

6. In the British Electoral system each prospective political candidate must pay a deposit to the electoral office to be duly nominated. If they do not obtain more than a threshold or minimum amount of votes on election day, they do not get their deposit back, which can be a source of shame for candidates who wish to be taken seriously.

same theme of mediating repatriation through political power resurfaced in the activities of Jah Lloyd and Black Heart referred to above. Their party has consistently lost its deposit. The fact is that Sam Brown and Jah Lloyd and Black Heart were isolated from the mainstream of Rastafari. Political activism has never sat well with the movement, not since the 1930s and 1940s. The 1938 general strike not only shut down the entire country but also set in train the process that brought about adult suffrage and limited self-government in 1944. The Rastafari at the time were active participants in both the strike and the subsequent national elections (Chevannes 1994, 146). But it was their disillusionment with politicians who they felt betrayed their trust once they got into power that turned them away from engaging in local politics and refocused their eyes on Africa. General Rastafari skepticism toward "politricks" began with this early experience.

Is there any hope that such skepticism could be abated in the future and that Rastafarians could become parliamentarians as has happened in the Republic of Trinidad and Tobago, where the junior minister of national security was a dreadlocked Rastafarian, or in New Zealand where a Rastafarian was elected member of parliament? In the course of becoming routine, such a development is entirely possible. However, it is so remote that contemplating it is vain. Politics in Jamaica, what with its link to gun violence and corruption, has become so discredited that it is difficult to see a movement like the Rastafari, nurtured on its caustic criticism of "Babylon," the establishment, embracing it without itself being contaminated and losing its value.

Where Rastafari sense of repatriation seems to be going is not toward local politics, not toward some miraculous repatriation, but toward the spiritual meaning of repatriation. Apart from the fact that those who have chosen to settle in Sheshamane or in any other part of Africa, for that matter, are relatively few, there is strong evidence to suggest that the movement is trending toward reconciling the hope of return with a life in Jamaica made more meaningful by its realization of a spiritual connectedness with Africa. Remarkably, the first to come to this conclusion was Claudius Henry himself. After his release from prison on parole in 1967, he gathered up his remnants and embarked on a development program targeting their needs. He claimed to have visited the emperor, who told him that Africa was in Jamaica and there was no need to fight for repatriation. When and how he visited the continent he did not say, but after two attempts at miraculous repatriation his goal now was to develop Africa where he was. Perhaps because he was already discredited among the general population of Rastafari, this remarkable insight did not resonate with the brethren until decades later, when more affluent members of the movement began to visit Ghana and a liberated South Africa, both of which have enjoyed close ties with Jamaica, as well as other Anglophone countries from West and Southern Africa. Tours of the Elmina slave-holding castle, with the ghosts of its horrors still felt, including its door of no return, have provided them with moving, spiritual experiences. The hospitality, also, that they receive from Africans who have heard of Bob Marley and yearn to visit Jamaica leaves them with a sense of wholeness as recognized sons and daughters of Africa. African Rastafari do not hanker for home; they are already home. What many long for is the visit to the place where this vision began, where it was nurtured, and where its greatest prophet lies buried.

Such recognition does not remain only at the level of the person. The African Union has understood the importance of the African Diaspora for Africa itself, thereby elevating the status of the descendants of the enslaved.

Conclusion

The internal adjustment that the Rastafari movement as a whole has had to make to their belief concerning the natural phenomenon of death is the most convincing evidence of a process of routinization underway. From a stance of resolute denial of the necessity of death for the truly faithful to acceptance of its inevitability is quite a distance. There was a time when the word "dedaz" (dead things) was commonly used by the righteous to heap scorn on meat eaten by the unrighteous. While there is no reason to suggest any change in food ways, it can no longer be said that the Rastafari have no truck with death. All that remains to be done is for the movement to develop its own liturgy of the final rite of passage. Until one emerges, the Ethiopian Orthodox Church will continue to oblige. For one to emerge, however, the Rastafari will require state recognition, which is unlikely as long as the sacred herb, ganja, remains illegal.[7]

Where repatriation is concerned, the process also continues. The spiritual trend—not that the others are not spiritual—will grow, because Rastafari has in large measure succeeded in forcing a change in the mazeway of Blacks.

7. This could change if government implements the recommendation of the 2001 Ganja Commission to make the use of ganja for religious purposes permissible.

Part 2 The Globalization of Rastafari

The Lantern and the Light

Rastafari in Aotearoa (New Zealand)

EDWARD TE KOHU DOUGLAS
and IAN BOXILL

The Rastafari movement came to Aotearoa in the last quarter of the twentieth century, when Maori human rights activists were borrowing ideas and rhetoric from overseas Black consciousness and Native American protest movements (Sharp 1997, 8).[1] In particular, Rastafari beliefs came to Aotearoa through the music of Bob Marley in the 1970s, a period that coincided with the reemergence of Maori nationalism and a subsequent Maori renaissance. Marley's lyrics brought to the Maori a message decrying "suffering" under a continuing colonial regime; they have resulted in some of Rastafari's staunchest and most sophisticated converts. Moreover, Rastafari's essentially spiritual and prophetic nature may have made it especially appealing to a people who have traditionally held these attributes in high esteem.

This article was previously published in a special issue of *Ideaz*, vol. 7, 2008. Used by permission.

This work was supported by a research grant from the University of Waikato, when the authors were in that University's Maori Development Centre.

The authors wish to acknowledge Oliver Dragon from Grenada, who video-recorded some of the reasoning sessions with the Ruatoria Dreads when he was a graduate student at the University of Waikato.

1. Aotearoa is the Maori name for New Zealand. The word "Maori" is used for both singular and plural forms.

Perhaps the most remarkable aspect of the movement in Aotearoa is that it has taken root without direct or sustained contact with other Rastafari. Maori commitment to Rastafari is further noteworthy because its essential Afro-centrism has been rejected and placed in a New Zealand context. Aotearoa Rastafari have accepted a Rasta identity in response to life crises caused by the power of Anglo-Celtic assimilationist politics and culture and the conflict of identity that has arisen as a result. As Rastafari, Maori in Aotearoa have a sense of belonging to and identifying with a wider group of similar people.

Aotearoa contains a number of Rastafari groups of varying size and commitment. The largest Rastafari community in Auckland has several hundred adherents.[2] While some groups are deeply involved with the religious and philosophical aspects of the movement's teachings, others are little more than reggae fans, groups of marginalized people, or defiant ganja (marijuana) users with dreadlocks. Influenced by the music and lyrics of Bob Marley and other reggae musicians, thousands of Maori and Polynesian teenagers and young adults wear their hair in dreadlocks and their clothes decorated with the *ites* (the red, green, and yellow colors of Rastafari), but more as a fashion statement than to signify their connection to a congregation or gathering of Rasta.

In this chapter we focus on the Ruatoria Dreads, a fluid community of about one hundred Rastafari notable for their syncretic beliefs and practices.[3] Living in the most easterly part of Aotearoa and in the heartland of their Ngati Porou *iwi* (tribe), they are deeply religious and have accepted Rastafarian beliefs not to replace but to augment an existing damaged identity. Their beliefs give political and spiritual expression to their desire for release from oppression and their hope for redemption within a secure Maori identity. After a brief historical overview of colonization of Aotearoa and the social context surrounding the growth of Rastafari, this

2. Called the Twelve Tribes of Israel, or Gaddites, they were led by a Jamaican musician (Hensley) who came to New Zealand in 1981, married a Maori woman, and stayed on proselytizing young Maori and Island Polynesians.

3. There are different groups amongst Ruatoria's one hundred Rastafari. The most numerous are the Ahi-ites, whose leader is Te Ahi o Te Atua (the Fire of God).

chapter explores the meaning of Rastafari in Ruatoria, focusing especially on distinctive beliefs and practices such as cannabis use, facial tattooing, and local changes to typical Rastafari symbols. We also briefly explore relations between the Rastafari and the rest of the community.

The Historical Context

Colonization and Religious Resistance

Maori were almost totally isolated from the outside world until the final quarter of the eighteenth century. But the first European explorers were quickly followed by resource exploiters, traders, Christian missionaries, and from 1840, large-scale British settlement. Literacy was highly desirable for trade, so Maori took to it along with a gradual acceptance of missionary Christianity. From about 1832, Maori perceptions of themselves were transformed by rapid religious conversion and the intrusion of colonial governance. Rapidly rising literacy in both Maori and English and in trade introduced the money economy of British colonialism.

Initially Maori had welcomed British settlers to Aotearoa as their equals, but instead they were overrun by rapacious, land-greedy settlers who considered themselves the natural successors to the land and resources of a people whom they believed to be depraved and dying natives. The settlers sought to create "Britain in the South Seas," while Maori struggled as their society and culture were set against a vastly different and powerful intruder. By 1860 British settlers (termed *pakeha* by Maori) were in the majority. As Sinclair (quoted in Asher and Naulls 1987, 27) notes, much more was at stake than just land:

> The rivalry that developed between the races was more than a naked contest for land, important though it was. It was also a contest for authority, for *mana* (influence or power), for authority over the land and the men and women that it sustained. Above all, there was the question of whose authority, whose law was to prevail.

As British settlements expanded through a constant demand for more land, wars and disease led to the growing economic marginalization of

Maori. Anglo-Celtic ethnocentrism, backed by British law, allowed British settlers to confirm what they had believed all along: they were superior to all other peoples.

By the end of the nineteenth century, Maori numbered fewer than fifty thousand, a mere 5 percent of the colony's total population. Today Maori constitute approximately 15 percent of a total population of 4 million.

Religion as a Form of Resistance

The new economic order and technological transformation wrought by colonization were accompanied by political subjugation to a settler society that denigrated Maori beliefs as both heathen and fanciful myth. Maori responded defiantly with guerrilla warfare and various forms of more passive resistance, including withdrawal. Syncretic messianic movements became very popular; they appeared to be the only hope of redemption for their followers. These religions drew partly on the authenticity of Maori tradition and partly on the Old Testament. Maori leadership has always had a strong element of prophecy, and a dozen or more local messianic leaders arose during the nineteenth century to lead their followers from the bondage of mission teachings and settler subjugation to a "new heaven."[4]

By the mid-nineteenth century, Maori had largely abandoned their indigenous religious system in favor of Christianity, but by century-end many had turned to messianic versions of it.[5] Many in the Ngati Porou tribe followed a prophet named Te Kooti Arikirangi Turuki and the Hahi Ringatu (the church of the upraised hand) that he founded. Te Kooti was a profoundly religious man who was hounded, captured, exiled, and incarcerated by the colonial government because he opposed further British settlement.

The Ringatu church Te Kooti founded has no buildings of its own. It conducts its services in communal meetinghouses on *marae* (kin-based village communities), but unlike most other religions, its services

4. See, for example, Elsmore 1989.

5. Currently almost one quarter of all Maori belong to a messianic movement or church.

are conducted in the Maori language. Many congregations of the Hahi Ringatu thrive today, especially in eastern regions of the country. Ringatu congregations are linked together in a loose federation of adherents. One such group is located in the Ruatoria district that we will turn to shortly. They are seen by outsiders as the most "authentically Maori" religious faith practiced today. Prophecy is important to their beliefs.

In spite of extensive Maori assimilation into European society and culture and extensive intermarriage between Maori and pakeha, conflict between pakeha and Maori worldviews continues. Land loss and opposition to political domination and assimilationist policies all eroded the visibility and practice of Maori culture (Spoonley 1988, 8). In political and economic life, Maori remain on the margins of a largely Eurocentric society. On all the usual social and economic measures, Maori fare worst with low educational attainment, poor health, high unemployment, low incomes, and poor housing. During the structural adjustment programs of the 1980s, 40 percent of the Maori labor force became unemployed. Even a decade later, Maori unemployment rates are two to three times higher than the national rate, and despite income support through unemployment benefits, one in three Maori children lives in poverty.

As a result, many Maori teenagers and young adults join potentially violent gangs, especially the Black Power and Mongrel Mob gangs, which have groups or "chapters" in most parts of the country. In towns and cities and in prisons, gang members actively recruit younger "prospects." Gang behavior is generally antisocial or criminal and involves burglary, assault, and drug manufacture, consumption, and sale. Both the Mongrels and the Power have made their presence felt in Ruatoria. During the 1980s, when the Ruatoria Dreads had begun to consolidate their presence, Ruatoria and surrounding farmlands experienced a spate of property crimes, cattle theft, boundary-fence cutting, and arson of farm buildings. Almost all of this petty criminality was unjustifiably blamed on the Dreads.

Maori culture, already transformed irrevocably by Christianity and British colonization, is being transformed once again by a growing contemporary interest in Maori language and culture, especially among urban Maori youth. British and American popular music and culture, especially from the Black Diaspora in America and Jamaica, have also been embraced as an additional way of symbolically emphasizing Maori identity as "Blackness" in opposition to mainstream pakeha and hegemonic New Zealand culture with its White, Anglo-Celtic, and Anglo-American symbolism.

In that changing cultural context, Bob Marley projected Rastafari deep into the heart of Maori youth; his message appealed especially to those active in the *tino rangatiratanga* (sovereignty) movement. The viewpoints of those involved in Maori protest movements of the late seventies matched the themes contained in Rastafarian religious philosophies and the Maori religio-protest millenarian movements of the previous two centuries (Levine and Henare 1994, 196). In fact, the Ruatoria Rastas consider Robert Nesta Marley as a twentieth-century inheritor of the prophets' role, the prophet of Jah Rastafari.

Marley visited Aotearoa in 1979, at a time when Maori political activism was reawakening. His very presence had an immense impact, especially on Maori and Polynesian youth. Reggae music expressed their discontent as indigenous people and their experience of colonial domination. The expressions of protest, despair, and rebellion in Marley's lyrics were seen as a voice of the philosophy of Rastafarian religion.

The Ruatoria Dreads refer to Bob Marley as the prophet Brother Bob, but the rest of New Zealand society perceived Rastafari beliefs and practices as foreign, heretical, and unacceptable. Rastas conjured up negative images centered on their exotic outward appearance of dreadlocked hair and beards and their involvement in marijuana growing and smoking as well as other outlawed and iconoclastic activities. Yet to the young, especially young Maori, they conjured up a different image: still exotic, but dynamic, defiant of the established system, part of the broader world of oppressed colored peoples, with a sophisticated, popular, and vital new musical form that had lyrics explicitly rejecting the dominant White society and culture (Turner 1991, 7). Dread beliefs remain deeply grounded in protest against the injustices of European colonization; the Rastafari interpretation of the Bible as a prophetic text of emancipation continues the practice of resistant Maori prophetic movements of the previous centuries, such as the Hahi Ringatu and Hahi Ratana.

In sum, Rastafari was initially carried to Aotearoa in the music of Bob Marley. It then developed against the larger background of Anglo-Celtic colonization, displacement and marginalization of Maori, rapid social change, religious resistance to oppression, and the revitalization of Maori culture and politics starting in the 1970s. We turn now to a closer portrait of the Ruatoria Dreads.

Ruatoria: Its Location, Its People, Its Rastas

Ruatoria is an isolated market town in the Waiapu Valley. It is the most easterly town in New Zealand and lies just west of the International Dateline. With a population of little more than one thousand, Ruatoria services surrounding pastoral farms, *kainga* (nucleated tribal settlements), and smaller villages, the closest of which is twenty kilometers away. There are a mere five thousand people in the East Coast region, of whom about 80 percent are Maori. The local *iwi* (tribe), Ngati Porou, call their tribal lands Tai Rawhiti (the coast of the rising sun). Their sacred mountain, Mount Hikurangi (the tail of heaven), stands majestic and dominant in the landscape.

In the 1980s the Rastafari of Ruatoria came to national prominence after several civil disturbances, which included trespass and boundary fence cutting; arson of farm buildings, houses, and community buildings; and the slaying of two of their number. Although relatively small in number and in an isolated rural area, the Dreads[6] of Ruatoria are as a result of these crimes the most nationally recognized group of Rastafari in the land. In order to understand the context of the Ruatoria Dreads, it is first necessary to understand the Ngati Porou, the tribe of most Ruatoria Dreads.

Ngati Porou

Ngati Porou is one of the largest of the fifty or so tribes of Aotearoa. Its 60,000 members trace their descent through more than twenty generations from an illustrious and venerated eponymous ancestor Porourangi. Their traditional tribal boundaries encompass the East Coast region. Nowadays, fewer than one in five Ngati Porou live within its traditional tribal

6. Their preferred name for themselves.

boundaries. Estimates of the number of Rastafari in the Ngati Porou range widely from a hard core of thirty or forty to well in excess of five hundred. Our own estimates are closer to one hundred.

In estimating several hundred adherents, Ras Francis includes Ngati Porou living throughout Aotearoa, but maintaining ties with family in the tribal territory:[7]

> Ruatoria is the Rastafari capital in Ngati Porou, and probably Ngati Porou would have the most Rastafarians than any other tribe in the country. Well, you find that young Ngati Porou people living elsewhere identify with what is happening back here even though they are living in Auckland, they are dreading it up in Auckland; in the South Island the same. They are identifying with their *whanaunga* [tribal kin] back at home here. A lot of them had to go through tribulation too though; they were persecuted as those other young fellas.

Ras Francis's comments are an important reminder of the breadth of Rastafari networks in Aotearoa.

Social Tensions in Ruatoria

Until the arrival of missionaries and settlers in the first half of the nineteenth century, Ngati Porou lived a relatively autonomous, subsistence existence based on coastal and riverine fishing, foraging in the temperate rain forests, and practicing horticulture based primarily on the *kumara* (sweet potato).

As with other *iwi,* contact with the British brought a transformation to their lifestyle through the introduction of new technology. But there was a price to pay: settlement, first on the margins of Ngati Porou's lands, and then among them, led to the conversion of their communal land titles to individual Crown title, the clearing of their forest lands for pastoral farming, and alienation of more than half their tribal estate (much of it by missionary families). One hundred fifty years of European settlement and influence has led to continuous and intense competition for their land.

7. All respondents have been given fictitious names.

By the mid-twentieth century, Ngati Porou had fast outgrown their dwindling natural resource base. There were few work opportunities locally, and encouraged by government policies, many Ngati Porou left their homeland for distant towns and cities to trade their seasonal and largely subsistence lifestyle for permanent wage labor. Today, three-quarters of Ngati Porou live outside their traditional tribal boundaries, contributing to the country's unskilled and semi-skilled urban workforce. In the cities, Ngati Porou live alongside Maori from other Maori tribes and the more numerous, dominant pakeha. Changes to their lifestyles have been as profound as they have been rapid, not just to the migrants but also to the *iwi kainga* (the home people).

Many migrants have since returned. They came back because they preferred country to city life or could not afford to live in town. Others raised in cities came back to reclaim their sense of Ngati Porou identity. Most migrants and their families return for major social events, especially *tangihanga* (funerals), weddings, and reunions. Others have come back to Ruatoria to take over a family farm or business. Most return as often as they can just to "recharge their batteries," which gives them the reserves of cultural strength that permit them to survive and flourish in distant and essentially foreign environments.

The East Coast region is still their ancestral and spiritual home. Here their ancestors lived, loved, fought, died, and are buried. In their ancestral lands, every river, every mountain, every other geographical feature and locality carries a tribal name of historical and enduring significance. These lands, as much as the genealogies and relationships of the speakers and listeners, are referred to unfailingly in ritual speech making. Nonetheless, the people at home are fearful that such a large exodus during the latter part of the twentieth century will mean that many of these oral records will be lost to future generations. Preservation of Maori identity plays a critical role in Ruatoria Rastafari.

Rasta and Maori Identity

Although there is a strong sense of historical continuity in Ruatoria and the East Coast, quite profound changes have occurred. The Maori language, only a generation ago the preferred language of communication in the region, has been replaced by English. Bilingualism has retreated in the face of increasing English monolingualism among younger adults and children and, consequently, as the language of communication between elders and their descendants. About 70 percent of Ngati Porou earned income is supplemented by dependency on the state through unemployment or sickness benefits or other welfare payments.

The tribe is still predominantly (but increasingly nominally) Christian. Anglicanism is the tribe's most popular religious affiliation, although other congregations there include Catholics, Brethren, Assembly of God, Mormons, Baptists, and Baha'i, in addition to two Maori messianic churches, the Hahi Ratana and Hahi Ringatu.

When the lantern of Rastafari first shed its light on Ngati Porou two decades ago, it was sustained by younger people, mainly in their twenties and thirties, and continues to glow. These young people were figuratively wandering in the wilderness without firm roots in the culture of their ancestors and marginalized by a mutual rejection of the pakeha majority and its culture. Though some have questioned how Rastafari identity and Maori identity can fit together, Dreads have no trouble distinguishing Maori identity from a Rastafari way of life. An incident related by Ras Daniel makes this point:

> This fellah said to the Dread, "How can you be a Rasta and be a Maori?" And the Dread said to him, "Same as you can be a taxi driver and be a Maori." It's a way of life, eh?

Ras Caleb takes the point even further, noting that Rastafari are proud of their Maori heritage but not limited by it.

> We are a living force of God's people; a new generation of Maori descent. You know, we are proud of our Maori descent; we know that the *reo* [language] is not number one, God is.

The reasons these youth give for becoming Rastafari vary, but generally include references to musical influences, questions of identity, reading about Haile Selassie, and spontaneous realizations.

Becoming a Rasta

REGGAE. The Rastafari both in Ruatoria and elsewhere in Aotearoa acknowledge the influence of Bob Marley's music and other reggae singers in bringing them to their faith and helping them to maintain and reinforce it. They refer to reggae music as messages of the third world brought to them through the music of Brother Bob, Brother Tosh, and other reggae artists.

To Sister Rachel, for example, music is an arm that can reach right across the world. As she puts it,

> Even though you're here you can send your message across the world with music. They have managed to convey to us a clear message, that we don't forget who we are, that we have got no need to try and be anybody else but ourselves.

As Ras Benjamin explained, the message conveyed by reggae is especially edifying when it is combined with reasoning and biblical interpretations of what they considered appropriate social behavior.

> Through the music, it opened my eyes to the real truth, eh? When I read Isaiah that made me look, the things that he [Isaiah] was talking about happened over there at that time is the same thing that was happening here in our time. They go and get drunk all day. Man sleeping with man, all this sort of carry on. Women were falling. Man giving up their families just for lust of the flesh, you know to go with another woman who'd left her family to be with this man—adultery and fornication. It is bad in Ruatoria, is one of the worst places in New Zealand for it, but through me being Rasta it's avoided me from all that sort of a thing. Drinking, I don't drink now, although I've only just given up cigarettes and that.

Ras Francis, raised on the East Coast, had gone to find work in Auckland, New Zealand's largest city. By the time he returned to the family farm near Ruatoria in 1977 or 1978, he already identified as a Rasta and believed that Ras Tafari (Haile Selassie) was the second coming of Jesus Christ. He said that he read about Rastafari all on his own and was not in contact with any other Rastafarians. For Ras Francis, Bob Marley brought the message:

> The message of Rastafari came through the music of Bob Marley. I think music was the first thing, and secondly was the message that was coming through. It wasn't really all about Rastafari at that, but there was running down the system and talking about how the Whites were oppressing; the experience that the Blacks were having with their White oppressors and how they were expounding "hold on to your culture," "don't be afraid of the wolf pack," and all those sort of things.

Francis also spoke of his experience with Bob Marley in person when he attended Marley's concert in Auckland in 1979: "Bob Marley's concert was really moving. It was like a spiritual experience, like going to see an evangelist, that's what it felt like for me."

IDENTITY. Although Ras Caleb also noted the importance of music in his becoming a Rasta, it was also clear that questions of identity underlie the decision. Ras Caleb had been associated with Rastafari from age thirteen, more than twenty years ago. His connection was primarily through Marley's music, and secondly through rejection of the Eurocentric presentation of Christianity and embracing a marginal identity (along with other Maori youth) of being "a sufferer," as mentioned in Marley's lyrics. In his early twenties he accepted the philosophy of Haile Selassie as the Messiah who "would come to us in our time."

> At first just listening through the music when I was a teenager, it was just the appeal, [to] my inner well-being, eh? Everything about Rasta was what I believed. I do not believe that Jesus Christ was a pakeha with blond hair and blue eyes. If you read the Bible properly you'll know that God's chosen people were the Black from the beginning and he would come to us in our time as a Black man. He is the Christ, the true Christ. I never believe anything the pakeha said because they say one thing and then mean another.
>
> Our people are not free, you know since [pakeha] been here our people have been oppressed; you know, like the teachings of our God, our respect towards spiritual things our ancestors knew. Our people have the

> spiritual *mana* [authority]. pakeha came here to bring us the teaching of their God, of Jesus Christ, who was to come to us in our time. I was supposed to be a so-called Christian when I was young, you know, to believe in the pakeha Jesus and all this is, but everything is White, eh?

Ras Daniel talked about his reasonings on the meaning and relevance of Marley and his music to their own lives.

> Brother Bob and Brother Tosh, and all of them in their beginnings, they're saying genuine, they're wailing with the chants eh? that's the feelings of the people. When we had a listen to your Brother Bob, and we sat down and we focused ourselves on our own people we can see where the Bro. was coming from. Like the system trying to overpower the people themselves eh, but the people were getting too far gone, becoming too dependent on the system, and became part of it. Whereas, we just stepped back and sort of jumped out of the system.

READING ABOUT HAILE SELASSIE. Another Dread, Ras Arama, was in prison when his girlfriend gave him a book about Haile Selassie. On his release he left it with another brother who had been in a gang. He too is a Rasta now.

> I think she just got the book 'cause she knew I was right into reggae, just the reggae music. I just loved it eh? And when she got this book, the book told me that there is a Christ and he is Black and if you feel it you will know it. Who knows it will feel it eh? If you believe in him, then he will tell you. I like the music and I like what the message was. I didn't know really what the reasons was saying about the Christ had been revealed. You know I didn't really see that side of the reasons, not until I was given the book and it had to do with Haile Selassie I of Ethiopia. He had been crowned okay, the world had seen it, it was on record.

Similarly to others, Ras Arama's story also involves a rejection of paheka religion:

> I have been through church and God wasn't there; I didn't feel him eh? But it was through Rastafari—he had everything, he had the freedom I

> wanted, he gave me a sign that I knew. I believe the power of God had to be, and it was Selassie I that got me through that.

SPONTANEITY. Ras Benjamin, aged twenty-seven, said that he had grown up a Rastafari. He believed that Jah came and revealed himself to his Maori ancestors and influenced them to such an extent that Rasta had always been there within him.

> Well Rasta has always been there, never, never left me. It's always been there inside me, inside everyone. I realized this when I was young, well from my learning when I had been an adolescent. Well I've been with Rastas, you don't join it, it joins you eh. From fourteen, He enlightened my life; I was an adolescent, a mischievous little snotty-nosed fella.

Another Ruatoria Dread, Ras Gideon, lived in a converted shearing shed about twelve kilometers from Ruatoria. The interior walls of his home were wooden and on them he had written more than forty Biblical texts with a felt pen. He showed us around his home, reading aloud many of the texts as we moved from room to room. We asked him, "You were a member of the Nyahbinghi, you were one of the first, how did that come about?" His response shows a more spontaneous conversion:

> Shucks, I don't know Bro. It was just like we've been Rastas all our lives, myself was more Rasta than half of those brothers over in Jamaica and overseas. It sort of like we take it to heart. . . . I used to be in the Blacks [the Black Power gang] before I became a Rasta. But this one day there, I just threw my patch down and woke up the next morning and I was praising the Lord. The Scriptures and revelations spoke of the uprising and anointing of one that they called the Lion of Judah.

At the same time, Ras Gideon stated that Ras Tafari was a spirit within him that had existed from earliest times. He said that Ras Tafari was not just with him, but within all Maori, because part of their nature and the values that Jah espoused were values that were part of Maori culture. The difference between himself as a Rasta and others was that the spirit of

Jah Rastafari had been awakened within him, whereas it still lay dormant within others, or they were led astray by other churches.

> The people are getting all upset with the system, eh? They are seeking something different; that difference that they're seeking was always there. In the beginning it was the unity, the understanding of being a person. We have always been Rastafarians, eh? Their beliefs have always been a part of our culture. As a people you change, some of them were here and deceived into their change by the denominations that they call church groups.

Dread Beliefs and Practices

The beliefs and practices of Ruatoria Dreads are based on three streams of consciousness used to explain the realities of their lives: the rhetoric of Maori self-determination, the Hahi Ringatu messianic religion, and traditional Rastafari symbols and practices. Chris Campbell introduced this combination of ideas to Ruatoria; he had learned of and adopted them while in prison. Back in Ruatoria, Campbell practiced as a Rasta and other locals followed his example, forming the collective group that calls itself the Dread. Campbell was also a staunch defender of *tikanga Maori* (Maori culture) and a land rights activist. He often questioned the legitimacy of the Treaty of Waitangi (which formalized British settlement) and local land ownership titles (McLeod 1988, 71). Campbell saw the separation of Maori from their land as oppression and subjugation, against which Rastafarian philosophies were opposed. The dispossession of indigenous people from their land heightened the dislocation of their identity as *tangata whenua* (people of the land). As people of the land, Maori physical and spiritual identities were inextricably linked to it. Thus, most Ruatoria Dreads are deeply dedicated to a spirit of self-determination and independence.

The Dread's philosophy of self-determination leads them to be true *tangata whenua*—people who live off and with the land, who live their *tino rangatiratanga* (sovereignty). As Ras Daniel puts it:

> People have got to learn and understand to break that dependency which they have on the system and to become independent. And the only way to

> do so is to occupy the land instead of giving it to sheep and cows. *He aha te mea nui? He tangata, he tangata, he tangata.* [What is the greatest thing in the world, it's people, it's people, it's people.] Because people have had their *mana* [authority] taken, that they can't provide the simplest things necessary of life for their families, which is food, clothing, and shelter.
>
> Now the system is structured so that it hinders everyone's chances, especially Maori people, and the other indigenous peoples of the world from standing up. You know people have got to learn to live with one another, that is our only hope as a people. It's *kotahitanga* [unity] eh? but you know, not unto no individual plan, but unto the divine plan eh? In order to have *kotahitanga* everyone must partake, you can't have people sitting on the fence eh? And by doing so it gives each individual a chance to clear the *mamae* [pain] they have on themselves, with their neighbors, with themselves and what they create. We are all allowed a time in the darkness then comes the time of the light, so that in order to understand bad, you've got to once tasted good.

Some Ruatoria groups have taken concrete steps in being self-reliant. The Ahi-ites, a subgroup of the Ruatoria Dreads, have formed a charitable trust with the help of relatives, friends, and some government officials. Members of this Kirikiritatangi Trust (which takes its name from an ancient martial arts training ground nearby) grow corn, beans, potatoes, and other foods for home consumption, to give away to older people, and to supplement their incomes. Members also conduct skills training courses for younger affiliates and regular health and well-being classes for them. Recently they have been able to run two-day field projects on rammed earth and adobe and earth-brick construction, which drew over a hundred participants from much further afield than the East Coast region, half of whom were not Rastas.

The Dreads' spiritual beliefs are firmly based on Maori tradition, Te Kooti's Old Testament teachings, and the teachings of Garvey and Marley, which they liberally quote to illustrate and justify actions. But there is also a sense that these ideas have to be interpreted by individual reasonings. As Ras Arama explains:

> You live your life according to how you feel it's right to yourself. I've been through gangs and gang warfare, fighting for something that's on the

> back, the [gang] patch. I see man getting killed for that. That's living a life of vanity. "Judge not least ye be judged, cursed is a man that kills another man. Let him repent" because Jah never put us on earth so you could go round killing each other over a little bit of colly [marijuana] or something like that. He got killed, because he was dipping, taking the colly, giving it to someone else. These other fellas, that was their profits eh? They were looking at the dollar sign instead of the peaceful side of the herb.

Ras Gideon reiterates this point:

> Being into Rasta I'm not saying I'm perfect, no one's perfect, we can do our best 'cause we're not here to live up to what another man can say. The only one who can tell us is that one inside us and that's the spirit of holiness that's in us, that God has given us to guide us in this time. Until He comes and brings on that destruction of all wickedness which is about to commence. I mean He can wipe me away—man, that's it, hellfire for me too. We don't know if we're going into His place [after death]. We can only hope that what we're doing as mere humans is right in His eyes.

Ras Francis believed that Ruatoria and the Ngati Porou were awakening to something new, to a change that would challenge the old belief systems, and he likened that to the period when Christianity was introduced.

> When Christianity was first introduced here the people went through the same thing. Well, Ngati Porou as a people when religion [Christianity] first came here, it wasn't accepted readily, and any other reform of any kind. Ngati Porou have sort of been cautious in letting that sort of *wairua* [spiritualism] in. I suppose a lot of it is a lack of knowledge. If it wasn't told to them by their mothers and fathers, then who are they to listen to others from outside?

The Dreads' regular gatherings display a mix of Maori and Rasta protocols and objectives, combining eating together with low-key demonstrations of what are considered to be appropriate domestic and community behaviors. The structure of the Dreads' meetings reflect normal Maori gatherings. They start with *mihimihi* (speeches of greeting) acknowledging all present; they include singing both *waiata* (Maori sung poetry) and reggae songs and are followed by reasonings about a range of topics from Biblical texts to issues of the day. Unlike some other Rastafari groups, here both men and women are encouraged to speak out on topics ranging from revolution to gardening to childcare and to sing praises to the god they call Jah, and to the Emperor Haile Selassie I, whom they call Ras Tafari.

In the opening speech at a Sabbath meeting of the Dread, where about thirty people from the Dread community had gathered to eat and reason together, Ras Gideon followed the normal protocols of Maori meetings by opening with *mihimihi*:

> At the time of thanksgiving, being together eh, under the banner of the most high, *Kia ora* [greetings]. It's good to see the I'n'I; good to see the *whanau* [extended family]. Good to see the Jah still dreading with I'n'I guarding I'n'I in our words, giving us the encouragement to praise His holy name, to witness the words that are going around and around about us, to see the *kotahitanga* [unity] coming back into the movement that I'n'I can dread on.

Because young children were present, the Dread did not smoke ganja until the food had been consumed and the reasoning session had begun. By then the children were outside playing.

In recalling one issue discussed at a recent Sabbath meeting, Sister Rachel spoke about the need for the Dread to help each other to live better lives. She spoke about the relative deprivation of some of the group and their deprived upbringings, lack of appropriate role models, and inappropriate family relationships.

> You know, whether great or small, we all have a part to play. For some of the Dreads, they don't know the family life. So for the children and the women there, we can offer them, teach them, what it's like to have children, to care for the children, for the women to be treated properly by the men and likewise for the men to be respected by their women. You know it's all part of the learning for us to live together, because some of the Dreads they come straight out of prison and they don't know what it's like to have a family life to have people that care for them.

Ras Daniel spoke about not confusing the message with the messenger. He said that all too often the Dread are judged by their outward appearances, so what they have to say is dismissed by others in the town. He likened that to a lantern and its light:

> It is not the lantern that is important, it is the light it makes eh? Just as [it's] not so much what title is on the door, that's really not important. What is important is what's being said. The message is the same. There are two ways a problem can be dealt with—peace and war. Only one of them works. Now if you exhaust all your passive resistance eh, well, what is left? The tools we pick up today eh, they are not weapons of violence but instruments of freedom eh, and the difference is we don't use them to enslave eh, but to fight for our freedom eh? The philosophy which holds one race superior and another inferior has finally and permanently been discredited eh? What I'm talking, these things eh, we yearn for peace we do, but we can't countenance the injustice eh?

To the Ruatoria Dread, the Rastafari symbol of Babylon represents the presence of evil in many forms and the supporters of that evil. For example, prisons and the recently built $750,000 courthouse in Ruatoria were referred to as Babylon intruding into their homeland. Most of the Dreads have been in prison, where they used their time to read about Marley, Garvey, Jah, Haile Selassie, and Rastafari and to debate their ideas and feelings in reasoning sessions with other believers. As Ras Francis explains, prison lends itself to reasoning:

> In prison you meet a lot of people who don't recognize any authority of any kind. And you know, religion is not one of their favorite subjects let alone talk about God. It's an easy place to talk about oppression when you're in prison eh? There's not much else to talk about; the misery and being in bondage when you're locked up in prison and you feel it. That's just the way it is.

Several examples of Rastafari practice and symbolism in Ruatoria show how syncretic the approach of adherents is and how the apparently foreign doctrine of Rastafari has been adapted to fit the prevailing circumstances of young men and women of Ngati Porou. Along with Ras Daniel we liken these examples to beams of Jah's light from the lantern of Ngati Porou culture that shine out into the surrounding darkness. These beams are cannabis, facial tattoo, and repatriation to Africa.

Rastafari Practices and Symbols

CANNABIS. When reasoning, the Dreads smoke marijuana (generally they use the Jamaican name "ganja"). Reasoning sessions usually involve reading and discussing Biblical texts to understand their meaning and intent. Many texts are committed to memory and liberally quoted.

In explaining the role that cannabis plays in Dreads' lives, Ras Arama argued that using cannabis helped him to deal with the reality of their daily existence, to deal with external as well as internal social interactions, and to deal with the sense of oppression, hopelessness, and continued exploitation of Ngati Porou by pakeha.

> When you smoke the herb you make peace with yourself as well as creation and others around you. I smoke every day. It does not get in the way of reality, I know what reality is, it's oppression. It's oppression—we have read it in the Bible; Rastafari is freedom from the world as it is. We don't just say nah, nah, it's cool man, you know, you grown dreadlocks and smoke a bit of marijuana and call yourself a Rasta man. No, no there's more to it than that. Rasta is God.

Sister Rachel confirms his reasoning:

> We know for a fact that amongst ourselves and others that when you use the herb it brings us to a point of reason; where we are not yelling and screaming and we are not fighting; where we can sit down and we can talk. That's how we use it, for that feeling. That's the healing of the nations. Because it is used worldwide you can go right around the world and everywhere you go they use it.

Ras Arama tries to live by Biblical law and justifies the use of marijuana because in his interpretation of God's law, marijuana use is not sinful.

Although it might be against man's law, that law is not reputable because it permits other activities specifically declared sinful in the Bible.

> I don't see harm in cultivating a bit of marijuana in my backyard, it's not a sin against God. It's only a sin against the law of man that we are supposed to live our lives with, abide by. [That] is the same law that legalises homosexuality—an abomination to our God. To them, they say, "Oh it's all right to go and jag that other guy down the road, because when we pass it through legislation we free it." The law is doing things like that, setting people in different classes, first class, second class, third class.

But marijuana also represents independence and sovereignty to the Ruatoria Dreads, who feel they have the right to grow what they want on their land. Generally the Dreads are good providers for their families. Unlike some other Rastafari, they are not strict vegetarians, so besides growing marijuana and vegetables for home consumption, they continue to survive by selling excess marijuana and employing the subsistence activities of their ancestors: fishing several times a week, hunting feral pigs and deer in the nearby mountains, and cultivating their cooperative food gardens.

Although they strive for independence, many Dreads receive government subsidies. Some feel that the dole they receive is part reparation for the extensive land alienations that Ngati Porou have suffered. All of them find justification for their iconoclastic and apparently antisocietal actions either from the Bible, from the teachings of Te Kooti, or from a sense of unjust deprivation by pakeha government policies both past and present.

> And we tell them no, we've got every right to be on the dole because we're being oppressed in our own land. We're not free to do what we believe to be right. Like the land is ours, we want to cultivate a bit of colly-herb. We want to put the *kumara* [sweet potato] in, well put the *kumara* in, plant the *kamokamo* [type of squash] whatever, so we can live without having to rely on the system all the time. Because if we don't, they are going to lock us away somewhere.

MOKO (FACIAL TATTOO). In pre-Christian times, adult Maori males were tattooed as a sign of their status. Because the tattoos were begun in early adulthood they were also seen as a rite of passage into adult roles. *Moko* were intricate lines and swirls that identified the wearer's ancestral lineage and also their achievements or those of their ancestors.

Christian missionaries successfully stopped the practice of tattooing of all but the highest-ranking males before the end of the nineteenth century, and of women by about 1940. Only a handful of women who took the traditional *moko* survive today; all are well past eighty years of age and are greatly revered. But in the past two decades a small but growing number of women have taken the *moko* each year. *Moko* among men has taken a little longer to revive, but increasing numbers of young men, especially gang members and Rastafari, have had their faces tattooed in the past decade.

Facial *moko* is the hallmark of the Ruatoria Dread. Most men and women have *moko* after the style of their ancestors (women with their lips and chin tattooed and men with full-face tattoos). Besides the traditional style *moko,* the Rastamen have engraved on their foreheads one of the many names of God; whether that be Jah, Rastafari, Lion of Judah, or names in Maori such as Io (the supreme), Te Kupu (the word), Te Timatanga (the beginning), Aroha (love), and Te Ahi o Te Atua (God's fire).

The facial tattoo serves at least three important purposes for the bearers. It identifies them as Rastafari, as Jah's chosen people. According to the Bible (Rev 7:3) those with his seal on their foreheads will be saved from destruction and will survive the cleansing. It also reinforces their tribal/kinship links as Maori, as one of the first people (both in terms of being indigenous and in being from the original Garden of Eden). To Eurocentric New Zealand society it identifies them as someone unwilling to submit to the assimilation pressures of Babylon. Thus, *moko* is another item in a one-hundred-sixty-year catalogue of resistance.

Ras Arama saw reason in the Bible to have Jah and Io tattooed on his forehead, but neither of his parents were pleased when he had his face tattooed. His mother was very upset and his father said that he would go mad for breaking the sacred rules surrounding traditional *moko.* As time has passed and they have seen how Arama lives, he feels that they now understand his viewpoint.

> My *wairua* [spirit] led me to getting my face tattooed years before any other Dread was tattooed. It was just I had read it in the Book. I never ever regretted getting God's name tattooed on my forehead. How could I? How can I deny it? I believe that no man can express this sort of love of God unless he was of the same belief as me. No, when he's ready, his *wairua* will lead him on that path because it's a big step—to do what we done. When I dedicated my body to God as his true church, my mother was very offended. I told her because I love God and because I'm Maori. She hit the roof, she couldn't dig it. Then my old man said I was going to go *porangi* [mad]. Because what I had done was *tapu* [taboo], I should have done it the old way, like our ancestors. But I said I did not do it for them, or for the old way, but for Haile Selassie I, God. Because I done it for him, he was going to protect me against any spiritual wickedness that could come to me, and he has. That was nearly ten years ago. They're coming to realize the truth; that I've prospered. I used to be a drunken little gang member, compared to what I am now; dreadlocks, non-smoker, non-drinker and smoke the herb and stay home and be with my family.

Ras Caleb reiterates the point and emphasizes that the *moko* shows other people what is in your heart:

> Yeah, yeah, He knows you got it in your heart, but how do you show that to another man? You put it on your head, eh? Put it on your head so that man can see you know who you are. You can see who I am. I've put him right across myself. People here have accepted it now because we are part of all the families here. All of us belong to big families. Well it affects a lot of the families.

Ras Francis does not have a face *moko*. His response to the obvious question was:

> I don't need to have a *moko*. As far as I am concerned, well it's already tattooed on the inside, here on the heart. I know what I believe and I don't need to write a little note to myself. I am basically comfortable with the way I am, I have never had to find any other way of affirming my being Maori. I don't see it [*moko*] as an identity crisis for them. It's an

> opportunity for them to take something that's theirs, belongs to their ancestors, and is something tangible that they can have for the rest of their life.

Non-Rastas in Ngati Porou are ambivalent about Rastafari *moko*. On the one hand *moko* are admired because they are an undeniable and irreversible statement of being Maori. On the other hand, in traditional times only persons of high rank would have *moko,* as a decision of the tribal collective. Rastamen are considered unsuitable candidates. Some people in Ruatoria had hoped that once tattooed, Dreads would be less Rastafarian than before. Ras Francis, who is in his forties, expressed the generally held Rastafari view that the face tattoo makes the brethren even more committed to Rastafari, but likewise even more committed to their Maoritanga. Ras Arama had a similar perspective.

> You know, when you write Ras Tafari on your forehead, it's there for life. What the *moko* does is emphasize that we can still be Maori, without losing our identity and belief in being Maori. We didn't have to go through any identity changes to be Rastafari, in fact what Rastafari did was to reinforce the Maori identity and take it to another level. You know that's a commitment for life.

REPATRIATION. Two traditional Rastafari ideas that the Dreads rethink are Repatriation and the Garden of Eden. Maori have traditionally traced their origins to Hawaiki, their original tropical homeland; after death they will return there. As it is, this is a belief that has been modified by Christianity but still remains intact in twenty-first-century Maori society. In funeral orations the spirit of the deceased is enjoined to travel to the most northerly point in New Zealand, to Te Rerenga Wairua (the jumping-off place of spirits) from there to journey on to ancestral Hawaiki. At reasonings, Mount Zion and the Promised Land are localized. Ruatoria's Dreads accept that Mount Hikurangi, their sacred mountain, is also their Mount Zion.

For all of Ngati Porou, Mount Hikurangi is symbolic of their tribe, its land, people, and prestige, even though much of their land has been alienated. Dread reasonings about the Bible tell them that Jah will wrest it back from Babylon and return it to them. Their land was taken unjustly, so Jah will return it; they await Jah's intervention. Ras Arama explains: "The Father has to come and return to us what was ours in the beginning, it will be also ours in the end. This land here is a Holy Land, this land was here from all time." Also according to Dread reasoning, the first man came from Mount Hikurangi, the place where God said "Let there be light." "That's where he stood, on Mount Hikurangi when the world was one. The East of Eden, the Garden, this is it."

Mount Hikurangi is the first place in Aotearoa to see the light of each day. Once the International Dateline was established, technically it became the first place in the world to see each day. As incorporated into Rasta belief, Mount Hikurangi is the original Mount Zion. This belief is justified by Ruatoria's Dreads through their interpretation of Biblical verses from Genesis where God separated the waters under heaven into one place and dry land emerged (Gen. 1:9). Then God created the lights of the firmament to divide the day from the night and to create signs, seasons, and years. These are the sun, moon, and stars (Gen. 1:14–18). The Ruatoria Dreads, who quite explicitly identify as practicing Rastafari, do not view Africa as their Promised Land; when Jah comes they will be restored to their own lands, not repatriated to Africa. As they are already in their Promised Land, repatriation will be its return from the pakeha. Mount Hikurangi, their sacred mountain, is their Mount Zion and Jah's coming will demonstrate that to all the world. Unlike Rastafari elsewhere, the Dread of Ngati Porou do not expect to be repatriated to Ethiopia or anywhere else. Ras Arama rejected Africa as their ultimate destination.

> People say Africa. Africa no, Haile Selassie yeah he will come from there, but the East is where he comes from the last time. He's widening his spirit and all his angels come in behind him. Any time zone, whatever you want to call it. I believe that God's bringing every nation here. All nations will be gathering on the mountain to see his light eh, just like that, one day. They want to see his light hit here first; but that light might be too bright for them eh? They'll be looking to see the light, and next minute that light was Jah. The brightest light in there, that's Him, that's Him there, the

> brightest light. In one second man, the world done, their wickedness gone, cleansing. We'll be all clean.

It is also clear to the Ruatoria Dreads that when Jah comes the third time, only a small number of his people will be chosen to abide with him. Their interpretation of the Scriptures make it clear that only 144,000 will be saved, and they will be those who bear God's seal (his name) on their foreheads. If there is to be any return, it will be to whence each tribe originated. But there is a duality in their beliefs. Some expect that they will go to Te Rerenga Wairua and back to Hawaiki pamamao (far distant), but others expect that when Jah comes again, they are already well placed because they will be free from the bondage of the pakeha. Jah will return them to the original Garden of Eden in Waiapu Valley, their "Land of Milk and Honey."

For the Dreads of Ruatoria, repatriation meant freedom from colonial bondage (the Babylon that Garvey wrote about and Marley sang about). Pakeha would be swept away from their consciousness and they would be joyful with their bounteous Garden of Eden returned to them. As Ras Caleb explains:

> Well in the Psalms it says "Ethiopia shall stretch forth her hands" because God will reveal Himself. Selassie come from Ethiopia—it's in the Bible. You can't refuse what was said in the Scriptures. But it doesn't say in the last days where he will come from in wrath. It just says he'll come from the east. Matthew 24 says that the light come from the east to the west, the coming of the son of man.

When elaborating on the location of the Promised Land and its meaning to different peoples, Ras Holah said:

> The Promised Land will be the New Jerusalem, New Heaven when the cleansing has taken place. It is here; it has to be right here because Jah first brought his light here on the first day. Only God knows where his Promised Land is, man is only just sort of saying. The Jamaican, the Rastaman in Jamaica 'cause they descended from Africa, naturally they will see Africa is their Promised Land. The Aboriginals from Aussie they'd say Australia is the Promised Land, their homeland eh? The Apaches and the

> brothers over in America they would say that there was their Promised Land. But when you check it out, I have only just come to understand this, I always thought because I believed in Rastafari, it was Jamaica. But when you get to read [the Bible], deep within there's something that will tell you something different, yeah the East. Well, no place is furthest east, this is as far as you can go and this is it.

Community and Outside Relations

Some Ruatoria Dread were openly scornful of the Twelve Tribes, who speak of their repatriation to Africa. As Ras Daniel put it,

> The Twelve Tribes are international; they are a different faction of Rastafari, they have got their own agenda as to what they believe is right. They believe Africa is their repatriation, where they are going, back to Africa. But you see out of Africa came the Garden of Eden; you can't tell me this is not the Garden of Eden, that this is not the furtherest east.

The Ruatoria Dreads differ from the Twelve Tribes significantly, and though there has been contact between the two groups, it has not been positive. Exploring links with the Twelve Tribes in Auckland, both Ras Francis and Ras Daniel talked of negative encounters, especially due to what they took to be the cultural presuppositions of the Twelve Tribes. As Ras Francis said:

> Some of them came to stay with me when I was living in Wellington, but man they're false, you know, laying around, talking like a Jamaican, denouncing their Maoritanga [Maori culture] you know. Saying that they were establishing the house in the Rising Sun. But a whole lot of things we fell out about, when they came here, they came right through the *pa* at Hiruharama [a small village five kilometers from Ruatoria; its name translates as Jerusalem]. [I said] all your belief systems and you've got no time for *te pa o te Atua* [the village of God]. They are a hundred disillusioned people.

Ras Daniel suspected the Twelve Tribes were more interested in money than anything else.

> We haven't got the Twelve Tribes here [in Ruatoria]. They have their prophet Gad or something and they talk about repatriation to Ethiopia. Old Hensley [the founder of the Twelve Tribes in Aotearoa] was here, but he done the dirty on them. So the old dollars got to his mind.

Relations with non-Rasta groups have often been even worse. When the Dreads first began to receive the light of Jah's lantern, they were mocked, denigrated, resisted, and shunned. When buildings in the township and barns were burned down, community feelings against them ran high. Although Rastamen were almost certainly responsible for some of these acts, especially where they involved land alienated by outsiders (i.e., by Babylon), they were unfairly blamed for all criminal activity in the area. As Ras Daniel puts it:

> Well you go anywhere and when they ask you about "Oh where have you been? Oh Ruatoria?" And they'll tell you all about us and they haven't even met us. And it is all negative eh? They just pass it on; they are like parrots. They believe in lies.

Matters are made worse because some illegal activity is associated with people who adopt a Rasta style or who have different beliefs but call themselves Rastas.

All of the Dread in Ruatoria have experienced hostility, rejection, and doubt from their relatives and neighbors. But they accept the suffering that comes from outside as fulfillment of prophecy, even as they acknowledge that they are still misunderstood by the wider society. Ras Daniel explains:

> The Lord was saying we would be hated for it eh? [Hated] by everyone for doing these things. And I don't see any other church that has been hated as much as the Rastaman. All we ever wanted to do was be culture men eh? From right back then, but we had to go through all that trouble with the *whanau* [extended family]; now it took us ten years just for Babylon to leave us alone. They saw us as terrible fellas eh? But now when they look at what are we doing, in all that time we struggled against each other. To them, we're just niggers, we're just niggers in their game of life they play. We are just their little flunkies, they look on Rasta as being druggies and

> dopers and good for nothing eh? But Rasta is a way of life and it is not all dope. I am a Rastaman who lives day by day. I say I am a Rastaman because I believe that His Imperial Majesty is our way into the kingdom. He is the Son; he is the Father and the Son.

There is a strong belief in the community at large that the Ruatoria Dreads are only "playing" at being Rastas. That is to say, some members of the community believe that the Dreads' Rastafarian appearance is simply defiance or an excuse to smoke drugs. Like most other New Zealanders, the rest of Ngati Porou believe that smoking marijuana leads to the use of "hard drugs" and that all gangs, whether they are Black Power, Mongrel Mob, or Rastafari, are just a front for drug abuse and criminal behavior. As a result, the Dreads continue to exist on the periphery of their tribal community, both physically and spiritually, while still living among Babylon.

But not all community relations are bad. For example, the Kirikiritangi Trust's field projects have attracted a number of non-Rastas. Even more importantly, about ten weeks before we began to interview in Ruatoria, Ras Gideon and a band of his close followers began to attend the Tekau-ma-rua (twelfth of the month) service of one of the local congregations of the Hahi Ringatu.[8] Initially Ringatu adherents had thought that the Rastafari were attending because services were conducted in the Maori language, and this would give them an opportunity to improve their own fluency in Maori, a language that is becoming more and more the preserve of generations over fifty years old. Most of the Dreads in Ruatoria along with other young adults in the community are not fluent in Maori.

"That was OK," said the leader of the local Ringatu church, "perhaps through the language they will come to the Messiah's message." However, Ringatu adherents were pleasantly surprised that the language was not the Dreads' only interest, indeed not even their prime interest. Ras

8. On the twelfth of each month, congregations are "locked-in" for a twenty-four-hour service, the Tekau-ma-rua. During this time they participate in a patterned form of worship by taking turns at reciting and singing set prayers based on the Psalms, other Biblical verses, and songs written by the church's founder, Te Kooti. The delivery style is more akin to pre-Christian Maori *waiata* (sung poetry) than hymns.

Caleb explains that the Rastas saw a similarity between the Hahi Ringatu's founder, Te Kooti, and Rasta icons, like Marcus Garvey:

> You see when the soldiers chased Te Kooti [just] as they chased Garvey out of town eh, Marcus Garvey. Now the works of Te Kooti, the soldiers were sent to stop the man that ties the land together, to stop him, because he is tying the people together as one. Now that's what part the Ringatu church plays—the *whakakotahi te iwi* [uniting all the people]; and you ask the difference between Rastafari and these things? There is no difference.

Other Ringatu were also surprised at the Dreads' depth of study, knowledge, and understanding of the Bible, especially the Old Testament, and their willingness to share their "reasonings" with others of the Ringatu faith. This perception has begun to turn community attitudes around. Among the Ringatu, Rastas are not seen wholly in negative terms; their presumed association with trespassing, arson, horse and cattle theft, and many other antisocial or criminal activities in the community has been questioned, and the beginnings of acceptance, if not understanding, are under way.

Conclusions

Alienation is a major theme of Rastafarian movements worldwide, and the Ruatoria Dreads are no exception. Listening to Bob Marley's songs and reasoning kindled their interest in Rastafari and the messages of freedom, spirituality, and anticolonialism that the music contained. Among the Ruatoria Dreads there is also a strong sense of moral propriety and independence. Other than growing and smoking marijuana, there is little that they do that is unlawful; nonetheless, they consider their relations with the outside community to be strained, which they demonstrate by the fact that three of their numbers have been killed in the past two decades and the police (Babylon) have failed to secure convictions against the killers. One of the men killed (Chris Campbell) was their acknowledged leader at the time, considered to be a person with prophetic powers. Today he is revered by the Dreads as a martyr to the cause of Maori liberation and redemption. Nonetheless, their exotic religion and appearance has ostracized them from their own relatives and unfairly demonized them as the bad men of the community.

Rastamen in the West Indies have found reason in the Scriptures not to cut their hair, shave their beards, or tattoo their skins; likewise, they observe many dietary prohibitions as determined by Biblical teachings. In Aotearoa in contrast, Rastamen, besides having dreads, usually shave and have tattooed *moko.* Their consumption of pork and shellfish, although proscribed in the Bible, is rationalized as part of their ancestral and Ringatu teachings, a faith they say they hold as strongly as their Rastafarian consciousness. To the Dreads of Ruatoria, their beliefs and practices are a syncretic combination of Rastafari and Ringatu and an expression of their desire for *tino rangatiratanga* (sovereignty), all three elements promising sovereignty and self-determination within the context of their Ngati Porou land, kinship, authority, and spirituality.

The Rastafari Presence in Ethiopia

A Contemporary Perspective

JAHLANI NIAAH

The rationale for this chapter emerged out of a concern that despite the increased visibility of the Rastafari character and way of life in the Diaspora and within Africa, there is yet to be any comprehensive assessment of the role that the movement plays in the African sphere. In this regard I examine the development of the Jamaican Rastafari presence in Ethiopia within the context of repatriation and the activities of the incoming population. The chapter concludes with an assessment of the Rastafari contribution (and potential contribution) to further advance Pan-African agendas and as an indicator of a commitment to African development.

Data have been gathered from secondary sources, archives, and Mortimo Planno's papers as well as interviews that I conducted in Jamaica and Ethiopia between July 2006 and September 2008.

The literature on Rastafari cannot ignore the work of Walter Rodney, who, though not identified as a Rastafarian, is considered a student of the movement and one of its biggest allies with respect to praxis.[1] Rodney, an African diasporan intellectual, reminds us that the African Caribbean intellectuals have not always ignored the Pan-African situation. Rodney integrated the trans-Atlantic world in reconstructing and analyzing the political economy of Africa, Europe, and the Americas, and he was able

1. See Rodney 1990, 1981. See also Campbell 2007; Waters 1999 [1985]; Lewis 1998.

to take his grounded understanding to impact and teach the "ordinary" citizenry. His intellectual activism and devotion to transforming the legacies of colonialism to advance the African liberation movement worldwide brought about his assassination in 1980 in Guyana.[2] Freedom fighters such as Rodney, Malcolm X, Martin Luther King Jr., and Bob Marley represent a trajectory developed from the work of Marcus Garvey in understanding the importance of constructing a united African sphere. All of these individuals were cognizant of the importance of their work impacting all but especially the grassroots.

If within the pantheon of African diasporan activists there is a loudest voice it would be that of the Rastafari as a collective, Bob Marley as an individual, and reggae music as the medium. Kwame Dawes (1999) identifies a reggae aesthetic as having emerged out of Jamaica since the 1970s and further suggests that in order for there to be an accurate accounting of the Caribbean as an economic, social, and political space from that time onward, one has to be *au fait* with the text and discourses of reggae music to truly interpret and understand these discourses. However, the reggae music identified by Dawes has been largely engineered and imbued with its "political" significance through the work of the Rastafari faithful, its chief exponent at the global level, with Bob Marley being the face of both the movement and the music. Despite the seemingly well-meaning intention of affirmative consciousness of Africa and things African, the movement suffers severe handicaps in being taken seriously within the context of being an official partner in the drive for an African renaissance, in spite of its undeniable track record of performance, in particular with regard to global *conscientization*, relating the plight of Africans both at home and abroad. Indeed, it is well established that the Rastafari movement and Bob Marley in particular have done more to advance the cause of Pan-Africanism in a couple of decades than that achieved by nearly a century of Pan-African activism.[3]

Rastafari and reggae as voices of the people have largely been taken seriously only by the youth, and as a result many are seen unfavorably as

2. See Campbell 2007 and Lewis 1998.

3. See Campbell 2007.

having appropriated an alien Jamaican cultic faddism, an influence undesired in older, more traditional societies. The case of a South African youth and his family provides a poignant example of what seems to be an extreme case of cultural confrontation. In South Africa, the family of a Xhosa youth who embraced the Rastafari faith forcibly initiated him into manhood, which included circumcision and ingesting the foreskin. The youth's father complained that African traditions were being dishonored because the Rastafarians "misled his son . . . they are not his family or part of his culture," he argued.[4]

In addition to regarding Rastafari as an "alien" culture that evolved in the West, the aesthetic of the dreadlock and the sacramental usage of cannabis (ganja, dagga) within the congregation and sympathizers concern many individuals, especially as they relate to youth. In Durban in 2006 one could still see it reported in headlines: "Dreadlock Boys 'Turned Away from School,'" the reason being "because of their 'untidy' locks." On this matter the South African Human Rights Commission said, "The schools should avoid rigidity when setting their uniform codes but should find ways to accommodate pupils whose religious requirements clashed with school uniforms."[5]

Bob Marley is also a part of the media's fascination. There are headlines that honor him: "Bob Marley: The Legend Still Lives," yet complicating the scrutiny of these contributions are ridiculous statements such as, "There is a legend that when Bob Marley died, eight new species of lice were found in his dreadlocks. It is 24 years since Marley died, but the legend still lives on."[6] In 2006, a story about the Africa Unite Ghana celebrations titled "'Weed for All' at Bob Marley's Birthday Bash," described "thick smoke from the numerous puffs" hanging overhead, yet "for all that

4. Melanie Peters, "Rastafarian Circumcised Against His Will," *Sunday Tribune*, July 4, 2004. http://www.iol.co.za/index.php?set_id=1&click_id=139&art_id=vn20040704124240917C136839.

5. See Noloyiso Muchunu, "Dreadlock Boys 'Turned Away from School,'" *Mercury*, Jan. 20, 2006.

6. See Titus Serunjogi, "Bob Marley: The Legend Still Lives," *New Vision*, Feb. 3, 2006.

'getting high' there were no awkward incidents of note."[7] These issues, seemingly antisocial components, place the movement both in Africa and the African Diaspora at risk of devaluation of its function and achievement as a popular vehicle for meaningful social evaluation, engagement, and change.

Regarding the importance of Rastafari to the youth globally—in particular in Africa and its role of giving voice to the redefinition of the Black self—the significant contributions of Minda (2004), who focused on Ethiopia, and Dovlo (2002), who looked at Ghana, support these claims.[8] Minda, through the lens of sociology, looked at the adjustment of identity experienced by diasporan settlers in Shashamane, in particular as it relates to the first generation of children born in Ethiopia. To this extent Minda's work is similar to that of Savishinsky (1993). Dovlo (2002) is interested in the religious movements and communities that emerged in the African Diaspora and have returned home to Ghana, from the point of these being "alien" to contemporary African spirituality. These studies all in some way reflect the social tension that often surrounds the phenomenon of Rastafari, with little emphasis on a wider range of positive contribution brought and derived by Rastafari. Moyer (2005) provides us with a compelling case of the Rastafari/reggae phenomenon operating in Dar es Salaam among street youth. Despite the limited geographical range in Moyer's study, both Moyer and Dovlo show that more studies of Rastafari-inspired youth culture are needed beyond Tanzania to regions where similar phenomena can be observed.

Today it is estimated that the movement exists in some shape or form throughout most African nations but, in particular, repatriates are anchored in Ghana, Ethiopia, Malawi, Benin, and South Africa, where it is estimated that the largest population of Rastafari exists in any single

7. "'Weed for All' at Bob Marley's Birthday Bash," 2006. http://www.musicinghana.com/migsite/news/read.php?cid=.

8. Dovlo, it should also be noted, draws on the work of Neil Savishinsky (1993), who did a detailed study of the spread of Jamaican Rastafari culture among youth in Ghana and Senegambia. Savishinsky provides a good historical and sociological record that this current project will benefit from.

location.[9] But though the persona that Rastafari represents might be conspicuous as well as speculative with respect to its genuine influence, it is undeniable that the music of reggae and some of the outward aesthetics of the Rastafari are swiftly on the rise within the African continent in general. This influence can be traced back about three decades and is largely based on the cross-fertilization of Jamaican Rastafari artists such as U-Roy, Jimmy Cliff, Peter Tosh, and Bob Marley. Through their touring of Africa they influenced genres such as Afro-pop as well as continental artists like Fela Kuti, Alpha Blonde, and Hugh Masekela. More recent permutations have emerged through dancehall music, realized in musical forms such as Kwaito in South Africa (see Stanley-Niaah 2007).

Back-to-Africa: Early Rastafari Journeys to the Continent of Africa

> it is not
> it is not
> it is not enough
> it is not enough to be free
> of the whips, principalities and powers
>
> Brathwaite 1973, "Negus," 222

Brathwaite, through the Ge'ez word for the ruler-King-Priest, "Negus," captures poetically the voice of Rastafari at the time when its voice sounded to have dialogue with the wider society in the early to mid-1960s. Long before there was the postcolonial postmodernist there was the Rastafari manipulating "word-sound" power to dissolve and reconfigure hegemony. The Rastafari movement originating out of Jamaica is internationally recognized as one of the loudest voices on issues concerning human liberty and dignity, the legacies of slavery, and the aspirations for human and Pan-African advancement. This voice is derived from a penchant for existential hermeneutics that is expressed in testimonies delivered in poetry, song,

9. Unofficial estimates suggest that more than 2 million members of the movement live in South Africa.

other forms of orature, and "cultural action."[10] In the words of one scholar, "Rastafari has become the memory of the Jamaican [African] people," and thus has become chronicler as well as key advocate, echoing ideas of issues unresolved within a society, in need of *collective reflection.*[11]

This reputation belongs to a tradition of thinking and leadership spawned by Ethiopianism, ritualized and fine-tuned as a way of being in Jamaica after the coronation of Emperor Haile Selassie I (whose name is Amharic for "power of the holy trinity") of Ethiopia in November 1930. Further, among the Rastafari the Ethiopian Amharic language is the harbinger of truth and a repository of uncolonized spirit and history of an African past lost by many during slavery. The word "Rastafari" was inspired by the Ethiopian emperor, developing out of the combination of two Amharic words: "Ras," a title given to a prince or noble, translated to mean "head," and "Tafari," a given name meaning "creator" or "one to be feared." By virtue of the trans-world constellation of the movement (i.e., its source of inspiration being Ethiopia and its operational location being in Jamaica and throughout the African Diaspora), Rastafari from its inception could be seen to have a built-in international potential and appeal (see Kitzinger 1969). Its first preacher, Leonard Howell, put in place a foundation that remains intact to this present time. This foundation related to championing the cause of Africans wherever they found themselves. Howell brought news of Ethiopia, the Great War, and what he interpreted as the coming of a new prosperity for Africans. Approximately one generation later (1950s–1960s), after successive encounters with the police and incarceration in a mental asylum, Howell retreated into a world of silence, and the expression of Rastafari became more urban and focused on a new young and militant-minded youth population (Boanerges, Prince Emmanuel, Mortimo Planno, Sam Brown, and Count Ozzie were among the emergent youth). The identity of the dreadlocked Rastaman took primacy.

10. Chevannes argues cultural versus political action as one of the key strategies utilized by the Rastafari (1994, xi–xii).

11. See Chevannes (2006) for discussion of this view.

Howell's strategy of communal living at Pinnacle in St. Catherine was destroyed by the authorities in 1954. The young dispossessed felt they had no choice but to confront the system that discriminated against them, while dwelling in the urban squalor and refusing to accept the society as being of their choice. Howell's communal organization transformed more toward a politico-religious agency in the urban space, and as one theorist suggests, it is in this marginalizing urban space without means and without employment that the impetus for repatriation grows strong (see Yawney 2001). The Rastafari were able to vocalize the captivity, longing, and experience of exile in Jamaica, within the expression of musical anthems, such as those on the 1973 Bob Marley album *Catch a Fire.*

More than a decade before *Catch a Fire,* Mortimo Planno was the first dreadlocked Rastafarian to emerge as an ambassador and plenipotentiary of the faith through the fact-finding mission to Africa:

> The Mission was granted audience with H.I.M. Emperor Haile Selassie I. at the Imperial Palace, Addis-Ababa. We were introduced to H.I.M. . . . who told us he knew the black people of the West and particularly Jamaica were blood brothers to the Ethiopians and he knew that slaves were sent from Ethiopia to Jamaica. He said that we should send the right people.[12] The Emperor said Ethiopia was large enough to hold all the people of African descent living outside Africa and he would send a delegation to the West Indies. . . . H.I.M. thanked the delegation and presented each of us with gold medals. (Government of Jamaica 1961, 15–17)

Ethiopia had been extending invitations for Africans in the Diaspora to work in Ethiopia for several decades. In 1922, H. H. Tupakin delivered a message from the Ethiopian sovereign to the Universal Negro Improvement Association (UNIA) convention for its members to "come home" to where their race originated, and they may be lifted to their "highest plane of usefulness and honour" (see Niaah 2005). When the government of Jamaica decided to send a mission to Africa in 1961 to look into the prospects for

12. In 1927 His Imperial Majesty Ras Tafari sent an emissary, Dr. Workneh Martin, to solicit workers from the Diaspora.

repatriation, its first official stop was Ethiopia, where it had been alleged that land had been given for that purpose. The need for a mission to Africa arose out of the advocacy of the Rastafari brethren who had approached the University of the West Indies to conduct a study of the movement. The outcome of the study was a report that recommended, among other things, "an official mission to visit several countries of Africa, and seek permission for Jamaican immigration" (Smith, Nettleford, and Augier 1960, 35). Among the members of the mission were three Rastafari brethren, Douglas Mack, Fillmore Alvaranga, and Mortimo Planno. This was the first Jamaican Rastafari exposure to the international community.

Jamaican Rastafari have spawned a Diaspora that has globalized significantly since the birth of the movement more than eighty years ago in Jamaica. After the coronation of the emperor in November 1930, Italy's invasion of Ethiopia 1935, the formation of the Ethiopian World Federation (EWF) in 1937, and the subsequent issuance of the Shashamane land grant, Rastafari from the Caribbean and Jamaica in particular have had ambition and active involvement in the construction of a vision of returning to Ethiopia and Africa. The delivery of the cosmological "overstanding" or vision of returning to Africa has been a fundamental point for critiquing the internal logic of the Rastafari as well as their philosophical and evidential integrity. Within the movement itself various mansions and unaffiliated individuals have grappled with fulfilling their desire for repatriation in the wider context of African reparations. This has led to a significant number of the movement's members engaging various strategies in realizing this return, ranging from Ethiopian volunteerism from the Americas (1935–41), to government assistance missions (1961 and 1972), to personal provisions missions,[13] to music tours and Nyahbinghi trods.

In 1961, before the movement was really known outside of Jamaica, Planno was included on a Jamaican government tour of five African states

13. One example of personal provisions is the Mystic Revelation of Rastafari who in 1965 went on a private mission to Ethiopia via the United Nations in New York where they staged a protest concerning repatriation. Afterward, they went to Ethiopia, where they spent six months and had audience nine times with the Emperor (interview with Sam Clayton, 1999).

and also traveled to the United Kingdom and the United States. On that tour Planno used the opportunity to teach about the new faith of Rastafari as well as to update these various communities on the status of the Back-to-Africa movement (as it was commonly known).

In 1972 Planno returned to tour Africa with yet another delegation. While in Zambia, an article about him appeared in a local paper and subsequently appeared on the front page of a Jamaican newspaper:

> **Selassie as God? Zambian says Planno is "Talking through his halo"**
>
> Lusaka (June 28, Reuters). A member of the West Indian Rastafarian religious sect who urged Africans to give up Christianity and rediscover their own god was politely told he was talking through his halo.
>
> He is Mr. Mortimer [*sic]* Planno a member of the Jamaican delegation led by Jamaican Minister of State in the Ministry of Foreign Affairs, Mr. Dudley Thompson on a tour to strengthen cultural ties with Africa. (*Daily Gleaner,* June 29, 1972, 1)

Not everyone had the same opinion about Rastafari as represented by Planno. Planno received an invitation from Bankie Forster Bankie, a Nigerian high court judge, who had met him in 1972 when the mission toured Nigeria, to return on a private mission in 1979. Of Planno, Bankie (2003) writes:

> Along with Kwame Ture, Planno was one of those rare persons who lived by that precept of revolutionaries "One of the struggle, all for final victory" . . . What Ture and Planno shared was a vision necessitating direct political action. Both were leaders of significant schools of progressive thought, whose ideas will endure for the foreseeable future. Ras Planno was the first African I met and interacted with who had unwavering commitment to radical progressive African nationalism.

Bankie and Planno maintained communication until Planno's passing in 2006. Planno's visit to Nigeria had caught the attention of some of the youth, particularly those who had heard of the Rastafari movement and its music. By that time Rastafari reggae superstar Bob Marley's reputation had successfully taken Planno's argument that struck the Zambians in

1972 "as talking through his halo" to the world, commencing a growth in the awareness of the movement in Africa generally. For his work musically Bob Marley was to develop a bridge with Africa as well as a fan base. After the trip to Nigeria in 1979, a steady stream of letters came to Planno over the next four years (Marley's de facto central advisor on the continent of Africa), from fans and followers of Marley's music and spirituality. The following letter to Planno provides an example:

> Hi Planno,
>
> Your Movement once spread to Nigeria and I know you did come but it was halted and wasn't given much publication. We agitated to the press, staged many riots in schools because we saw that it was the right move to complete freedom. It was not until June this year that a popular magazine—The Spear—could publish the address of Bob Marley.
>
> Tell us more about the Rastafarians Movement. Many of us are very interested and are even going by the name Rasta . . . we are still novices—more information Please.
>
> Larry, D
> Imo State, Nigeria
> July 25, 1980

Planno's trip to Nigeria in 1979 was sponsored in part by Bankie and Bob Marley. Bankie had visited Planno in Jamaica in 1976 seeking to recruit reggae acts for the Second African Festival of Arts and Culture (FESTAC).[14] He was not able to attract Bob Marley at that time, however, and Jimmy Cliff took on the invitation. Bankie hosted Planno in Nigeria for a few months while arranging for his meeting and engaging his faith and knowledge system with the African community. Planno was given voice in the Nigerian print media, namely *Spear Magazine,* which proved critical in providing a framework for fans and initiates to connect with Jamaican Rastafari and reggae icons subsequently.[15] One such fan wrote Marley the following:

14. The Second African Festival of Arts and Culture was held in Nigeria in 1977.

15. Planno kept over one hundred thirty such letters written by Nigerians and a few Ghanaians, currently located among Planno's papers.

Do you know that your Rasta reggae music has become a music of life remembered of Black Africa Southern Africa Apartheid Massacre. Your latest music "Survival" had rock niggers wild seeking to know you real . . .

Victor, Y
Abeokuta,
Nigeria
July 7, 1980

Knowledge of the Jamaican Rastafari movement began to spread in Africa, especially after the *Survival* album featuring the single "Zimbabwe," followed by Marley's performance of the song at the ceremony ending British rule there. Marley succumbed to cancer and died about a year after he performed at Zimbabwe's independence celebration (April 1980). In the months leading up to his death Nigerian fans expressed concern about Marley's health:

This letter is just to know your present condition of health. And ask some few questions.

I am a student of a technical school. I have been hearing your records and tunes.

A while ago I watched you on t.v. at Kano State of Nigeria where you sing your exodus.

First; can you give me the idea of what shall I do in order to become a musician and how to come to Jamaica myself father is not rich enough. And please give me a little histories.

Secondly; can I write to any Jamaican musician with this address.

Thirdly; Why don't you want to visit Nigeria like some other Jamaican musicians.

I stop here. Please I am looking forward for your reply. Thanks.

Yours Faithfully
Emmanuel A. I.
Awka, Nigeria
April 1, 1981

That letter is one of several thousands of letters sent to Bob Marley in Jamaica and is part of a select set of letters that originated from Africa, mostly Nigeria, all expressing similar sentiments. Marley died one month after that letter's date, and his death generated more letters expressing grief and condolences to the family of the reggae king:

> I have read about the sudden death of . . . Bob Marley and believe it or not I am having a heart attack as there has never been a musician I loved like the late Bob Marley.
>
> What pains me most is that we here in Nigeria who are lovers of Bob Marley had expected [his] death to flash all the international magazines especially "Newsweek" and "Time" but to our utmost shock these magazines failed us. When John Lennon of the Beatles group was shot his pictures and stories occupied the whole "Time" and "Newsweek" but what more of Bob Marley who was superior?
>
> My explanation and indeed that of all Bob Marley's fans is that it is because Bob Marley was anti-imperialistic, anti-colonialism and anti crazy-baldhead so they feel they can't pay tribute to him 'cos he wasn't in their good books. I never hated white men before but it seems I am going to start 'cos of Bob Marley's death. . . .
>
> Bassey, U.
> Kaduna, Nigeria
> June 14, 1981

Reggae king Bob Marley, new Rastafari plenipotentiary extraordinaire, effectively bequeathed the Rastafari vision for African unity that he embodied in his music and lyrics to the continent of Africa, the African Diaspora, and his Rastafari children.

Shashamane as a Case Study of Rastafari in Africa

Let us now consider the Rastafari community of Shashamane in Ethiopia to assess how the West Indian–Jamaican Rastafari have relinked Africans abroad with the continent of Africa.

This is by no means trivial. Indeed, a case can easily be made that one of the most significant places in the history of the African Diaspora is Shashamane, in part because of the uniquely prophetic way that it came into being and because of its subsequent history. Shashamane was a gift from Emperor Haile Selassie I for the African Diaspora, the scattered children so to speak, who had come to hold the Ethiopian struggles, at the time of the Italian-Ethiopian war (1935–41), dearly in their hearts and minds. This land grant actualized the desire carried in the loins of the Back-to-Africa movement in their search for a resting place to recompose their centuries-long struggles to return to the Homeland.[16]

Shashamane Town: Origin, Location, and Demographic Composition

Legend has it that there once was a woman named *Shasha* who established a house of hospitality (*mane*) for people traveling through the region—hence Shashamane. These lands bordered by the Melcoda and Shashamane Rivers were a part of the royal land holdings said to have been first given by Menelik II in the early twentieth century for Blacks in the Diaspora who wished to return to Africa.[17] Today it is a medium-sized junction town 250 kilometers south of the capital city Addis Ababa, and 25 kilometers north of the Oromo city of Awassa. Shashamane by virtue of its location may be considered an important dormitory town for travelers exploring the Great Rift Valley (which dominates the south of Ethiopia) or who are en route to Kenya (which is approximately 8 hours away by asphalted road). At about

16. This was not unusual, and in recent times the Falashas (Ethiopian Jews) have fulfilled this ambition of returning home to Israel (in two waves of migration in 1985 and 1991) after more than 3,000 years of separation. The repatriation must be seen as different from the resettling and dumping of maroons and other Africans liberated from slave traders and coerced from the United Kingdom in Sierra Leone in the late eighteenth century as well as the formation of Liberia in the early nineteenth century from liberated Africans who originated from the United States. Garvey's Liberia settlement project would have been of the closest significance to the current Shashamane project under discussion (see Campbell 2007, 212–28).

17. See *JAHUG: Jah Rastafari Nyahbinghi Order Theocracy Reign,* vol. 5: Alpha and Omega. Ed. Carl Gayle (Repatriation Productions, 1980; reprinted June 1992).

1,700 meters above sea level, the region experiences mild temperatures, and its fertile lands are suitable for the cultivation of a range of crops, including cereal grains, mixed subsistence agriculture, and large-scale production of specialized crops. Over the past sixty years the community of Shashamane has attracted diasporan Africans from the United States, the West Indies, and Europe as well as non-Africans from Europe and Asia. Though gifted to diasporan Africans in general, the entire region has become known within Ethiopia as "the Jamaican Rastafari Community." The area is rural and primarily occupied by Ethiopian peasants who farm the land. Population estimates for the town range from about 50,000 in the 1990s to in excess of 100,000 presently.[18]

Historical Consideration of the Settlement of Shashamane by Diasporic Africans

It is significant to note that the Rastafari presence in Ethiopia predates the emergence of reggae music as a tool for evangelizing the movement. The first settlers (the husband and wife team named Piper from Montserrat) arrived sometime in the mid-1940s. They were the first administrators responsible for overseeing the distribution of homesteads to incoming settlers. Toward the end of the 1950s an African American minister named Rev. Robinson settled as well, and in the 1960s a number of Jamaicans started to arrive, especially after the government's mission to Africa that confirmed the existence of the land grant and its acceptance of those diasporans interested in settling there. Mama and Papa Baugh, Brother Brissette, Brother Moodie, and Brother Solomon Wolfe are among such personalities who arrived in the 1960s to settle. However, it is perhaps the story of Brother Noel Dyer, who walked to Ethiopia from the United Kingdom (a journey that took one year), that most captured the imagination of those familiar with the settlement. Most of those who arrived in Shashamane were connected to the Ethiopian World Federation (EWF), initially the institutional framework for gaining access to the land grant.

18. I have also been told of population estimates of 290,000 by local authorities.

Through a combination of means, including attempts framed by local chapters of the EWF, members desirous of returning to Africa could be assisted. Locals 43, 37, and 15 were among the most outstanding in such attempts. Up until the end of the 1960s there were only about twelve families living on the 500-acre land grant.

Two years prior to the start of the revolution leading to the deposal of the imperial Ethiopian government in 1974, the Twelve Tribes of Israel (TTI) embarked on a highly organized strategy to repatriate its membership to Shashamane Ethiopia. Through a lottery system members were asked the question, "Are you ready?" If their answer was yes, the TTI provided passage and "settling in" and "start up" funding. The main objective for which the TTI had been established was to "gather members interested in repatriating to Africa." Over a period of twelve years (1972–84), twenty-eight members (twenty-three men, three spouses, and two women) were sent to settle on the land grant. To date (2011), three have died and eighteen remain. One individual moved away from the land and went to live in Addis, and six individuals returned to Jamaica. More than half (at least twelve) of the individuals who remain have established unions with Ethiopian women, mothers to approximately half of the eighty-five children born to these repatriated members on the land.[19] Over the years, the systematic infusion of members facilitated the transplanting of a significant (dominant numerically) presence of the TTI in Ethiopia. This helped to support a fledgling settlement of a few families at a time when the revolution disrupted the paradigm of returning to Zion. The crop of mostly young (early 20s) skilled individuals were able to form a framework to maintain hold over the principle of the land grant, now threatened by the Derg's revolutionary land nationalization policy and the overturning of Emperor Haile Selassie's provisions for repatriation.[20] Prophet Gad sent several teams and missions

19. Data for this section developed from field notes corroborated and expanded through the data collected by Angela Heron, who lived and worked in the community of Shashamane in 2004 and in 2007–8.

20. The Derg administration, though it embarked on a so-called Red Terror approach, left the Rastafari in Shashamane relatively untouched. Mengistu in fact is cited by individuals as commending the Rastafari for their true patriotism in Ethiopia. Also see *JAHUG*, 5: 25.

to deploy the group with efficiency (builders, farmers,[21] teachers, electricians, trained individuals, as well as couples). The largest group deployed at any one time numbered twelve.[22]

The earliest set of the TTI were well timed and constituted a militant and technically prepared group to cope with the issues and realities of revolution as well as the task of pioneering. They helped to secure territory that was then becoming nationalized and less receptive to the idea of a handful of Rastafari living on a five-hundred-acre imperial land grant. The deposal of Emperor Haile Selassie I provided challenges for the Rastafari since they had enjoyed a special regard from the sovereign. Questions emerged within the community as to how they were to proceed after his removal. Members of the TTI who arrived at this turbulent time indicated that the Prophet Gad told them that they were to go and hold the land for those who were to come in the future, and so from the outset they saw themselves as a sort of garrisoning force at a troublesome time for Ethiopia and the movement in general.

A Millennial Perspective Regarding the Settlement of Shashamane

In 2006 when I first visited Ethiopia the timing of my trip was driven by the almost apocalyptic expectations within the Rastafari community regarding the Ethiopian millennium and the deluge of Babylon as we know it. September 11, 2007, the dawn of the Ethiopian millennium, was awaited with great anticipation. Indeed, September 11, 2001, was viewed widely within Rastafari circles as an indication of the downfall of Babylon. For a number of years prior to 9/11, the members of the movement were preparing themselves for going into Africa and Ethiopia or, to put it differently, to come out of Babylon into Zion. My trips in 2006 and 2007 were to provide me with a platform to view and interpret these activities.

21. Most individuals do some measure of farming.

22. This included Flipping, Zebulun, Rueben and Naphtali, Bunny Joseph, Pinkie Zebulun, Moses Issachar, Brother Levi, and Judah. Some who went but did not remain include Allan Skill Cole, who was not sent through the TTI but was connected, and Ian Coore, who also connected to the TTI but was not sent by them.

Since the centenary of the birth of Emperor Haile Selassie in 1992, the Nyahbinghi as well as the Bobo Shanti Mansions have turned greater attention toward Ethiopia and have embarked on missions to develop their traditions and repatriation plans. As a result, there are now present active representatives of the three major mansions (Twelve Tribes of Israel, Nyahbinghi, and Bobo Shanti) with established organizational locales (headquarters, tabernacle) operating on the land. The end of the Derg administration of Ethiopia in 1991, the centenary of His Imperial Majesty's birth, and the Western millennium helped to pull attention back toward Ethiopia in particular for Rastafari.[23]

Presently, the points of origin for new arrivals are primarily the United States, the United Kingdom, and Canada. The presence of former nationals of Trinidad and Tobago is said to have increased significantly in the past decade. Many of the individuals interviewed had been living for some time in Europe or North America, accumulating resources to return home to Africa. Some lived there for a few weeks or months, although some had more extended stays, living and working up to retirement age in order to secure adequate resources including pension and other benefits to take to Africa.[24] In recent time another option, becoming an investor, has also served as yet another settlement strategy, which is significant because the bureaucratic red tape of settling is often better dealt with in this way.

23. Some argue that the idea of repatriation has been replaced by a "make Africa where you are" concept.

24. The earliest TTI returnees did not stop for any length of time in the north, which is where the ports of connection for Africa are located. The experience of the more recent migrants, however, is somewhat different; some reside in the north for up to fifteen years before traveling to settle in Ethiopia. In the case of some of the recent settlers from Trinidad, a two- to five-year stay in the north was noted. Some settlers operate in the "go and come" mode, which is to not permanently relocate at one time but instead gradually settle in. This latter model is seemingly gaining precedence. For example, the Nurses of Israel is one such group, building through western linkages a health center on the land and routinely contributing medical and other emergency supplies. Jamaican and other Rastafari who migrated to North America use these spaces to work and to funnel these and other resources to Shashamane. For example, Rastafari in Washington, D.C., are using this location as a way of securing funding to develop the school there in the community.

Rastafari Demographics in Shashamane

Most of the repatriated Rastafari chose to live either in Addis Ababa or in Shashamane, where there are about four to five hundred settlers, about half of which are Jamaicans and the remaining from about seventeen other nations, including Trinidad and Tobago, Barbados, Guyana, Antigua, Dominica, Martinique, Montserrat, and St. Kitts as well as Germany, New Zealand, Japan, and Ireland.[25] Recently there has been the development of a new community in the town of Bahar Dar, and there has always been a fair representation in the Addis Ababa suburb called Hyatt. The Ethiopians largely see all Rastafari present in Ethiopia as Jamaican irrespective of their country of origin. This imposed dominant Jamaican identity is sometimes to the displeasure of the other nationalities and is perhaps one of the only areas of potential disharmony within the movement in Ethiopia. This identity can work favorably, for example, when Bob Marley or the Ethiopian nationalism of the Jamaican Rastafari is the reference point, or unfavorably, if the cultural "foibles"[26] introduced to the youth are being highlighted as undesirable influences. Since the staging of the Bob Marley Africa Unite concert, an increase in the wearing of dreadlocks and the display of other aspects of the movement's culture have been observed among youths in Addis Ababa. Further research into this development, though interesting, is prohibitive at this time.

Fulfilling the Rastafari Creed: School, Shelter, Water Security

One of the principal organizational structures operational on the land grant in Shashamane is the Jamaican Rastafari Development Community (JRDC), a formally registered NGO since 2001, with specific interest in health, sports, education, and agriculture. This community has been the

25. Estimates by the Rastafari community suggest that there is about twice the number of the Shashamane community (or about 1,000 in total) living in Ethiopia. Erin MacLeod (see chapter 4) indicates that over twenty different nationalities are present.

26. Tourist guide books suggest—as is the local belief—that Shashamane is now a central source of ganja production and consumption.

primary source for the development and management of the school on the land that caters to the children of the Rastafari settlers as well the wider Ethiopian citizenry. The school, which has been operational for more than a decade, has a feeding program, and provides books and uniform supplies in addition to a full curriculum. It is considered to be one of the leading all-age institutions in the region, with particular strength in English language instruction, which is the language of high school and postsecondary training. At one point its enrollment was in excess of six hundred students. Unreliability of funding, much of which comes from fund-raising activities in Jamaica, the United Kingdom, and the United States, continues to threaten the institution's survival.

Another major aspect of the investments and activities of the Rastafari community in Shashamane is the development of hotels in the region, owning approximately one hundred fifty rooms (this constitutes about 90 percent of the rooms in the region). There are also other hotels planned for the land as new investors have been working to improve road networks and provide greater accessibility, which the community now enjoys. At a more informal level, many Rastafari households have the capacity to provide bed-and-breakfast–type facilities or to transform some section of their domestic space for the purpose of assisting those who come as visitors (and to earn cash).

The EWF is also actively involved in the service of the wider community, and since 2002 it too has registered as an NGO and has been the driving engine behind the implementation of "rainwater-harvesting systems." Some 165 water-harvesters have been constructed serving more than 3,000 people. The project has received strong support from regional Ethiopian farmers' associations as well as the German and British Embassies.[27]

New arrivals are engaged in a range of occupations, such as shopkeeping, operation of small restaurants, and handicraft or clothing manufacturing, among other activities. As the investment in the land increases, more large-scale commercial developments have been undertaken, especially

27. The data related to the EWF's project come from research by Erin MacLeod (see chapter 4).

hotel services, entertainment, music, and Internet and other small businesses, many of which take place from homes. The developments have included community administrative services—the community is a pioneering one and therefore there is little in place—and the Rastafari have had to develop them, including, perhaps ironically, a police station.[28]

Jamaican West Indian food ways have also emerged. The operation of restaurants, cook shops, and juice bars are significant parts of the movement's business activities. Jerk, curry, escoveitched fish, oxtail, and natural juices—sour sop, sorrel, carrot, "front-end lifters" (or natural energy drinks)—now abound. The consumption of ganja and its related rituals has been given greater significance because of the presence of the movement. The development of a vocabulary of "Ital" food is absent. Noteworthy, however, is the introduction of solar food processing and the cultivation of soybeans on a large scale, which are some of the new innovations being pursued by members of the movement.

Bob Marley has emerged as a Rastafari hero in Ethiopia and his face and music have taken on a national prominence. Indeed, in Shashamane there is a Bob Marley stadium under construction. With regards to entertainment, the reputation of the movement for reggae music production has made this one of the major activities on the land. The first generation of Jamaican Ethiopians have emerged with a musical fusion locally described as jam-haric, and this forms a part of the linguistic expression of the youths in general on the land grant.

Problems Concerning Rastafari and the Promised Land

The primary problem expressed by persons who have returned to Ethiopia to settle has been one of representation within the society and the right to citizenship for those born on the land or in Ethiopia. The current

28. Historically, Rastafari have had an antagonistic relationship with the police, who are often styled as "Babylon" and viewed as one of the central symbols of oppression. Shashamane, however, has an unusual reputation for burglary, bag-grabbers, and other types of petty violence and theft.

situation regarding diplomatic representation is therefore a central lobby for the movement.[29] Currently, the accredited representative for Ethiopia is located in Abuja, Nigeria. This imposes problems of an obvious nature. The acceptance of the Ethiopian-born generation and their issues of identity and belonging are also emerging, and this presents challenges to the sustainability of the movement's understanding of the repatriation vision (Minda 2004).

Citizenship

The issue of citizenship for African diasporans is a provision that is arguably the core of this chapter. How do we receive in Africa those of her children dispersed centuries ago? Ethiopia has made little headway on this matter, and this is further exacerbated by the fact that the Rastafari population constitutes a small community (numerically insignificant in a country of more than 70 million) and because the majority of migration into Ethiopia comes from its neighbors. The needs of a constituency such as the Rastafari constitutes somewhat of a unique situation.[30] Philosophically, Ethiopians argue that "You are born an Ethiopian and you stay an Ethiopian, you can't become Ethiopian." What this translates to is, after years of living in Ethiopia, repatriated Jamaican Rastafari can at best hope to acquire residential privileges, but their children must secure citizenship of their parents' country, which is Jamaica. In other words, being born in Ethiopia does not automatically entitle Ethiopian citizenship to the children of the Jamaican Rastafari. In the same way that citizenship is restricted so too is ownership of land, which is primarily for Ethiopians, although it may be made available for use by foreigners if there is a significant investment.[31]

29. Jamaica established an embassy in Ethiopia in 1970 but closed it in 1992, just about the time when the community in Shashamane was about to grow more rapidly.

30. Especially given the fact that the population classified as immigrant is less than 100,000 or 0.7 percent, 90 percent of which is Somali and Eritrean. See chapter 4.

31. Ibid.

Overall Assessment of Rastafari Repatriation at Present

Boyce Davies and M'Bow address the issue of an ongoing denial of the concept of citizenship for Africans in the West that leads to a sense of statelessness and alienation. This is a part of the epistemological understanding of the Rastafari nation, an international community that perhaps best exemplifies the idea of "an international African identity" (Boyce Davies and M'Bow 2007, 19). In this community of Africans in the Diaspora, repatriation increasingly is envisioned as an option or life ambition, for some. The phenomenon of Rastafari repatriation to Africa is underresearched. Yawney identifies repatriation as a continuum "beginning with the recognition and reclamation of one's identity as an African, moving through several levels to physical repatriation to Africa" (2001, 4). An individual Rastafari might be located at any point along this continuum, which could range from studying African history, learning an African language, developing skill of service to Africa, and so on. It is Yawney's observation about the repatriated Rastafari that is most critical as an entry point into the potential of Diasporas. Yawney states:

> At the community level . . . the repatriation continuum is developing linkages between African communities both in the Diaspora and on the continent. Various Rastafari groups in the Caribbean, North America and the UK have already organized to mobilize resources in support of communities of Rastafari settled in Ghana, Benin, Ethiopia and Malawi. The politics of repatriation are such that these globalized communication networks transcend national boundaries to define an African community without perimeters. In other words, the repatriation continuum serves to define a community of resistance using networks to strengthen African linkages between the Diaspora and Africa. (Yawney 2001, 134)

Yawney's assessment of the Rastafari Diasporas within Africa helps to locate such communities as offering an outstanding promise for harmonizing and strengthening Pan-Africanism, especially by virtue of the homogenous and centralizing principle of Rastafari that binds these communities and helps to establish their agendas and purpose. This tendency toward communities of repatriated Rastafari is likely to increase, Yawney believes, as the political climate in the West becomes more hostile toward the movement's ideals. To this extent, Shashamane provides a microcosm of issues, realities, and experiences that could be encountered on a larger scale for repatriates.

Conclusion

- The Rastafari constitute a modern Ethiopianist movement representing a celebration of a return to Africa/Ethiopia/Zion as a part of a larger memory of unresolved issues emerging from colonialism and slavery; this is comparable to the Falashas of Ethiopia, who sought a return to Israel after 3,000 years of separation.
- The presence of the movement in Africa and Ethiopia is not only that of a commitment to repatriation but also demonstrates a commitment to African nation building.
- In recent years Rastafari and reggae have begun to influence the African youth, primarily through the work of Bob Marley and his legacy.
- The desire for back-to-Africa/Ethiopia over fifty years fueled a range of strategies to realize the visionary ideals of the movement in Africa.
- Over the past thirty-five years the strategies of the TTI have demonstrated the greatest degree of success with respect to the consolidation of attempts to succeed with the development of the Rastafari community in Shashamane.
- With the approach of the Ethiopian millennium there was a reemergence of the commitment to return to Ethiopia/Africa.
- The small community of Jamaican Rastafari in Ethiopia has acted like "yeast in the dough" and has created major impact on the overall African/Ethiopian society with regard to community development and cultural influence.
- As with most diasporic groups there remain unresolved issues relating to the settlement, citizenship, and land access.
- Not withstanding the above, the communities in Africa and Ethiopia continue to impact the society in which they find themselves in significant ways, making them a most outstanding contributor to the society.

Water Development Projects and Cultural Citizenship

Rastafari Engagement with the Oromo in Shashemene, Ethiopia

ERIN C. MACLEOD

> It's the legal recognition that's lacking in our situation. What country in the world could you go to and spend thirty or forty years and not be a citizen? Have second and third generation children who are not citizens? This is the only one I know. It's unbelievable—we have children born here who've never left Ethiopia and are asked to get Jamaican passports . . . It's ironic that we should be in such a situation. People like myself, professionals who have been here twenty years legally, who have applied for citizenship are just fobbed off, fobbed off, fobbed off. To us it's ridiculous. We know it's an issue that has to be addressed and has to be corrected.
>
> —RAS TAGAS KING, Addis Ababa, September 2007

Ras Tagas King describes the situation for Rastafari repatriates in Ethiopia. For the past half century, Rastafari have been settling in Ethiopia, most specifically on land Emperor Haile Selassie I granted the African Diaspora in 1948. This land is in the Shashemene *woreda,* a town 250 kilometers south of the capital. Why, after all this time, is citizenship such a problem? Why, as King, a construction professional living with his family in Addis Ababa, asks, are residents of Ethiopia, residents who contribute to the economic development of the country, not provided with access to citizenship? Why are their children denied this right? How do the Rastafari function under these circumstances?

The Rastafari are a unique community in Ethiopia. Though some research has been done on the Rastafari themselves in Ethiopia (notably Giulia Bonacci's work [2007] on the history of the community from the time of the land grant up to the turn of the century), there has been little discussion of the relationship between the Rastafari population and the wider Ethiopian community. It is this relationship that creates the environment in which the repatriates live. In this chapter, I look specifically at the issue of citizenship and the connection between Rastafari initiatives and cultural citizenship within Ethiopian society.

In 2003, according to Bonacci's work on the history of the Rastafari community, the immigration minister analyzed the legal situation of 121 repatriates living in what is referred to as the Jamaica *sefer*—the area of Melka Oda, a former village that is now a part of the Shashemene *woreda*.[1] Of these individuals, seventy-seven were in the country under a tourist visa, thirteen had a business visa, and thirty-one had residence permits—not one was considered an Ethiopian citizen under the law.

At a community development meeting held at the Municipal government offices in Shashemene on November 21, 2007, this issue was raised. One of the Rastafari representatives

> expressed surprise that there was no classification for the Rastafari Community who have been looking to be accorded the same rights as Ethiopians, since [they] argue that they are Ethiopians, who have returned after being away for hundreds of years. He made the appeal that [the Rastafarians] should not be treated as foreigners, but wished to be classified as Ethiopians returning home, noting that in many countries to which people migrate, classification is attached.[2]

As regards the Ethiopian government, it would seem that, on first glance, the country does indeed allow for foreigners to become Ethiopians,

1. Amharic for "Rastafari village." The Ethiopian community in Shashemene, and beyond, commonly refer to Rastafari as Jamaican, regardless of nationality or race. In a slight deviation from the other contributors to this book, I use the spelling of Shashemene that duplicates the transliteration standards of the Wolf Leslau Amharic dictionary.

2. Minutes of Community Development Forum, 2007. Shashemene, Ethiopia.

much like the other countries referenced by the Rastafari representative. It is even in the constitution. Article 6.2 of the 1995 constitution of the Federal Democratic Republic of Ethiopia states that "Foreign nationals may acquire Ethiopian nationality" (Ethiopian Government 1995, 78).

This should effectively mean that foreigners desiring to become Ethiopian should eventually find themselves in possession of an Ethiopian passport. As it presently stands, however, this is simply not the case. In article 33, the constitution states that "Ethiopian nationality may be conferred upon foreigners in accordance with law enacted and procedures established consistent with international agreements ratified by Ethiopia" (ibid., 91–92). What, then is the problem? There is simply no system in place. No citizenship process has been developed as yet. Due to the reality of Ethiopian political history, in which there has been a shift from constitutional monarchy to communist dictatorship to the form of democracy that exists now, the lack of government movement on issues such as land rights and citizenship places the Rastafari in a position whereby they have been living in Ethiopia for decades without access to any process in which citizenship can be gained.

Another part of the reason there are no political or other processes to help newcomers integrate is that Ethiopia is not a country for which immigration is a common concern. In 2005, only 0.7 percent of the population was classified as immigrant from an external nation. Of that number, over 90 percent were from neighboring nations, the huge majority coming from Eritrea and Somalia (Shaw 2007, 5–6). The Rastafari are not only a marginal group within Ethiopia but also within the small group of immigrants to the country.

Though in 2002 an Ethiopian Expatriate Affairs General Directorate was established as part of the Ministry of Foreign Affairs, with the purpose of "working closely with diaspora Ethiopians and facilitating their activities in Ethiopia" (Belai 2007), there is no office to assist the integration of newcomers to the country. The Ethiopian Diaspora has services and support in repatriating to Ethiopia,[3] but since immigration to the country is so

3. One need only to walk down Bole Road to see the involvement of repatriated Ethiopian citizens. Businesses are run by Ethiopians who immigrated to America, gained success, and have now returned to their home country to help contribute to the economy. As Tadiwos

rare, these same services are not available to any other foreigners, including Rastafari, and there is no ability to gain Ethiopian citizenship.

With Ethiopian citizenship comes access to land; without it, it is impossible to acquire or lay claim to any piece of land. After the Selassie-era government fell, on March 4, 1975, the incoming Derg regime issued proclamation 31, which nationalized all rural lands and declared them the collective property of Ethiopians (Bonacci 2007, 390).[4] The results of an agreement between the communist government and the Rastafari, who were present in Shashemene and living on the granted land, meant that a fraction of the land grant remained the property of the Rastafari who were already there.[5] Bonacci reports that the same amount of land that was allotted to Ethiopians was allotted to each Rastafari family: 10 hectares each. With eighteen families, this meant that 180 hectares were made available; however, the government also declared that "No land [would be] available for new arrivals until the provisional military government [was] satisfied that the project had been completely and effectively developed" (qtd. in Bonacci 2007, 393).[6]

Government ownership of land was maintained as policy by the present Ethiopian Peoples' Revolutionary Democratic Front (EPRDF). Again, according to the constitution, land is a "common property of the Nations, Nationalities and Peoples of Ethiopia and shall not be subject to sale or other means of exchange" (Ethiopian Government 1995, 98). The use of that land, for residential purposes, is permissible only for Ethiopians. Foreigners can

---

Bekele, who left his adopted city of Boston to return and run a swanky spa in Addis—appropriately named the Boston Day Spa—says, "Ethiopia is growing, and I want to be part of its development" (Thibodeaux 2005).

4. "Avec la proclamation n° 31 du 4 mars 1975, toutes les terres rurales furent nationalisées et devinrent propriété collective des Éthiopiens." My translation.

5. Ivan Coore discussed this agreement in a presentation at the Crossroads International Association for Cultural Studies Conference, held July 2008 at the University of the West Indies, Mona.

6. "Aucune terre ne sera disponible pour de nouveaux arrivants jusqu'à ce que le gouvernement militaire provisoire soit satisfait que le projet actuel ait été complètement et effectivement développé." My translation.

make use of land only if there is a significant investment in the country—whether for business or humanitarian purposes. Even though the Rastafari cannot buy additional land, they most certainly are not leaving Ethiopia.

Nick Stevenson argues that citizenship should be seen as a social practice "in which the emphasis is less on legal rules and more on norms, practices, meanings and identities" (2003, 331). Jan Pakulski has argued that "cultural" citizenship should be viewed in terms of satisfying demands for full inclusion into the social community (qtd. in Stevenson 2003, 333).

These ideas of cultural citizenship for Stevenson, however, are related to the ways in which "transnational spheres of governance, instantaneous news, and global networks amongst new social movements . . . undermine or at least call into question, the correspondence that citizenship has traditionally drawn between belonging and the nation-state" (2003, 333). Given the contemporary connections between nations and cultures, through technology as well as new unions and treaties, the sense of national identity has become less related to a specific country of birth. This concept of cultural citizenship has, therefore, been utilized in the context of globalized Western societies. The Rastafari experience in Ethiopia demonstrates a way in which this concept can be used in a non-Western, supposedly nonglobalized environment.

Ethiopia is not a homogenous country with a consistent sense of national identity. Uniquely independent, save for five years of Italian occupation in the 1930s, there are eighty different nationalities represented in the Ethiopian population. Though Ethiopians have many different identities, with the advent of the EPRDF's controversial establishment of specific ethnic regions in 1991 the issue of identity has become all the more fraught.

Through interviews with Ethiopians in Shashemene and beyond, there is a wide-ranging sense of what it means, in the new Ethiopian millennium, to be Ethiopian.[7]

This may not be a so-called developed, Western society, but it is a nation for whom cultural citizenship—what Toby Miller suggests "concerns the

7. The topic of my dissertation research was the Ethiopian perception of the Rastafari population. As part of my research, I interviewed more than seventy people.

maintenance and development of cultural lineage through education, custom, language, and religion and the positive acknowledgment of difference in and by the mainstream"—is of utmost importance (Miller 2001, 2). Miller insists that this version of citizenship is necessary because "citizenship is no longer easily based on soil or blood. And the state is no longer the sole frame of citizenship in the face of new nationalisms and cross-border affinities that no single governmental apparatus can contain" (4–5).

This may be true for Western societies, but it is also true for Ethiopia in which so many different groups coexist under the banner of Ethiopia. The Rastafarians, themselves, within Ethiopia, represent over twenty different nationalities. Ethiopia is negotiating relationships between various cultural groups, especially in environments such as Shashemene, where internal migration to the town has led to it being quite a polycultural environment, as recorded by Gunilla Bjeren (1985) in the early 1970s and reestablished over recent months of new research (personal conversation, November 2009). Rather than instantaneous news or transnational governance making nation-state less relevant, it is the reality that Ethiopia has always been and continues to be a nation of nations.

Therefore, the concept of cultural citizenship is an ideal framework for analysis of the ways in which the Rastafari of Ethiopia engage with the experience of being in Ethiopia. Living on the outskirts of Shashemene, which is a crossroads market town to which various people of various backgrounds come, the Rastafari are increasingly confronting spiritual, economic, and cultural divisions with development and investment into Ethiopia. Through the denial of official citizenship, as a result of the political and legal environment in which the Rastafari live, this community has been forced to focus "less on legal rules and more on norms, practices, meanings and identities" (Stevenson 2003, 331). The Rastafari in Ethiopia have been developing and continue to develop various initiatives that work, in multiple ways, to achieve cultural citizenship, thereby attempting to integrate the Rastafari into the community of Shashemene and wider Ethiopian society. Rather than fighting against a structure that has denied citizenship for so long, the Rastafari community is working with whatever opportunities are legally available but focusing more on activities that develop this sense of cultural citizenship and belonging.

Within Shashemene, one can observe the growth of business initiatives. In addition to small businesses that line the road leading into the town, Rastafari have established two flagship local hotels. These hotels attract tourists to the area but are also used for weddings, municipal events (the Ethiopian Millennium Celebrations were held at the Rastafari-owned Rift Valley Hotel), and conferences. Rastafari have established a tofu factory as well. This business is of particular interest because it connects the Rasta practice of eating vegetarian food with the Ethiopian Orthodox practice of fasting. Company literature suggests that the tofu be used for fasting meals.

Humanitarian initiatives such as the Jamaican Rastafarian Development Community School are evident as well. The school has more than 450 students, the majority of which are Ethiopian. The education of these youths is subsidized. The school is known throughout Shashemene as a high-quality institution. All of these business and humanitarian initiatives are important in developing the relationship between the Rastafari and Ethiopian communities; however, for the purposes of this chapter, the Self-Sustainable Water for Life Community Based Rain Water Harvesting Project undertaken by the Ethiopian World Federation (EWF) will be discussed.

This is a project that is particularly important within Shashemene in terms of the relationship between the Rastafari and the growing Oromo community—who are the main stakeholders of this project—as well as the need for clean water. There is a river running through Shashemene, but due to a combination of factors, including a decrease of rainfall and the use of river water for agricultural projects outside of the town, the river has shrunk and is visibly dirty. People still wash clothing in and make use of the water from this river. Access to clean water is becoming increasingly difficult; in May 2008, the Ethiopian government reported drought and crop failures in areas near Shashemene (Bengali 2008), and as recently as April 2011, areas surrounding Shashemene were reporting water shortages.[8]

The EWF, the organization behind the rainwater project, was first established in New York in 1937 by Malaku Bayen with the following

8. *Humanitarian Bulletin*, April 25, 2011. UN Office for Coordination of Humanitarian Affairs. http://reliefweb.int/sites/reliefweb.int/files/resources/Full_Report_319.pdf.

major goal, according to the EWF Web site (EWF 2008): "The Ethiopian (meaning all Black people), World (everywhere), Federation (autonomous groups working together), desiring to do all we can to restore the continent of Ethiopia-Africa to her former state of complete independence and self-reliance thereby effecting a social and economic betterment of race everywhere."

The goal, as outlined here, is for the African Diaspora to work together for the development of Ethiopia. "Autonomous" groups located all over the world therefore interface with each other and converge on Ethiopia. In the interest of bringing this goal to its fruition, in 2002, the EWF was registered as an international nongovernmental organization (NGO) with the Ministry of Justice of the Federal Democratic Republic of Ethiopia.

Working alongside the local municipal government, the regional Oromo government, and four farmers' associations, the EWF's project has resulted in the construction of 165 water harvesters that serve 3,240 people. They are now about to sign a second tripartite agreement with the Oromo government to provide a further amount of these rainwater-harvesting systems. The project has also received the support of the German embassy and British embassy and has three main goals:

1. Improving the availability of water to the community in and around Shashemene.

2. Effectively using members of the community as a major factor in helping to teach the benefits of rainwater harvesting.

3. Encouraging educator teams in the project to set up their own small-scale businesses dealing with rainwater collection systems.

It is important to juxtapose these goals with the goals of the EWF as stated in the preamble to the organization's constitution. The political goals of independence and self-reliance are still evident in this humanitarian project. The very name, Self-Sustainable Water for Life Community Based Rain Water Harvesting Project, indicates that these goals are clearly part of the initiative.

In addition, the EWF's project also works to bridge the Rasta and Ethiopian communities. A 2007 EWF report on the project presents a detailed understanding of Shashemene and acknowledgment of the "melting pot of various nationalities" that exist in the area.[9] It details the need for fresh water and in particular the role of women in the procurement of this water. Reading the report of the project's first two phases, dated June 2007, it is evident that the EWF is functioning according to the results-based management techniques often used by NGOs within Ethiopia and the so-called developing world.

Clearly describing the expected outcomes and using the results-based-management language of impact—detailing the social impact and underlining specifically the impact on gender equality—the EWF's report presents a comprehensive depiction of a sustainable development project in line with the mainstream of international development work. At no point in the report is there an indication of the culture of Rastafari, the desire for citizenship, or the desire for integration into the community. This may be an indirect result of the initiative, but it is most certainly a desired result.

Tagas King, the EWF's representative in Addis Ababa, manages the project alongside B. J. Moody in Shashemene. He recognizes how this project has improved relations within the community:

> As an international NGO, we are the implementing agent, also the forefront of these projects, so we seek the funding from various donors and we implement the project in conjunction with local authorities in Shashemene. This is the way that we are trying to improve the relationship with local authorities by humanitarian development—giving them these things and providing orientation with how to maintain them. They have really appreciated it—they have said to us we want to make this as wide as possible meaning that every family that has a tin roof should have a rainwater harvesting system.
>
> This project also highlights the plight of women. The women are the ones who have to be fetching and carrying this water and it consumes the majority of their time during the working day. By giving them a rainwater

9. This information and further information about the Self-Sustainable Water for Life project was gleaned from a 2007 report compiled by the EWF as well as from interviews with Ras Tagas King and an EWF representative in Shashemene, Berthal James Moody (Brother Moody) on September 5, 2007.

> harvesting system right there, at their house, it means that the time that was spent fetching and carrying can now be dedicated to other things. So it's a very important project, it's been well appreciated and it's helped to improve the relationship. (Personal interview, September 1, 2007, Addis Ababa)

For the recipients of the water harvesters, support for the project is clear. "The water harvester is a great help," said one female beneficiary in a January 2008 interview. "I give thanks for the EWF. The eleven people in my household use the water for cooking, cleaning, coffee, and so on and so on. There are many, many uses! I thank God for the Rastafari community. Let God help them. The government cannot do what they are doing." Another woman, interviewed in January 2008 as well, described to me the impact of the water harvester on her own family as well as the wider community. "Before, I had to go far to fetch water. It took a long time. Now it is in my own yard. The neighbors can use the water as well as my family. I give thanks."

On many levels, this project allows the Rastafari to connect with the Ethiopian community on a governmental level and also on a local, interpersonal level, specifically with the Oromo people, who are members of the four farmers' associations. The fact that the main stakeholders of the project are Oromo farmers is of additional importance to the issue of cultural citizenship. After all, Shashemene is located in the region of Oromia.

Scholarly work by Asafa Jalata details the narrative of Oromo oppression—a narrative of colonialism by the Amhara, as represented by Emperor Haile Selassie I. According to Jalata, "Oromos . . . have been dominated and exploited by Ethiopian racial and colonial dictatorship respectively since the last decades of the nineteenth century" (2008, 363). Specifically addressing the Emperor, Jalata describes how "the Ethiopian colonial state and the Ethiopian settlers in Oromia did not tolerate any manifestation of Oromo consciousness. The Haile Selassie government banned the [Macha-Tulama Self-Help Association] in 1967, and its leaders were imprisoned or killed" (374).[10] As well, for Jalata, the Ethiopian government has always desired to take land from its rightful owners, the Oromo people. "The

10. The Macha-Tulama Self-Help Association was an Oromo cultural organization, established in 1963. See Jalata 2008 for details.

main reason for [the Ethiopian government's] colonial expansion," writes Jalata, "was to obtain commodities such as gold, ivory, coffee, musk, hides and skins, slaves, and land" (366).

Asafa Dibaba, a Oromo cultural scholar, agrees. As Dibaba described in an interview I conducted in September 2007:

> Ethiopians are hospitable, but, practically, on the ground may be different. There are problems with granting land already owned by people that worsens the relationship between newcomers and the already indigenous people . . . I think that from outside, one can infer problems . . . When you look to [Selassie's] line, on his father's side is Oromo, his mother Gurage . . . it doesn't give sense. This person put into bondage his own people, from his father's side. Then to be the one who freed Africans? I'm not happy with this.

Dibaba refers to Selassie's ethnic makeup—half Oromo, half Gurage. This means that Selassie, to Dibaba, acted as a colonial leader over his own ethnic group. Dibaba directly connects this factor to land rights. From this perspective, Selassie simply cannot be viewed as a liberator. If one views the former emperor in this way, and then goes ahead and makes use of land originally owned by those oppressed by the Emperor's government, it "doesn't give sense" for Dibaba.

After 1991, when the EPRDF came to power and introduced what is referred to as "ethnic federalism" (Hameso and Nebo 2000), the region of Oromia was established. The working language of this region is Afaan Oromoo, and the regional government grants permission for all land use in Oromia. Through the work of Asafa Jalata and in conversation with Asafa Dibaba, it becomes evident that the Oromo might have concerns about the Rastafari use of this land.

Local farmers provide a practical commentary on the land issue. In January 2008, I conducted interviews with Oromo farmers living and working in the Melka Oda area, the same area where the Jamaica *sefer* (Rastafari village), is located. In the words of Leenco Ibsaa:[11]

11. All names have been changed. The interviews took place in January 2008 and were translated from Afaan Oromoo.

> The Rastafari have money and they give the money to get the land and the farmers give the land towards them. This has a negative and a positive side. The negative side is that when the farmer gives their land for them the farmers move away from the town to the rural area where there is no town, no clean water. The positive side is that when one Rastafarian person is here, he has money. When he brings the light and the water for him, the society in the area gets to use from him.

Usman Leenjiso described apprehension about the long-term effect of selling land. "In our society, some people sell their land to them to get money," he said. "This is a great problem. The farmers in our society have their children and if they sell their land, they will become landless."

The concern about land is voiced alongside worries about the impact of Rastafari in Shashemene. Usman explained his sense of the reasons why the Rastafari come to Shashemene and his views on their presence:

> Historically, during the regime of Haile Selassie, he gave them five gasha of land because he had a strong relationship with them. When the regime of Haile Selassie was replaced by the Derg, the Derg didn't like Rastafari. They didn't let them build houses. They stayed during the Derg regime, and, after the EPRDF came to power, there was democracy so they built houses and established their school. Their great problem is that they start something and they don't finish it.

Leenco referenced the use of land in relation to development projects, and, in using the verb "to take," presents his complaint about the lack of progress on a hospital project in an all the more pejorative way. "They took land by saying that they would establish a great hospital for the Shashemene town ten years ago," he said, "but now it is still in the beginning stages."

Echoing Jalata and Dibaba, farmer Bunna Mohammed spelled out one of the main issues regarding acceptance of the Rastafari. "In the Oromo region, Oromo people don't like Haile Selassie. Generally, most of our society doesn't like him." Concurring, Usman said that "during the reign of Haile Selassie, here in [the Shashemene area], there is a separation between the Oromo and Amhara people." In addition, drug use is troubling to the farmers. Leenco explained: "They have changed the norms of the culture of the young generation. For example, they use marijuana or the other drugs and the young participate. Unnecessary attention is therefore given to us. For instance, Shashemene town is given a bad reputation for drug abuse and crime."

The water-harvesting project, however, serves these same people who have concerns about Rastafari and their involvement in the community. In a documentary meant to showcase the success of the water-harvesting project, produced in 2008, the EWF makes it clear that their project serves the Oromo community—the presenter, Ras Tagas King, makes a point of telling the viewer when he is talking with Orominya speakers as opposed to Amharic speakers. When I interviewed recipients of the water harvesters, there were representatives of both Amharic and Orominya (Afaan Oromoo) communities. This is a project that has a clear aim and demonstrates visual progress in the form of the harvesters themselves. It does not involve the use of land; in fact, it helps to increase the use value of land already available to the farming community. Furthermore, the project presents the Rastafari as development workers as opposed to a different cultural group with a different belief system and misunderstood cultural practices.

The Rastafari are making use of a strong humanitarian project from a position that is well understood by local inhabitants. In Shashemene, international and local NGOs are active. The Swedish International Development Agency has opened two youth centers, and Habitat for Humanity also has an affiliate in the Shashemene community.

A fundamental difference between the Rastafari and traditional NGO workers is that they will remain in the community. The issue of sustainability is a given because the Rastafari wish to remain in Ethiopia. As the chapter epigraph states, Rastafari have been in the country for decades and plan to stay not for months or years, like traditional NGO workers, but for a lifetime. This desire to remain in Ethiopia creates a large potential for the Rastafari as humanitarian workers. The Rastafari faith encourages the development of Africa, and those individuals who choose to live in Africa can make a difference in the community by ensuring the long-term viability of projects, thereby increasing the likelihood of sustainability.

Rastafari humanitarian projects, such as those undertaken by the EWF, utilize economic capital to engage in development—much like a traditional NGO does—but the economic capital is then converted into symbolic capital: cultural citizenship capital. The Rastafari make use of their position as "foreigner," which is similar to the "outsider" role of an international NGO, and in this way they gain stock in cultural citizenship. They are working within the community on a relevant community project. Within the water-harvesting project itself, there is evidence of an increasing "positive acknowledgment of difference," a factor of cultural citizenship as indicated by Toby Miller (2, 2001). If the Rastafari can be viewed in an increasingly positive light, their level of acceptance in the community will increase, thereby increasing the power of their argument for citizenship.

The potential, therefore, for concurrent Rastafari integration and Ethiopian community development is great. As the rainwater project demonstrates, the Rastafari gain cultural citizenship capital by making use of the capital they earn as foreigners engaging in NGO work. In the face of the seemingly impossible goal of political citizenship, the Rastafari have gained something perhaps more valuable: a level of acceptance within the Ethiopian community.

Ato Demisse Shito, the mayor of Shashemene, in an August 2007 interview explained that because of the great potential of the Rastafari, the Ethiopian community must move to view the people referred to as "Jamaicans" as different than other foreigners. Underlining the constitutional restrictions for foreigners, Shito explained the limitations on Rastafari in Shashemene: "They can invest their money. They can participate in development for the city. They can participate in the city. But there are no rules or regulations regarding these people."

The mayor, however, described the uniqueness of the Rastafari. "They are different from others," he said. Turning to me, a white, non-Rasta woman, he exclaimed: "They are different from you also! They are mentally, spiritually and have other attachments to Ethiopia. By social relationships and marriage they are related to us; this cannot be changed. Some of them know the languages of the area as well. They are part of our city and part of Ethiopia even though they come from many parts of the world. But the legal constitution is needed."

Though the mayor is saying that the Rastafari should be viewed as "different" from "regular" foreigners, they are still not Ethiopian. As much as he recognizes their contributions and validates the mental and spiritual connection Rastafari have to Ethiopia, his comments demonstrate a lack of potential for Rastafari to be fully accepted without government legitimacy. Thus, beyond the bureaucratic impossibility of citizenship, the mayor also presents a perceptual problem created by the lack of categorization for Rastafari. Although the efforts of the Rastas to be accepted are being well received, the fact that they must inhabit the position of foreigners to engage with the community presents a reality of liminality in which their identities are culturally and politically unstable. Perhaps the mayor is right, and the only way this can be changed is by legal changes allowing for citizenship. In the absence of this possibility, however, it is clear that the Rastafari will continue to strive for cultural citizenship—an alternate and perhaps more meaningful acceptance.

"A New Christianity for the Modern World"

Rastafari Fundamentalism in Salvador, Bahia, Brazil

JANET L. DECOSMO

This chapter will describe the beliefs of a number of "religious" Rastafari (also called "orthodox," "fundamentalist," or "Protestant" Rastafari) interviewed formally and informally in an urban barrio known as the Pelourinho in the city of Salvador in Bahia, Brazil. The research took place during Carnaval in February 1997, 1998, and 1999, during the summer of 1997, and continued about once a year for the next ten years. One of the informants told me that Rastafari was "a new Christianity for the modern world"; hence the title for this chapter.

As elsewhere, Rastafari in Bahia may be described as a continuum of beliefs and lifestyles, ranging from religious fundamentalists on one end to antireligious individualists on the other. Nevertheless, Bahian Rastafari of all stripes see self-expression through art, poetry, and music as having the power to liberate. Some express a desire to be politically active, while others refuse to participate in politics but use the system when it benefits their cause. All wear dreadlocks. Most eat meat. Some smoke ganja and others do not. For the orthodox Rastafari, smoking ganja is always in the context of informal communal reasonings and is seen to be a way to discover divine truth within themselves.

As is the case in other parts of the world outside Jamaica, Rastafari made its way to Bahia in the seventies by way of reggae music; in particular, the music of Bob Marley and the Wailers. Although reggae music in Bahia represents cultural resistance against the system, it does not necessarily represent the views of orthodox Rastafari. For the orthodox, reggae is not only a form of social protest and a tool of consciousness-raising and liberation; it also provides a means for religious evangelism.

Thus, there is a clear distinction between those reggae musicians who are Rastafari and those who are merely "dreadlocks." Many of the orthodox Rastafari describe themselves as evangelizers or "students of the spirit of Jah's word." They stand opposed to racism, oppression, and injustice as well as to indigenous forms of Bahian religion and culture such as Candomblé and Carnaval, despite their African origins.

Candomblé is one of several Afro-Brazilian religions found in Bahia. Characterized by members who are possessed by African spirits known as *orixás,* the most well-known group within Candomblé uses Yoruba dress, rituals, and language.

Regarding the latter, in Bahia they have a saying that Carnaval is "the festival of the devil blessed by God" (Wafer 1991, 10). Orthodox Rastafari would agree with the first part of the statement, but not the last. They take part in what they consider to be a Babylonian festival encouraging the weakness of the flesh, only to proselytize through reggae music. From the tops of their mobile trucks band members call out to people "in the name of the Father, Son and Holy Spirit" to be strong, to stay away from crack, and to not succumb to the desires of the flesh and Babylon.

Like the rest of Brazil, Bahia has a long history of economic hardship, political repression, and racial discrimination. Rastafari (and practitioners of Candomblé before them) have been discriminated against and brutalized by the police, especially during the period of military dictatorship in the sixties and seventies. Brazil has long existed in a state of denial about racism. Since there has been a long history of miscegenation and a resultant interracial amity, the myth of racial democracy is predominant. But after studying the 1980 census, Afro-Bahian activist Abdias do Nascimento wrote: "In contrast to the image of 'racial democracy,' the data cited show a clear racial hierarchy in terms of income and educational opportunity. At the top are white men; next, white women; third, Black men [including Blacks and Browns], and lastly Black women" (do Nascimento 1989, ix). Thus, as Kim Butler maintained, in Bahia "poverty, violence, and lack of opportunity . . . disproportionately affect people of African descent" (1998, 160).

The 1991 census (which used colors as racial categories) reported that of Salvador's population of 2,075,273 inhabitants, 14.5 percent were "black," 64.2 percent were "brown," 20.4 percent were "white," 0.1 percent were "yellow," and 0.2 percent were "red" (indigenous) (Kraay 1998, 9). One of my informants who would be classified as Brown but who identified with the Black oppressed, told me the following: "Here in Salvador, the *mestiço* [a daughter or son of Black and White] is used to say 'no' to the authentic Negroes. In Bahia people use *mestiços* to be 'captains of the bush' (soldiers who would go after escaped slaves). They use the *mestiço* to 'educate' us, to keep us mentally enslaved." Thus, the rhetoric pertaining to racial harmony does not reflect reality.

The historical significance of the urban barrio of Pelourinho is that it served as the location for public whippings and beatings of African slaves (the word Pelourinho in Portuguese means "whipping post"). The average monthly income in the area, where approximately 75 percent of the population is illiterate, is about $120 U.S. dollars. In regard to illiteracy, I observed a sign maker having to recarve a beautiful, hand-painted wooden sign for a bar because he had misspelled "Pelourinho" by leaving out the "u."

Unemployment is high (about 80 percent of Salvadorans live in poverty), and impoverished street kids roam the streets begging for money in this popular tourist area. However, those who have problems with alcohol abuse, prostitution, and crack remain largely invisible to tourists.

Moreover, there is no government welfare or "safety net" for the poor in Salvador. People get along as best they can, some depending on the charity of the many churches found in the area. But the churches merely apply Band-aids. Living conditions remain precarious. A fundamentalist Rastafari informant lucky enough to have a roof over his head provided me with the following description of the ghetto in Pelourinho in which he lives:

> The situation in Salvador, it's very poor. It's very precarious. Like the blood that is running in Zaire, in the old Congo republic, here in Salvador

> blood is being shed. People are hurting here. The activists, the militants, are very hurt and are repressed by the police. Movements dedicated to revitalization are being put down very strongly. The policeman goes into the street and fights with his dogs and guns. A majority of us don't have jobs, and we don't have a chance and opportunity. It is not given to us the right that we have, the right of surviving. We survive by miracles. We evoke the all-powerful God and we use the positive, supernatural powers. Like the people were fed for forty years in the desert, like our patriarch Moses, the leader of our people invoked the all-powerful God and the all-powerful God sent food to us. We don't have basic help of any kind. We are left. We are thrown and confined to the concentration camps that in Brazil they call *favelas*. These are concentration camps like Auschwitz. Here is hell.

It was not this informant's desire to repatriate to Africa to escape difficult living conditions. However, a connection to Africa is felt so strongly in Bahia that one of the well-known sayings about it is that "it is a place where the ancestors walk." There are three reasons for the potent African presence in Bahia.

First, slavery in Brazil was characterized by waves of newly arrived captives, replacing those who had died before they had a chance to reproduce. These continual, "fresh" infusions of Africans meant that African cultural practices were constantly renewed in Bahia. In other locations in the Diaspora where slaves lived long enough to reproduce and new captives were not brought over in such large numbers (or were restricted to one or two ethnic groups), cultural practices became more diluted. The sheer numbers of Africans imported into Bahia made it impossible for authorities to "control" them, especially in the urban areas.

Second, in the history of Bahia there have been many repatriates, beginning soon after emancipation in the late nineteenth century. Many of these trips were made for the expressed purpose of gaining the necessary information and skills to return to Bahia to found houses of Candomblé. For example, geographer Robert A. Voeks wrote that in 1888, "a black woman born in Cachoeira, Bahia, named Isadora Maria Hamus, moved to Lagos, spent eight years learning Yoruba and English, and returned to

Bahia to become a leader of a house of Candomblé" (Voeks 1997, 154). As Voeks put it, for Afro-Bahians, "Africa is not a vague mythical land. . . . It is a living reality, from whence many of the objects they use in their rituals are imported, where people they know have visited and . . . where their fathers or grandfathers came from" (153).

Third, the fact that the colonizers of Brazil were Catholic rather than Protestant made a difference in the degree of African cultural practices retained. Because of their belief in saints as mediators between the human and the divine, and also because of their acceptance of religious objects as having mystical sacred powers, Catholic colonizers showed greater tolerance of African cultural arts, especially the visual arts. In Jamaica, colonized by Anglicans, African cultural practices were not tolerated to the same degree that they were in Brazil. Even though the assumption behind the policy was "divide and rule," Catholic colonial governments in Brazil fostered brotherhoods segregated according to African ethnic affiliation. These islands of African space—where the bonds of oppression were temporarily loosened—were inhabited by people with similar languages and worldviews. Thus, they became areas where African language, customs, and ideas could legally be perpetuated.

Even for the casual observer, it is impossible not to think of Africa while one is in Bahia, especially in Pelourinho. There are African museums, exhibits, restaurants, fabric stores, *baianas* selling African food on the street corners, and images of Yoruba *orixás* everywhere in the public spaces of the historic district. As far as they are concerned, the Rastafari of Pelourinho already live spiritually in the midst of Africa and Jamaica. Thus, their goal is not to abandon where they live but to transform its Babylonian elements.

Because Afro-Bahians have refused to give up their heritage, cultural and religious pluralism has managed to prevail over acculturation to European norms. Black consciousness has been expressed in nonpolitical forms such as religious brotherhoods, samba schools, Carnaval *blocos* (groups), African religious organizations, mutual aid societies, and recreational clubs. Nevertheless, although Afro-Bahians have come quite a distance in the struggle, their concerns are still basically the same as they were four centuries ago. As Butler concluded:

> At their most fundamental level, Afro-Bahians' struggles today address the same issues that their African forebears faced when they first arrived in the sixteenth century. Countering the impositions of a slave society in which a small elite dictated the rights and prerogatives of others, Afro-Bahians have consistently fought for self-determination and equal access to sociopolitical power. Applying countervailing pressure against hegemony, people of African descent have used existing mechanisms, created new ones, and seized upon moments of sociopolitical transformation to find self-fulfillment and dignity in a society that once defined them as chattel. (K. Butler 1998, 158)

The twenty male informants were interviewed in and around Pelourinho, ranged in age from twenty-five to fifty, and held a variety of occupations. Many were musicians or artisans, some were office/factory workers, one was a professional, and a few were unemployed. In describing themselves and their beliefs, twelve could be classified as orthodox based on their use of terms and ideas associated with evangelical Christianity, that is, Jesus Christ having died for them; the Holy Trinity of Father, Son, and Holy Spirit; the apocalypse having already begun and the imminent return of Jesus to bring salvation and eternal life; and the need to proselytize or spread the word of God. Some described themselves outright as "Christian Rastas." One who did so divided Rastafari into Christian Rastas, Jewish Rastas, and Rastas who participated in Candomblé. I was told that there were also dreadlocks who were not Rastas as well as "baldhead," beardless Rastas, although I did not interview any of the latter.

Despite using the terms "Jah" and "Rastafari" frequently in their responses, the orthodox Rastafari considered Ethiopian Emperor Haile Selassie to have been a servant, prophet, or messenger of Jah rather than Jah himself. They placed no great emphasis on his image (I only saw one poster of the emperor the four times I visited). They told me they believed he was/is God in the same way that they themselves were God, with the difference between themselves and the emperor lying in the degree of inspiration by, or in the dwelling of, the Holy Spirit.

In their responses, some of the informants specifically used the name "Haile Selassie I." One said that when he used the term, he literally meant "the power of the holy trinity: Father, Son, and Holy Spirit." He said that the emperor was a symbol of the power of God prophesized in Revelations 5:5. (Revelations 5:5 reads "Weep not; lo, the Lion of the tribe of Judah, the Root of David, has conquered, so that he can open the scroll and its seven seals.")

Another informant explained his view of Haile Selassie:

> I consider Tafari Makonen to be a guide, salt, light. I'm also salt, I'm also light, like Jah lives in me and also lived in him [Makonen] because Jah is alive. According to the words of Jah, according to his ethical principles and social principles, he is God like we are God. The messenger Jesus Christ told us that we were God because we're manipulated by God the Father. . . . Jesus Christ, through Tafari Makonen, gave deep things to us. He taught us something wonderful. He taught us to be wise and to be able to translate the Bible to everybody else.

When offered a choice of defining Rastafari as a religion, a philosophy, or a way of life, many of the orthodox informants stated that it was all three. One said that Rastafari was "the feeling of men of all races for justice, liberty and spiritual harmony." Another said that Rastafari was not a religion or a philosophy, but "an attitude about life." He said: "The real Rastafari believes in the Father, Son, and Holy Spirit as the absolute God, and observes the commandments of Jah through his son Jesus Christ in the consolations and revelations of the Holy Spirit." He continued, stating that "Rastafari is the King with the Holy Spirit. I am a King with the Holy Spirit. Jesus Christ is the King of Kings."

A third informant maintained that "Rastafari is the King of Kings, the Seer of Seers, the Conquering Lion of the Tribe of Judah, the Majesty. He's everything in all. Amen." Yet another informant defined Rastafari as servants of Jah "who are sealed with the Holy Spirit and who are in harmony with the word of Jah. We only believe in the power of the Holy Trinity in the person of Jesus Christ, the true God, and life eternal." Some said that they had been "born Rastafari," but had "assumed the posture" in the late seventies or early eighties after being exposed to reggae music.

Following are several excerpts from the responses of three of the orthodox Rastafari. The first is Ras Carlos, a thirty-seven-year-old Rastafari who called himself a "psychotherapist, sociologist, and theocratic." He lived in a communal ghetto in Pelourinho haphazardly built of wooden shacks constructed inside the facade and three walls of a roofless, floorless, centuries-old historic building (which, he told me, the inhabitants owned). There was one small stand-pipe providing running water on the ground level. Ras Carlos's back and upper arms were covered with tattoos of Bob Marley and other images, about which he said:

> These tattoos are a letter; the name of this letter is "words of wisdom." With this letter what happens? People will not relate to me by the color of my skin; they deal with me because of intelligence, because of love. I am respected not by how I look outside but the kindness, justice, and truth of Jah inside of me. I'm a mural because on my body I go back to the roots of the African people, of the less fortunate poor ones. But even the very small can give a rich spiritual presence.

Ras Carlos's dreadlocks were wide and matted. He told me that Rastafari men looked like Jesus, which a lot of people did not accept. He said: "Some people ask me, 'Your hair is so soft, why do you leave it in such misery?'" Ras Carlos ate meat when he could get it, and he smoked ganja. He performed with various reggae bands. He told me he had a wife and children who did not live with him because his lifestyle, he said, was too difficult. He told me that whoever needed a place to stay was welcome to stay with him. His small house in the ghetto contained a table containing a few pieces of literature. Clearly, he was a man with a religious calling, a man on a mission.

Ras Carlos distinguished between "the dreadlocks without faith, and the dreadlocks with faith." He explained how he began to grow his locks:

> I identify myself as Rastafari because I transformed through Jah and the Holy Ghost the segments of Babylon that were inside of me. I started when I was eighteen years old, when I went into the army. I found some brothers who liked Bob Marley and who identified themselves with me because I had already heard Marley, and I had heard reggae music. And because of my own lifestyle and my environment I was touched by the Holy Ghost. Jah transformed my life, and I became his disciple, his lamb.

Describing himself as a man with mystical powers, he added:

> The people who hurt me are afraid of me because [they think] I am a demon. They don't understand the knowledge that is in me. They don't understand that Rastafari is the spirit of light; that I'm in the light of God. They do not understand what's written in the name of the master, Jesus Christ. I could drink anything that could kill me, and it wouldn't kill me. I could touch the snakes that spoke in tongues, I could put my hands on the hearts of people and cure them. Me, in Brazil, I live from miracles.

Ras Carlos vigorously condemned the capitalist system:

> I do not believe in capitalism. Capitalism was taken away from my life. To maintain this hair, I cannot invest in the system. Not a cent. I live from the powers, like Daniel, like Joshua. I live like Jesus Christ. I live spirit, because I *am* spirit. If I live in spirit, I have to walk in spirit. People do not understand why I do not need money to live. I do not need a form of government. I live theocracy.

About Candomblé, Ras Carlos stated the following:

> Candomblé is anticulture. Candomblé in Bahia is used to retain us, to hold us back in our evolution. . . . I hate Candomblé because I was part of the lower spirituality. I tried to find myself. I was involved with the prince of darkness, with this low culture. . . . When I lived for Candomblé I mutilated myself. I cut my own body, and I fed violence. Bang! Good boy. When I lived in Candomblé I tried to feed myself, being a bad man, taking away from the rich and giving to the poor, and Jah doesn't want a man to rob and to be violent. I was able to destroy and kill, and Candomblé didn't give anything good to me. Candomblé is the opium of the world. . . . It destroys.

About political power, Ras Carlos expressed hope for change. He said:

> When we get the chance to get in the government, in power, we're going to start a new program, planting and sharing and dividing. We are all partners on the land. Why didn't we have participation in Brazilian oil and gold? We are a people of the planet. Why aren't the universal riches of the world invested in us? We have to do that. When we ascend we have to give

> people what they deserve: dignity. What I understand by dignity is that man is an instrument for love, to love. Love your neighbor like you love yourself. Let's start this feeling, this mental posture, fraternity, to see in each human being a brother. Fraternity. To give up, extinguish, and banish away capitalism from the earth. No money. Culture of Jah, yes. Amen.

For Ras Carlos, the way to fight Babylon was through music. He stated:

> Jesus Christ has given me the consciousness that I'm a living fire, a living stone foundation, a tool to annihilate the system of lies. I want freedom, fraternity, sharing. No guns, atomic weapons (disarmament), heavy machinery. We have the music to fight this system of lies. In a simple clear way, money brings confusion. We can't prostitute the music. We have to be our own producers. All of you who have a boom box, a bass, a drum, a guitar, let's get together and do a project the same way Jesus did through Marley. We can do the same. If you don't want reggae, the beat of the heart, tell the truth with any kind of music—salsa, merengue, waltz, bolero, any music—but say the truth.

The next informant, Ras Ciro, was a friend of Ras Carlos and was a capoeirista and reggae vocalist and composer for a band, Amantes do Reggae (lovers of reggae). In his mid-to-late thirties at the time, he was light-skinned and had short, fine, thick dreadlocks. He had a small tattoo of a *berimbau* on his upper arm, and he ate meat and smoked ganja.

He lived with his Argentinean wife and two small sons in an apartment that he said they owned in a building inhabited by other reggae artists and friends. It had a communal yard behind it for washing, growing herbs, and reasoning. He told me that he worked about ninety hours a week teaching capoeira at four different locations in Salvador and taking care of his fruits and vegetables on a small plot of land (a *terreno*), which he said he owned in Pernambues (another barrio a short bus ride away). In order to accommodate all, he refused to charge his capoeira students; they lived mostly off the income his wife earned for teaching Portuguese to families working at the Argentinean Embassy.

I was able to visit the *terreno*. There was a small one-room structure there as well as a shallow well. Although eventually Ras Ciro would construct a building there to house his family as well as his capoeira academy, the location was mainly used at the time to grow food and for reasonings, which included smoking ganja, sharing food, and talking to passersby who ventured in, some of whom were in need of a place to stay. The room contained shelves with written materials on such topics as racism and injustice and religious tracks used by the evangelical churches. To explain their beliefs to outsiders who visited the *terreno,* Ras Ciro read from these tracts. One pamphlet he gave me was entitled "Racismo e desigualdade" (racism and inequality) and consisted of a speech given by Bahian Deputy Domingos Leonelli during a session held in November 1996, in honor of National Black Consciousness Day.

Ras Ciro had been exposed to evangelical Christianity as a youth, having been regularly taken to church as a child. He said that he and his two sisters played music in the church and that his father played bolero music. When I asked him to tell me about the "evangelicals," he replied that he, himself, was an evangelizer. I explained that I had meant the evangelical churches. He said he had rejected them because they were too commercial; what people needed was a baptism of fire, not water. He also objected to their prohibition of ganja.

In the first interview with Ras Ciro, after telling me that he was going to answer my questionnaire in a "very philosophical" manner, he proceeded to answer as if he, himself, were Jah. He volunteered no personal information about himself, which the questionnaire was designed to elicit:

> What is my name? His name is Jesus Christ, Jah Rastafari.
>
> My age is? He is the Creator, and nobody created him. He is the power not created by anyone, who created all the power, all the energy.
>
> Where do I live? Jah lives in the heaven of heavens. He lives with Jesus Christ and with the Holy Ghost and has his archangels and cherubim, twenty-four old men that are in the front of his throne and four animals that are around his seat, singing a song that we're going to listen to flow. Praised is Jah, the all-powerful God, the One that was, is and will be, All the Power. Amen.
>
> What is my profession and how do I support myself? Jah is Rastafari. His is the profession of love. He supports himself through his own spirit, through his creation.

> Why am I Rastafari? Because Jah Rastafari is the recognized Holy Ghost and he convinced us that that is the truth.
>
> When did I start with this? Jah started this a long time ago, before the foundation of this planet, when Jesus Christ was already here to recover the humans from this earth. Jah is all over. He is the head, we are the members of this large body. Jah is in all of us; he never leaves us. Amen.
>
> Are my family members Rastafari? Those who do not abandon father, mother, son, and daughter for Jah Rastafari is not dignified to be with Jah.
>
> Are there different groups of Rastafari? Only Jesus Christ saves. The Bible said, in the word of God, that many false or fake Christs would come, prophets would come to make themselves big, not to praise Jah Rastafari and his majesty Selassie I, the trinity power. He prepared the church that when those fake prophets came to create division of religions for reasons of money or even sensual divisions, that we run away from this kind of people. It's the will of Jah Rastafari that we live in this world but apart from these people who want to create this division, these different groups.
>
> What is the number of Rastafari in Bahia today? It's not an answer that I can give because only Jah can look into the hearts and change the hearts of each individual. Only Jah can look and know who is Rastafari. But the important thing is that his redemption plan is for everyone living on this planet: for the Greek, for the Jew, for the barbarian, for the African, for the South American, North American, European, Asian, Japanese. The plan of Jah is for everyone to unify in Jesus Christ. Amen. Glory to Jah. Rastafari.

When I inquired about Haile Selassie, the first time I was in Salvador Ras Ciro explained that "God took Ras Makonen to the glory and he is resting for the resurrection of the dead in the day the Imperial Majesty will come and embrace to his kingdom, to the right words, the lambs." On my third and fourth visits, I continued to ask him to clarify his views. I told Ras Ciro that some Rastafari say that Haile Selassie is Jah. He replied that Tafari Makonen was a prophet, not God, and to say that he is God is idolatry. He said that Jesus was/is the only Son of God. Haile Selassie, he said, is "the light of the trinity, the Holy Spirit of Jah Rastafari that is in all of us." Jah is "in us, in nature, in everything," he said. By contrast, Tafari Makonen was "a man, even a dictator." Bob Marley, Marcus Garvey, and

Tafari Makonen were all prophets. And although the emperor's words might be right and just, Jah's words are to be found elsewhere: in the Bible. Therefore he didn't seem particularly interested in reading the emperor's speeches, although he knew that the words to Marley's song, "War," came from one of these speeches.

Ras Ciro seemed only to have time to read the Bible. However, during a subsequent visit, he read passages aloud from a book entitled *Estudo Perspicaz das Escrituras* (study of scriptural insights) published in 1990 by the Watchtower Bible and Tract Society of New York (more commonly known as Jehovah's Witnesses). He had told me earlier that the apocalypse was "now," and that if a bomb hit him he would escape death and still live (presumably, as spirit). He also told me that there would be "a big victory—maybe in an hour or maybe in a thousand years. Only Jah knows." Then the struggle would be over and all would be made right.

Ras Ciro inscribed "Jah Rastafari, Selassie I" on everything that he designed or made. Outside his apartment in Pelourinho, the wall read, "Jah vive em nos" (Jah lives in us). Another wall read, "Selassie I, Espirito Santo, Jah, Jesus Christo." At a capoeira Angola practice with his students I was able to see the school's uniforms he had designed. They consisted of loose-fitting green pants with an elastic waist and a white T-shirt. On the front of the T-shirt was a rainbow of red, yellow, and green with a Star of David underneath it. At the top were the words, "Jah Rastafari Selassie I." In the red part of the rainbow was written "Academia De Estudos Da"; in the yellow part, "Capoeira Angola"; and in the green was written the name of the informant's well-known master teacher, "Joao Pequeno." Under the rainbow, the Portuguese words for "Jesus Christ Is Our Teacher" was written and, in very small print, the location and date of the academy's founding could be seen.

The *berimbaus* that he made were also inscribed with words important to his faith. A large Star of David with a fish in the middle of it was burnished into the gourd. Along its rim were three smaller stars and the words "Jah Rastafari Selassie I." At the top of the bow were the date of the instrument's making and an address in Pelourinho. In the middle, the words "Jah Rastafari Selassie I, Amen" were inscribed. Toward the bottom were the words "capoeira Angola" and his own name as instructor. Ras Ciro hoped one day to have his own capoeira academy, succeeding Joao Pequeno.

Ras Ivan was a forty-year-old friend of Ras Carlos and Ras Ciro. Whenever possible, he sang reggae songs "inspired by the Bible" in a group called Unidade Real (real unity). At the time unemployed and homeless, he told me that until his tools were stolen he was a craftsman, making jewelry out of coconut shell. He was separated from his wife and daughter. His wife was Rastafari and worked full-time in order to live in a comfortable environment—he told me that women had "no use" for unemployed men. He said that he had a house where assorted people stayed for various lengths of time (some apparently for years), but that the house apparently was not in or near Pelourinho. Consequently, he often slept and showered at Ras Ciro's apartment in Pelourinho or in the *terreno* in Pernambues.

Ras Ivan wore somewhat matted, thick dreadlocks, and he smoked ganja, consumed meat, and drank beer if offered. He was eager to collect and read everything in print on Rastafari, defining himself as Rastafari "because the person of Jesus Christ in accordance with the New Testament turned me into a son of God." He explained, "I, like any other being under the sun, was dead, and the spirit of Jah through Jesus Christ took the sins away from me and revived my spirit—I in Rastafari and Rastafari in I."

Ras Ivan stated that his band's reggae was "orthodox": "We play reggae because we believe reggae is the Song of the Psalms, the song of the kings, right? We play reggae, nyahbinghi, to say good things to the Creator of everything. We sing songs to everyone." He said that there were many dreadlocks in Bahia, but few Rastafari: "Some of them call themselves Rastas but when you see the practice you know they're not Rastas." Then he explained why the Bible is so important to him and his friends:

> The little information that comes to us from the rest of the continent, the rest of the world, sometimes it is changed and altered. That's why the Bible is our faith book, our ruling book in practice. Everything that's not in accordance with the teachings of the Creator, of Jah, it's not literally worth our respect. I think that men and women, white and black, yellow and green, should listen to the word of Christ and the book says everyone should believe. If you believe in the book you'll be saved; if you don't believe in the book you'll be condemned. But it's necessary that more people be recruited, not only people connected to evangelical denominations.

> We believe that Jah opened the door and Jesus Christ conquered the right of salvation for all men, for every living man.

Ras Ivan maintained that Rastafari was both a way of life and a religion. It is a religion, he said,

> because the literal meaning of religion is to keep yourself away from the corruption of the world. That's why we don't have communion with the world, because the world made Jah very upset. Because we're not citizens from below [his actual words were "under-down"]; we're citizens from above, sons of the Highest Above. Rastafari is the correct way of life. It's love. Love is the accomplishment of the law. Christ said, "I'm the way, the truth and the life." Allelu-Jah. Rastafari. Amen.

Like Ras Carlos and Ras Ciro, Ras Ivan defined Candomblé as a form of "low spiritism." He said: "Candomblé doesn't have any relation to the people of God, neither with the sons of God. Candomblé is idolatry. Candomblé divinizes strange gods, praises strange gods. And Jah, the true God of eternal life, the creator of heaven and earth, abominates idolatry. Rastafari, or the Son of God, does not bend his knee to idols. Rastafari are only afraid of the name of Jesus, in the person of Jah, Rastafari, Selassie I the First."

He equally condemned Carnaval:

> Carnaval is Babylon. The meaning of Carnaval literally is "party of the meat, of the flesh." Rastafari are afraid of the word of Jah. Jah tells us to walk not according to the flesh but according to the spirit. . . . In Brazil the great explosion of the flesh happens in Carnaval, everything happens—all kinds of crime, injuries, alcoholism, and many deaths that the media do not report—because the city lives through tourism. In Carnaval children are violated because of this immoral music that's out there. In Carnaval all kinds of transgressions, physical and also moral and cultural, happen. Carnaval, in truth, is an authentic cultural genocide.

Ras Ivan said about Haile Selassie:

> When he was dominated by the Holy Ghost of God in route to that discourse to the organization of the United Nations, he didn't go there as a normal man or a secular man. He came to talk through the Spirit of God. He was sent through God, from the Holy Ghost's spirit, to the nations. This discourse or presentation that later Bob Marley put music to [the song "War"], this discourse was to this people.

On a later visit, when I asked Ras Ivan to clarify and explain his views about Haile Selassie, I drew a diagram. I wrote "God" at the top of a piece of paper, put "Jesus" underneath to the left, and "Holy Spirit" underneath to the right. I then asked him to tell me where Haile Selassie fit in. He drew a circle around the three words and then drew two arrows: one to the right of the circle with the words "1 pessoa so" (one person only) written under it, and another arrow under the circle with "Haile Selassie I" written under it. When I indicated my lack of comprehension, he shrugged and said that I should "put on God's glasses and think like God thinks" so I could "understand these spiritual matters."

Ras Ivan's answer to the question of whether or not he wanted to repatriate to Africa contained a reference to a future time or place when Jah would bring everyone together after the apocalypse. Because of the strong body/spirit dualism of his beliefs, apparently this unification would only occur in spirit:

> I have a lot of interest in going to Ethiopia. I have a lot of desire to know the Maroons and the Rastas that live in the mountains of Jamaica. Yes, I'd like to know my brothers and sisters who live in Jamaica, who live in Grenada, who are in Martinique, who are in Surinam, who are spread all over the entire planet. However, one day all of us will be together. We are going to be meeting there, where there's no tears and crying, because the light of the celestial father, Jah, Haile Selassie the First and the Only, his light is going to shine every place, and our tears and differences here in Babylon will be extinguished from our minds and from our hearts. We know the redemption of our spirit has already been done because Christ paid a very high price to conquer the right of salvation for us. . . . Come then, Jah. Amen.

One purpose of this chapter is to share the views of some of the orthodox Rastafari in Bahia. Now, in discussing the significance of their viewpoints, I would specifically like to state, as I did in an earlier article, that Rastafari cannot be dismissed as an escapist religion (DeCosmo 1994). Religion can serve the status quo or oppose it. All three informants—Ras Carlos, Ras Ciro, and Ras Ivan—saw Rastafari as a type of "primitive" Christianity, a collection of individuals practicing the fraternity that could only exist without a church hierarchy and that stood opposed to existing religious authorities. The fact that they were poor, Black, and oppressed and wore dreadlocks and smoked ganja, but came out of a Protestant evangelical tradition, led them to identify themselves as evangelical Christian Rastafari. Although they expressed hope in a "big victory" wrought by Jah, in the meantime they took action.

In all its manifestations globally, certainly Rastafari has changed the consciousness of many Blacks, as well as Whites, the world over. The important question has to do with why, and how. Part of the answer, I would suggest, has to do with the affinity of Rastafari to what Robert N. Bellah called a "civil religion." American civil religion, according to Bellah, was based on the belief that America was chosen by God to be a "light unto the nations"—it was dedicated to the highest ideals and would redeem the world (1992, 36). Those Americans who subscribed to this belief belonged, at the same time, to a variety of religious denominations.

According to Randall K. Burkett, the same was true of the Garvey movement, which brought a "diverse group of clergy together with a much more heterogeneous group of social, political and economic (and even some anti-religious) radicals" (1978, 186). Many religious leaders who united under Garvey believed that since the White race had failed to redeem the human species, the Black race had been called upon by God to lead the way. Burkett explained that

> civil religion . . . is a "powerful motivating myth" predicated on a shared historic experience, and it possesses the capacity of calling [a] nation itself first into being, and then into judgment, in the name of the higher ideals to which it is dedicated. Further, the civil religion always stands in a somewhat ambiguous relationship with respect to particular religions; it

> can stand alongside of, exist in tension with, or subsume or at least seek to incorporate them. (ibid.)

Burkett wrote that Garvey

> unabashedly set out to create a new/old mythos, a coherent interpretation of reality which . . . moved to a new level of self-consciousness and consciousness-formation. . . . The panoply of symbols, the theology, the pomp and ceremony, the use of music . . . were advanced to demonstrate to all men and women of African descent their essential oneness in the struggle for survival in a hostile, white-dominated world. Garvey also demonstrated the power that would be theirs if that oneness could be actualized via self-respect, self-reliance, and faith in one another and in one's God. (ibid., 7–8)

For Garvey, social justice involved a fair distribution of power. Some critics of Rastafari lament the fact that Rastafari is most often identified with religion or culture rather than economics or politics, and therefore claim that it cannot yet be considered a "movement." They stress the necessity for Rastafari to infiltrate and change power structures through political action. This schematic distinction between popular culture and politics keeps resurfacing in the literature on Rastafari.

In this regard, I would like to suggest that perhaps Rastafari could be seen as an emergent civil religion that strives, through culture (that is, "conscious" reggae), to achieve the political goal of social justice. Cultural groups can create alternative spaces that, when they become visible, strong, and influential enough, can exert political leverage and begin to make changes to mainstream institutions. In this way the gap between culture and politics is bridged.

Although at present they lack what Max Weber would have described as a "world-historical" figure such as Garvey, it is evident that Rastafari, no matter where they are found on the planet, feel that they have been divinely called to a special task in the world. They are aware that some people consider Rastafari to be an escapist religion and reggae and ganja to be opiates, but these informants did not consider them to be such. (Ironically, as we have seen, because of their Christian evangelical bent, they considered the religious and cultural practices closest to African roots, such as those of Candomblé, to be the real opiates.) Lacking access to Babylon's political and economic structures, they publicly spoke and acted in their communities to try to uplift their fellow sufferers in the hope that, with the help of Jah, their actions, small and nonrevolutionary as they might seem to some, would become part of a larger pan-African vision of Black redemption that would uplift not only the Black race, but all human beings.

Thus, the orthodox Rastafari informants described herein had a mission. Their mission was not only to survive (which in itself was an accomplishment) but to shoulder the heavy burden and responsibility of educating and proselytizing, through whatever small means of self-expression available to them, the hope and potential of Rastafari. Whether it was feeding or housing a lost soul, writing graffiti on a wall, placing words and images on a T-shirt, teaching children in the streets, or singing reggae songs and preaching to the crowds during Carnaval, they were doing all they could in good faith. And they were doing it in the context of a Rastafari they considered to be "a new Christianity for the modern world." The belief that Jah was with them sustained them in the struggle.

Part 3 Rastafari Ideology, Philosophy, and Praxis

Rastafari as Philosophy and Praxis

LAWRENCE O. BAMIKOLE

The motivation for this chapter stems from the fact that philosophy is a multifaceted academic discipline. Gone are the days when philosophy was an exclusive preserve of the West. Today, there are different traditions in philosophy: Western, Asian, African, and Caribbean. However, there is still a certain ambivalence in regarding non-Western philosophies, especially African and Caribbean philosophies, as *philosophy*. Thus, Stewart and Blocker observed that "opinion is divided among philosophers whether there is any non-Western philosophy, and if there is, how many distinct kinds of philosophy there are. Many philosophers hold that there are three great original centers of philosophy in the world—Greek (or Western), Indian, and Chinese" (2001, 435).

The view expressed by Stewart and Blocker has, surprisingly, been supported by some scholars within the African and (possibly Caribbean) traditions. For instance, some African scholars who have been labeled as "African logical positivists" have argued that the African thought system cannot pass for philosophy until it undergoes the rigorous and critical testing that Western philosophy endured. Thus, within the Caribbean space, certain movements and individuals have put forward worldviews that reflect the realities of their space, but those views have not been recognized within the space as constituting a respectable philosophy in the purely academic sense. The view expressed here is similar to the observations made by two scholars working within the Caribbean tradition. Paget Henry observes that "Caribbean philosophy has been carefully embedded in the practices of nonphilosophical discourses almost to the point of concealment" (2000, xi). Bewaji observes that "there is a philosophical tradition in the Caribbean that bred the Pan Music, the Calypso Tradition, the Dancehall culture, the genius of Garvey and that there is a corpus of text that is 'Caribbean Philosophy' properly so-called, rigorous in content, fecund in orientation and apposite in its effort to comprise a self-knowledge discourse, and that this text has to be studied, used and taught in the Caribbean" (2005, 1).

Implicit in Henry's and Bewaji's observations is that the Caribbean has an autonomous philosophy of its own, independent of Western philosophy. Although Henry holds that such philosophy still needs to be thematized, Bewaji believes that such philosophy is already in its complete form, and the only thing that is required to be done is to use and teach it. In my opinion, the positions of the two scholars boil down to the distinction between the professional school and the ethnophilosophical school in (African) philosophy respectively. The questions that arise are these: What is philosophy? Are there universal (normative) features of philosophy? Can Rastafari qualify as philosophy in the technical and academic senses of the term? If the answer to the last question is in the negative, then can Rastafari be reconstructed to make it philosophical? Our primary aim in this chapter is to attempt a response to the last question.

Scholars from sociology, anthropology, and cultural studies have carried out extensive research on Rastafarianism, but to the best of my knowledge, there is still a dearth of literature on critiquing Rastafari from a purely philosophical perspective. My intention is to look at Rastafari as a potential philosophical tradition with the aim of reconstructing some of its basic tenets in such a way that they can stand the test of critical reflection, thereby elevating it from the realms of religion and ideology to a respectable philosophical position worthy of respect by academic circles within and outside the Caribbean space.

The Activity of Philosophy

Different scholars have given different definitions of philosophy. This suggests that the term "philosophy" is essentially contestable. The question of the definition of philosophy may in itself be considered a philosophical question. Here I present several positions that shed light on the nature of the discipline so that scholars may come to an agreement about what philosophy is or ought to be. The first position is to follow the etymological definition of the term. According to this approach, philosophy is coined from two Greek words: *philo,* which means love, and *sophia,* which means wisdom. Thus, philosophy is the love of wisdom. However, the word *wisdom* has been used by different persons without definite meaning attached to it. But what the ancient Greek thinkers referred to as wisdom is the knowledge of fundamental principles and laws, an awareness of that which was basic and unchanging, as opposed to those things that are transitory and changing (Stewart and Blocker 2001).

However, judging from the history of philosophy, this primary definition of philosophy has undergone many changes, to the extent that the basic ingredient of the definition is almost entirely lost. However, despite the changes, an intuitive element to the understanding of philosophy still exists, a kind of reflective thinking not based on brute facts but requiring a systematic thought process, making use of human reason to bear upon such facts.

Another way of defining the term "philosophy" is to adopt a usage in which the word is used in a broad sense and in a narrow sense. The broad sense of philosophy, which is also the nonacademic sense, is captured by the phrases, "I have my own philosophy of life" and "Every business has its own philosophy." What is implied in the broad sense of philosophy is that each person or business has a way of doing things that is governed by some principles. The same can be said of a whole society or culture. Insofar as each society or culture has its own idea of itself, its own conception of what the world is like in general terms, there is a sense in which each society or culture can be said to have its own philosophy. This is the worldview conception of philosophy. According to Stewart and Blocker (2001) this is one of the things sociologists and anthropologists study when they examine different societies and cultures. In my own judgment also, this is the kind of philosophy referred to by Henry and Bewaji in their works. However, Bewaji and Henry hold that this kind of philosophy is in itself discursive and rigorous.

Philosophy can also be defined in a narrow and more technical sense to indicate a particular methodology—"a specialized way of investigating and organizing ideas"—one that is "critical, logical, analytical, systematic" (Stewart and Blocker 2001, 433). Bertrand Russell also recognized this way of understanding the term "philosophy" when he observed: "The conceptions of life and the world which we call *philosophical* are a product of two factors: one, inherited religious and ethical, conceptions; the other, the sort of investigation which may be called *scientific,* using this word in its broadest sense"(1972, xiii). Russell tried to maintain a balance between these two views:

> Philosophy . . . is something intermediate between theology and science. Like theology, it consists of speculations on matters as to which definite knowledge has, so far, been unascertainable; but like science, it appeals to human reason rather than to authority, whether that of tradition or that of revelation. All *definite* knowledge—so I should contend—belongs to science; all *dogma* as to what surpasses definite knowledge belongs to theology. But between theology and science there is a No Man's Land, exposed to attack from both sides; this No Man's Land is philosophy. (ibid.)

From Russell's observation, the following may be inferred as to the nature and definition of philosophy. (1) Philosophy cannot be totally detached from the pre-reflective beliefs of individuals, societies, and cultures. (2) Philosophy is an active discipline in the sense that it is a continuous process of finding out how things are or how things ought to be. (3) Philosophy is essentially an activity carried out by human (autonomous) reason. These features of philosophy cut across societies and cultures, and this is one of the reasons why philosophy cannot be denied in any culture in both the broad and the technical senses.

This brings me to the earlier claim that philosophy is multifaceted. However, some norms are needed to govern the activity of philosophy wherever such activity is taking place. This does not suggest, contrary to what it is often believed, that a particular section of the world should arrogate to itself the originator of such norms. Furthermore, in observing such norms, the peculiarities of each tradition should be borne in mind. This way of conceiving the philosophical agenda strips philosophy of any kind of ethnocentrism, whether Western, Asian, African, or Caribbean. Such norms should include the fact that philosophy is a critical, reflective, analytical, and systematic activity, carried out by the aid of reason, which should aim at understanding and dealing with the human condition in the spaces where such activity is taking place. It is in this way that philosophy is construed as a "critical/moral practice" (Kiros 2001). It is this approach to understanding philosophy that underpins the title of this chapter.

The Worldview of Rastafari

In this section, I discuss two issues: first, the notion of a worldview, and second, the problem of identifying the features of the Rastafari worldview. With regard to the notion of a worldview, Lynch has this to say: "A worldview is an organic whole whose parts . . . can best be understood in relation to their functions inside that whole" (1997, 421). He goes on to say that "our world-view includes not only our beliefs and the concepts we employ in forming our beliefs, but the interests we have which help explain why we have those concepts, the values which guide those interests, and the underlying practices and capacities which limit and define our cognitive production and intake" (422).

Philosophical debates have ensued about the status of a worldview. The crux of the debate is whether a worldview or what is sometimes referred to as a conceptual scheme is fixed for all time or is capable of being revised. The debate is between those who support a Kantian idea of a fixed element of a worldview and those who support a Quinean view that a worldview is capable of being revised to take cognizance of current experiences. The middle way between these positions has been taken by Lynch, that is, the notion of *contextually basic* concepts. A contextually basic concept sees the elements of a worldview as "absolute" not in the sense of being fixed for every thinker, but in the sense of being presupposed by the lion's share of one's thought, as that thought might be in a particular historical circumstance (Lynch 1997, 420). We shall pitch our tent with this middle way of seeing a worldview. This is because a worldview has a double status, with primary and secondary elements. The primary elements of a worldview can be regarded as its "soul" in the sense that they represent features that are resilient to change, whereas the secondary elements can be regarded as the outer dimension of a worldview. These are the elements that readily undergo change. The idea of a worldview, as analyzed here, will later inform a critique of Rastafari.

With regard to the second issue, I acknowledge the fact that Rastafari is made of diverse groups otherwise known as mansions or houses (Chevannes 1998a; Barnett 2005). Scholars of Rastafari have identified some major groups: the Twelve Tribes of Israel, the Nyahbinghi Order, and the Bobo Shanti (Barnett 2005). The belief of these scholars is that there are hardly any essential characteristics common to these houses that can identify them as belonging to the Rastafari movement. Thus, Chevannes observed that "Rastafari is an acephalous movement. There are groups, quasi-groups and individuals, who while sharing the core beliefs, nevertheless remain separate and independent" (1998a, 31). In the same vein, Barnett suggests that because of the divergence within the Rastafari movement, much debate exists concerning what determines whether one is Rasta or not (2005, 75). In other words, Rastafari do not have identifiable commonalities that define them as a group. This position might present problems for identifying the worldview of the Rastafari as a unified system. One way of addressing this problem is to invoke the Wittgenstein (1988) notion of *family resemblance.* According to Wittgenstein, there is nothing common to a group of things or instances called by the same name other than family resemblances—the vague and overlapping likeness one sees between the different members of a family (Wittgenstein 1969, 31). What comes out of the Wittgensteinian distinction is that the Rastafari movement is made of groups with related and similar beliefs and practices, but none of these beliefs and practices can serve as identifying criteria that characterize a Rastafari, to the extent that if any of the groups does not possess them, then the group will not be regarded as genuine Rasta or Rasta in the first instance. Consequently, the worldview of Rastafari can only be identified by the beliefs and practices that the various groups share: the belief in the divinity of Haile Selassie; repatriation; adherence to some sort of livity; and reasoning.

Do elements of the Rastafari worldview actually constitute philosophy in the academic sense of the term, or there is need for reconstructing them in order to make them philosophical? An affirmative answer to the first question will commit us to embracing the ethnophilosophy school, whereas the second leads us to embracing the professional philosophy school.

Ethnophilosophy is a canon in (African) philosophy that aims at describing and documenting the differing worldviews of African people and presenting them as philosophy. According to the proponents of this trend in philosophy, philosophy is incarnated in the mythical and religious conceptions, worldviews, and lived ritual practices of ethnic Africans (Serequeberhan 1991). The proponents of the professional philosophy school claim that philosophy should be critical, analytical, and reflective. This trend criticized ethnophilosophy as folk philosophy belonging to a collection of people, which therefore falls within the purview of pre-philosophical activity.

My position between these two canons of philosophy is a conception of philosophy that takes traditional beliefs of a culture as ingredients or data for philosophical reflection. This reflection should not be seen in isolation from the situation and experiences of that culture. This is the conception of philosophy that some scholars have referred to as hermeneutics (Okere 1983; Smith and Blasé 1991; Serequeberhan 1991; Hallen 2002). According to Smith and Blasé, three major features of philosophical hermeneutics may be identified. In the first instance, hermeneutics argues that there is no absolute "bottom line" upon which to justify knowledge claims; hence, there is no possibility of certitude. What we come to accept as reasonable in terms of knowledge about our social and educational lives is the product of a socially and historically conditioned agreement. In the second sense, hermeneutics does not accept the idea that social reality is reality that exists independently of our interests and purposes. Reality is a social, and therefore multiple, construction. Finally, the goal of hermeneutics is not prediction and control, but rather to realize an interpretative understanding of the meanings people give to their own situations and their interactions with others. The investigator is an interpreter (second order) of the interpretations people have already given to their lives (first order). Next I apply the hermeneutics method of philosophizing to reflect upon Rastafari beliefs and practices, thereby fulfilling the primary task that Rastafari can be reconstructed to constitute philosophy in the technical and academic senses.

Rastafari as Philosophy

Hallen (2002) identified Okere (1983) as one of the first African scholars who has adopted philosophical hermeneutics as the canon of African philosophy. Okere criticized ethnophilosophy as not worthy of the label philosophy. According to Okere, at the most the collection of proverbs, wise sayings, and religious beliefs and practices of a given people can qualify as ethnography. Hermeneutics philosophers might work with such ethnographic materials to render them philosophical by interpreting them (using critical tools) and situating them within the past, present, and future experiences of the people. In order to defend my position in this paper, I refer now to the shared elements (identified earlier) of Rastafari as ethnophilosophy, which, in order to become philosophy, should be critically and analytically examined, using the hermeneutics method.

Belief in the Divinity of Haile Selassie

Chevannes (1998a) observed that the most important belief of the Rastafari is that Haile Selassie, the late Emperor of Ethiopia, is God, thus leading to the Rastafari claim that God is Black. In the same vein, Henry observed that the foundation of Rastafari theology is the mystical knowledge of the divinity of Haile Selassie (1997, 160). However, there appears to be divergent views among Rastafari regarding the divinity of Haile Selassie. Thus, Barnett (2005) claims that the original Twelve Tribes of Israel teachings hold that Jesus Christ was manifested in his second coming in the person of Haile Selassie; the Bobo Shanti hold that Haile Selassie is the father of Jesus Christ (who is Prince Emmanuel, the founder of the house, so far as the Bobo Shanti are concerned); and the Nyahbinghi Order holds that Haile Selaisse is the Trinity (Father, Son, and Holy Ghost). The Ethiopian Zion Coptic Church (a mansion that occupies a marginal status in the movement) does not accept the divinity of Haile Selassie I, although they still believe that he is of the Solomonic dynasty, thereby linking him with King David and therefore to Christ (Barnett 2005).

From these different conceptions of the status of Haile Selassie emerges the point made by Chevannes that this conception "gives to Black people a sense of being one with, of sharing in an attribute of God" (1998a, 28). This suggests some issues that are philosophically important. The first of these issues is connected with the hermeneutics method of philosophizing where realities are not separated from the interests and purposes of individuals, cultures, and societies; the second is the issue of identity in its multifaceted dimensions.

With regard to the first issue, it would be observed that the idea of God is not seen by the Rastafari as a notion that is totally outside their experiences in the world. God and his attributes have been understood within the cultural and social experiences of the group. The Black God is a God that is both transcendent and immanent. The transcendent feature is linked with his being divined, while the immanent nature is his being around with the people in their day-to-day activities. With these double attributes of God, the people can relate well with him in different experiential situations, thus giving sense to their understanding of themselves and their natural and social environments. This point also leads to another issue that the Rastafari are noted for: the question of identity. The issue of identity within the Rastafari ideology is a large issue that cannot be exhaustively dealt with here; however, I shall briefly discuss it, making use of the relevant philosophical literature.

There has been an ongoing debate in philosophical parlance concerning the relationship between individuals or groups of individuals and the basic norms of their community. This question has figured centrally not just in discussions of ethics and political philosophy but also in philosophy of mind and language (Boedeker 2001). The issue as put by Boedeker is this: Must someone be in some sense a member of a human community, trained in its practices and beholden to its norms, in order to have a "self"? Responses to this issue have divided scholars into the individualist school and the collectivist school. The individualist school claims that the self is robbed of its identity by clinging to the norms of the community, whereas the collectivist school claims that the self realizes its identity by participating in communal norms. However, from the literature on Rastafari, one can easily see that it is the collectivist's position that has been embraced by Rastafari. This choice has many implications for the Rastafari ideology. Henry's analysis (1997) of the relationship between Rastafari and Haile

Selassie may help to bring out clearly the point that is being made regarding this debate. Henry observed that the direct, mystical, and spiritual participation in the divinity of Haile Selassie is captured in the Rastafari use of "I" language. He observed that among Jamaicans, Rastafari are unique in their use of the pronoun "I," which has been substituted for the "me" and "my" that represent the old self before awakening to the divinity of Haile Selassie. "I" represents the new identity that emerges from participation in the divinity of Haile Selassie. In other words, the kind of identity involved in the Rastafari belief system is not the atomistic one that has been embraced by modern Western philosophy. The modern Western perspective of the self is exemplified by René Descartes's "cogito ergo sum" (I think therefore I am), whereas the African (Rastafari) perspective is encapsulated in John Mbiti's view that "I am because we are and because we are therefore I am." This is not too surprising; after all, the Rastafarians are offering a critique of Western culture and ways of life. With respect to the philosophy of language, the use of "I" language is connected with what linguistics refer to as honorific pronoun. When the self is understood in this way, there is the indication that the people to whom the language is applied share in the same social horizon and that they are bound together as such. This is also the reason for the Rastafari referring to themselves as brethren and sistren.

Repatriation

Connected to the Rastafari belief in the divinity of Haile Selassie is the doctrine of repatriation. Repatriation simply means the return to Africa. This "return" has been conceived in different ways by Rastafari. Some see it as a physical return, others see it as a psychological return, and yet others see it as a spiritual return. Our position on this matter will have to reflect the current realities of the Rastafari and the present space they occupy and other current realities outside their current space. In order to argue for this position, we need to focus once again on Wittgenstein's conception of a worldview. According to Wittgenstein our worldview is similar to a river bed, where certain "hardened propositions" function as the bed of the river, acting as the form that contains and guides the mass of our ever-changing belief system. Yet, according to Wittgenstein, "The river-bed of thoughts may shift.

But I distinguish between the movement of the river-bed and the shift of the bed itself; though there is not a sharp division between one or the other (Wittgenstein 1969, 15). What comes out of the Wittgensteinian position is that there has been a shift in the political, economic, social, and cultural realities of the world, including Ethiopia, the Zion of the Rastafari. Thus, it becomes important to revise or reinterpret the notion of Zion to be in consonance with the present realities of the Rastafari themselves and the spaces they occupy. The notion of Zion was derived from the Bible, which is connected to the Promised Land. The idea of the Promised Land is a situation where oppression, exploitation, deprivation, and discrimination will cease and where happiness (in Aristotelian terms) will be achieved. This appears to be a secular conception of Zion, and I think it is more reasonable to press this notion; after all, some mansions have interpreted Zion from this perspective. One problem with physical repatriation is connected to the point made by Henry that the social and developmental problems the Rastafari seeks to abandon in Jamaica and the larger Caribbean are as severe, if not more, on the African continent today (2000, 213). In other words, by insisting on repatriation, the Rastafarian is liable to jump from the frying pan into the fire. Though we agree that the current political upheaval in Ethiopia, where scores of Ethiopians have been massacred, lends that thought empirical validity, in terms of its philosophical sense, one can still urge that whatever the current situation, home is still home. This is the aspect of retention that gives a worldview its "hardened propositions." Thus, the doctrine of repatriation is more psychological than physical. My suggestion here, which has also been made elsewhere (Bamikole 2007), is that rather than pressing for physical repatriation, Rastafarians should appeal to the spirit behind the traditional norms in Africa, their homeland, which is summed up in the notion of African personalism (Sofola 1978). They should then inculcate such norms into their daily lives and transmit the same to other African Diaspora societies. This position has been buttressed by Garvey's slogan, "Africa for Africans at home and abroad." Williams interpreted Garvey's words to mean that repatriation should "start in the minds and hearts of our people; in our words, actions and deeds we must go back to Africa. We may never set foot on the continent in our time, but we can live and represent our heritage each day we live in the world" (2000, 20).

Livity

The notion of livity has both narrow and broad interpretations. The narrow interpretation is connected to the "Ital," the norms relating to diet, whereas the broad interpretation, according to some Rastafari scholars (Williams 2000; Semaj 2000; Barnett 2005), suggests a way of life, an ideal way of conducting oneself. For Rastafari, an ideal way to conduct oneself would be to sever from the ways of life of the West and to embrace a way of life linked to the Black God in the spiritual, political, social, and cultural senses. In other words, the notion of livity represents a form of liberation in the various senses of the term. This is another area where I think the Rastafari worldview requires a revision. Although the message that is being passed across is well understood, the question is whether, given the current realities of the Rastafari spaces, such doctrine can still be sustained. In other words, apart from for health reasons, can we still expect Rastafari to stick to natural diets, when local farmers are not producing enough food to feed the population and recourse has to be given to importing food items from abroad, especially from Western nations? Apart from diet, can the Rastafari stick to their modes of life in the face of situations where dress codes are being recommended for specific occasions within the secular society? In order for Rastafari to still retain their identity in the aspect of livity, a different philosophy has to be embraced other than the philosophy of primordial identity. It is along this line that the philosophy of multiculturalism becomes apposite. Multiculturalism advocates for the principle of recognition, especially in the pluralist society in which the Rastafari have found themselves. This recognition has to be negotiated with the other members of the society. This is the trend in the world, and the Rastafari cannot afford to discount this fact. The principle of multiculturalism respects the right of different groups to exist, but the different groups must be aware that this can only happen when there is cooperation based on such moral notions as equality, fairness, and justice. Although it can be argued that in reality, multiculturalism seems not to have been working well, this is a practical problem that can also be addressed by minority groups working in tandem with other groups in the society.

A vexing subject when discussing livity is the use of ganja. According to the Rastafari belief, ganja is a holy herb used during worship sessions. Conceived in this way, the use of ganja is comparable to the use of the Holy Communion in orthodox Christian churches. But just like the Holy Communion has its own problems with regard to how it is administered, the use of ganja also has its own problems with respect to its status within the legal framework of a multicultural society. Given current developments in social and moral philosophy, the reason for embracing ganja as an instrument of worship has to be revised to accommodate changing in worldviews. A contemporary position on this issue is related to the distinction that Rawls (1993) made between church and state, to the extent that the two represent distinct spheres of human action that should be kept distinct from one another. However, on a second look, it would be hard to make a rigid distinction between the state and the church because both are human institutions that work to ensure the well-being of persons. Given the fact that individuals and groups like the Rastafari have the right to worship, it becomes a moral issue whether their mode of worship can be allowed to have a negative effect on nonmembers of the group who are also members of a multicultural society. This position is a revisit of the classical position in legal philosophy regarding the question of using law to enforce morality. This chapter will not enter into the wider issues involved in this debate, but it suffices to point out the need for a possible revision of this aspect of livity in Rastafari ideology.

The Idea of Reasoning in Rastafari

The place of reasoning in the Rastafarian worldview is well captured by Homiak: "The Rastafari are men of words who address themselves passionately not only to concerns of identity and ideology, but to concerns of communal morality and responsibility. They come together to fashion continuous streams of 'reasoning' in which 'Jah is praised,' inspiration is received and ideology is reproduced; they are also a collective of individuals who speak to each other, about each other, and about themselves and their experiences" (1998, 130). Although the characterization of reasoning as depicted by the above view is in consonance with the concept of reasoning in philosophy, there is still the need to pay attention to the use of sexist language in the characterization. One thing that is clear, of course, is that reasoning is a male affair within the Rastafari movement. However, this should not be the case. In order to give a respectable status to the idea of reasoning in Rastafari, women should not be excluded. The exclusion of women from reasoning sessions is a reflection of the patriarchalism of the spaces where the Rastafari live. However, reasoning is a distinctive human ability. It involves making inferences, setting goals, and thinking about how such goals will be met. These are characteristic human activities, and one does not see any justifiable reason for excluding women from this human activity. The reason given in the literature that women are often too emotional to engage in the art of reasoning is weak because it must have been based on the Biblical view that women are of a weaker vessel (Williams 2000). The present realities point to the fact that women are becoming increasingly responsible not only at the home front but also at the social front and at the highest level at that. The current heads of state of Liberia and Germany are women. More importantly, Jamaica elected a woman prime minister, Portia Simpson Miller. Although some Rastafari might regard Jamaica as Babylon, my view is that such a view flies in the face of current facts.

Rastafari as Praxis

The ethical, social, political, and cultural dimensions of Rastafari have been well acknowledged by scholars both within and outside of the Caribbean. Although not speaking specifically about Rastafari, Stewart and Blocker have this to say about such movements as the Rastafari: "In several countries, there are revivalist movements that renounce the incursion of Western values along with Western technologies and urge the return to a purer, more fundamental set of values. Such fundamentalist movements, whether they are labeled religious or philosophical, are continuing to have a major impact on the political life of several countries" (2001, 437). Henry states, specifically about the Rastafarians: "The importance of Rastafarianism is not in the size of its following; indeed, the number of members is small. Rather the worldview and value system expounded has permeated not only Jamaica, but also a good bit of the Caribbean as well" (1997, 164). Yet another scholar observes: "Rastafari is still one of the most viable fronts from which we can launch a cultural revolution for the liberation of Africans in the Diaspora" (Semaj 2000, 24). These comments and others not included here are exemplifications of the importance of Rastafari as a cultural ideology. However, the question may be asked whether Rastafari has lived to these ideals in practice. Is there, for instance, a gap between the philosophy of Rastafari and how such philosophy operates in practice? Are there both theoretical and practical difficulties that have militated against the putting into practice of Rastafari ideas?

Chevannes (1998a) and Barnett (2005) observed that the diversities among the Rastafari have not enabled the movement to have the desired impact on the Jamaican society in particular and the wider Caribbean in general. This observation is essentially correct because, as the saying goes, there is strength in unity. Added to this observation is also the problem of the pluralist nature of Jamaican and Caribbean societies. The Jamaican and Caribbean societies are made up of different people divided along racial, social, political, and cultural lines. It then becomes difficult to sell the ideas of Rastafari across to the people with these characteristics. One way of overcoming these problems is that Rastafari as a movement should put its own house in order. Inasmuch as the different mansions share the same goal of reconnecting the Caribbean with its African roots, this goal should serve as a rallying point for all the different Rastafari groups. Thereafter, they can use this goal as a fulcrum to effect the necessary changes in their spaces. With that unity secured, they could reach out to some other racial groups to press for an alternative philosophy for their spaces. We have to note here that the Sino-Jamaicans and the Indo-Jamaicans also have traditions that are non-Western in orientation. What is common to a non-Western system of thought as a whole is the rejection of the Western and modern conception of persons as atomic individuals who usually see relationship between individuals as that of the market. This conception has as its alternative the view of persons as social beings who are closely knitted together in virtue of their personhood. Following from the rejection of the atomic conception of a person is also the rejection of the capitalist ethos upon which the conception is built. Insofar as this is the philosophy being embraced by the Rastafari, then through negotiation and dialogue with other races such attitude to life can be adopted to constitute a viable alternative to the Western ways of life that the Rastafari are critiquing.

When considering Rastafari as praxis, there is the need to recognize the fact that the Rastafari also live consistently with their philosophy of the Babylon/Zion distinction. It was pointed out to me by Ayotunde Bewaji that the reason why the Rastafari have not been identified with criminality in Jamaica may not be unconnected with their view that they are presently in Babylon, and committing any crime that can lead to imprisonment will amount to living in another Babylon! This situation will evidently lead to total hopelessness with regard to attaining their much cherished idea of emancipation into Zion.

Conclusion

It might be argued that what I have done in this chapter amounts to looking at Rastafari as a Caribbean tradition from the perspective of African canons of philosophizing and that we have assimilated Caribbean philosophy into African philosophy, thereby committing what Ryle (1949) called a "category mistake." Our response to this hypothetical objection may take two forms. First, the method of hermeneutics is not a distinctive African method of doing philosophy. The originator of this method was not an African in the first place. Even more important, the originator of a given methodology is not really the essential thing; what matters is the appropriateness and relevance of that methodology in the sense that it captures well the reality of the situation to which it is being applied. Second, since the Rastafari are urging a return to Africa and African ways of life, the method of philosophizing about Africa and African ways of life should also become important for the movement and its supporters.

Furthermore, I suggest that Rastafari should embrace a more robust notion of identity, one that spells out the relationship between themselves and others. In consonance with the view expressed in this chapter, the Rastafari have now found themselves in a world where cooperation with other people is sine qua non to securing their own identity. In other words, identity construction requires the recognition of our commonality with and difference from other human beings. As Allen suggests, "The process of relating to others, in terms of appreciating differences and recognizing commonality, is of greatest urgency for understanding the contemporary world" (1997, 19). The Rastafari and the Rastafari philosophy cannot afford to ignore this important message.

7

Exploring RastafarI's Pedagogic, Communicative, and Instructional Potential in the Caribbean

The Life and Works of Mutabaruka as a Case Study

ADWOA NTOZAKE ONUORA

Through a critical content analysis of contemporary RastafarI orature[1] (focusing on the life and works of Mutabaruka), I argue that RastafarI can serve as a form of reparation for the damages wrought by the colonial education system, consequently breaking the cycle of hegemonic colonial "downpression."[2] Hence, I present RastafarI as a vital communicative, pedagogical, and instructional tool for educating Afro-Caribbean youth to resist colonizing tendencies. Among the critical issues raised are: How is the colonial education in the Caribbean paralyzing our ability to charter a different developmental path? How can Afro-Caribbean peoples

1. This concept was borrowed from Asante who uses it to describe the comprehensive body of oral discourse on every subject and in every genre of expression produced by a people. It includes sermons, lectures, raps, poetry, and humor (Asante 1998, 84). When used in this chapter, the term refers to the body of artistic works used by Rastas to articulate their spiritual, ideological, and political positions.

2. In the RastafarI vernacular, "downpression" is used in place of "oppression" to signal pressure or hegemonic force applied from a top-down position to further marginalize those victimized. See http://www.castlebar.ie/board/0103/60392.htm.

ground their conceptualization of education in their own version of reality? What role does RastafarI spirituality, spiritual practices, and worldview play in paving the way for creating pedagogies of liberation within Caribbean societies in the new millennium? In answering these questions, RastafarI discourse is introduced as a framework for reimagining how education can be conceptualized in the Caribbean context.

The Scope of the Problem

Thoughts about transforming the educational system in the Caribbean are necessarily complicated by an understanding of the processes through which racialized knowledge hierarchies are created and maintained in postcolonial societies such as Jamaica. Attention must be paid to how mainstream schooling has fostered a culture of fear and complacency to move away from dominant Eurocentric status quo knowledge (Dei et al. 2000). This is so to the extent that Eurocentric epistemologies are positioned as commonplace and put at the forefront of curriculum and pedagogy, whereas Afro-Caribbean indigenous knowledge is relegated to the margins, devalued, or completely omitted from classroom spaces. Race thus becomes central to understanding how the hegemonic conception that Eurocentric knowledge is the only legitimate frame through which to see the world (Dei 1996, 100) results in the deligitimization of worldwide indigenous epistemologies. In fact, it is through this type of thinking that hegemonic regimes that espouse such epitaphs as "anything black nuh good" are maintained. These racialized knowledge hierarchies are often presented through the prism of Orientalism (Said 2003), wherein the body of knowledge located in the Orient (read: spaces outside Euro-America) is regarded as invalid and placed at the periphery, while dominant Eurocentric epistemologies are made the epicenter of Caribbean schools. In this regard, RastafarI gains significance as a counterhegemonic African-centered epistemology for challenging and transforming these asymmetrical power relations in schools.

Since its genesis in the early twentieth century, RastafarI has been characterized as a revolutionary movement. This phenomenon of late postcolonial Jamaican society has played an instrumental historical role in Africa and its Diasporas insofar as providing a platform for Africans to critically interrogate hegemonic power relations born out of plantation slavery, colonization, and neocolonization. As a philosophy of reasoning, it proffers a critique of dominant philosophical paradigms that position Euro-America as superior to Africa and other racialized[3] spaces (Christensen 2003; Said 2003).

Importantly, RastafarI ushers in a call for the affirmation of the epistemic saliency of indigenous African communities. For many displaced Africans, RastafarI serves as a rallying point from which to reclaim from the margins their histories, their cultural experiences, and their indigenous knowledge that has been the object of European bastardization and invalidation (Dei 1996). To this end, RastafarI has become an important part of the African people's journey toward spiritual and mental decolonization. Rastas, in advancing RastafarI (a once marginal ontology) as a knowledge system, have made a vital contribution to the Afrocentric quest for social justice and toward engraining "a philosophy of hope [and] empowerment for minoritized communities" across the globe (Brown-Spencer 2006, 108).

As was mentioned earlier, this chapter is an exploration into the pedagogical relevance of RastafarI for schooling and educating Afro-Caribbean youth. I work through the terrain of RastafarI orature (that is, dub poetry), citing various themes of resistance, reclamation, decolonization, and African liberation that emanate throughout the artistic works of RastafarI. I present RastafarI as a viable alternative mode of knowledge production, gesturing toward a transformative pedagogy embedded within. To this end,

3. The term "racialized" is used throughout this paper to describe the power relationships inherent in the process of scripting nondominant (read: Black) bodies. Through this process certain groups are designated as different and are subject to differential treatment on that basis. It entails the notion of biological determinism: the idea of particular human traits as biologically determined and thus consistent for all individuals within a particular group. For instance, in racially diverse societies such as the Caribbean, dominant (read: lighter skin/miscegenated) bodies impose labels or markers for those groups that are visibly different (based on phenotype) from them. It is on the basis of this racialization that individuals are fixed into subservient roles and subsequently marked or positioned for rewards or punishments. In essence, the process of racialization allows dominant thought, bodies, and systems of power to suppress racial and linguistic minority agency and resistance (Solomon and Palmer 2004).

I illustrate how RastafarI, with its emphasis on the redemptive power of *nommo* (the spoken or performed word), can serve as a vital pedagogic tool for emboldening Afro-Caribbean youth toward social transformation and finding "epistemological centeredness" (Mazama 2001, 388). I further contend that RastafarI can empower students to name, critically analyze, and challenge hegemonic "regimes of truth" (Foucault 1980) that pose a threat to Black/African and other marginalized voices in mainstream schools and society. By exploring ways in which the teachings and philosophies of RastafarI can influence educational practice in the Caribbean, I advance one way for Caribbean educators to acknowledge the vitality of indigenous African epistemologies and to see its utility as a launch pad for charting our own ontological pathways outside of the purview of dominant Eurocentrism.

Embodying and Enacting Resistance through the *Nommo*

According to biographical accounts (Morris 2005), Mutabaruka was born Allan Hope in Kingston, Jamaica, in December 1952. In his adolescent years, he began examining RastafarI after being drawn by the upsurge of Black consciousness in Jamaica and other parts of the world. During this time, Muta gravitated toward books that furthered his awareness about the historical and contemporary conditions of African peoples. Given the strong Afrocentric thrust of RastafarI, and its orientation toward the centering of African culture, history, and identity, it becomes easy to see why Muta would begin growing locks, altering his diet, and declaring himself a Rasta.

From an early age, Muta was heavily influenced by the ideas of Caribbean Pan-Africanist intellectuals such as Edward Blyden, C. L. R. James, Walter Rodney, and Marcus Garvey, to name a few of the most significant. His pieces illuminate the experiences of Black/African people born into circumstances of racial downpression and socioeconomic disenfranchisement stemming from imperialism, neocolonialism, and "mis-headecaytion." In addition to touring the world and taking African history to the streets (Lewis 1991, 73), he is the host of the prominent late-night radio talk show *Cutting Edge,* broadcast every Wednesday night on IRIE-FM (Jamaica's only twenty-four-hour reggae radio station). His program is also broadcasted to the world over the Web and reaches millions of listeners all over the globe.

From the above narrative, one could deduce that Muta embodies a pedagogy of Afrocentrism and social transformation. Commenting on the nature of his art, Muta states the following:

> My poems are to show you the problems that face us in the world and then motivate you to find the solutions to these problems—I don't think I could show people how to get out of their problems with poems, but at least I could motivate action. I write a poem, so that my poetry can be the . . . weapon of freedom. (Morris 2005, viii)

Still today, he is hailed as the most thought-provoking and controversial dub poet to have emanated out of the Jamaican space. With lyrics "always smoking" he continues to "edutain" youth all over the world about RastafarI, African-centered and alternative spiritual worldviews, and other social issues affecting the world.[4] Mutabaruka's narrative is illustrative of the central thesis of this chapter: That resistance is born on the bodies of Rasta artistes who through their individual histories, experiences, and the views espoused in their writings are actively engaged in a politics of reeducating and "re-righting" history from below (to borrow from Walter Rodney), thus "creat[ing] a voice for the voiceless and provid[ing] visibility and space for those who have long been marginalized and neglected" (Lewis 1991, 73).

That a reviewer once stated that Muta's "reading[s]" are also "reasoning[s]" is of major significance (Morris 2005). Informal gatherings known as "reasoning circles" predated reggae music (which is now the central medium for spreading RastafarI philosophies and teachings) as the earliest medium through which Rasta elders such as Leonard Howell, Sam Brown, Ras Mortimo Planno, and Emmanuel Charles Edwards transmitted their pedagogy of Black/African liberation. It was within these circles that the idea of taking education to the streets was actualized by Rastas. This tradition of dialoguing in ritual circles to produce and disseminate knowledge

4. http://www.iriefm.com.

of and for the downpressed is continued today through younger generations of Rastas such as Mutabaruka. Indeed, the notion of taking education to the streets through the "informal" is in and of itself oppositional and antihegemonic, in terms of moving us away from the nebulous dichotomy created between formal and informal education and valid and invalid knowledge.

Muta's individual exploration of books on Black/African history and culture is also of noteworthy importance. Such an autonomous undertaking on his part pales in comparison to the underlying message being sent that some of the most invaluable lessons are often learned outside of "formal" educational settings. His narrative thus serves as a testament to the fact that individuals "can find other arenas for enriching their mind" (Sackeyfio 2006, 100), to learn about themselves and experiences through their own lenses, and develop healthy habits necessary for one's personal growth. In this regard, the personal becomes political, as individuals can become empowered through drawing on various bodies of knowledge that speak to their personal experiences, rather than learning through and from disjointed representations of histories (a major flaw of learning within mainstream educational settings). In this way, they become more equipped to map the connections between themselves and the wider world.

Also of pedagogical significance is the fact that Muta writes mainly in the language of the Jamaican people. More importantly, he makes an effort to incorporate elements of the Rasta speech code throughout much of his work. One could argue that resistance is embedded in Muta's choice to break away from the linguistic hegemony of the Queen's English and other colonizing languages positioned as lingua franca. His choosing to perform in his native tongue gives primacy to narrative expressions and languages of indigenous and marginalized groups. The fact that his message carries across racial, spatial, religious, and linguistic boundaries debunks the Eurocentric "myth of Babel" (Roy-Campbell 2003, 94), which calls for the universalization of European languages because other variants of English (such as Jamaican patois) are seen as obstacles to progress and development. Arguably, Muta's choosing to perform and write in a politically charged language (Jamaican patois) is what has earned acclaim and his claim to fame. Notwithstanding performing in his mother tongue, he is still able to communicate his anticolonial message to people who, more often than not, speak a different language. He has succeeded despite potential linguistic barriers to the extent that his performances and lectures are well attended. His life story is illustrative of the fact that individuals need only share similar experiences of downpression in order to learn from and to band together across boundaries to resist forms of social marginalization. Muta's work is best described as "protest poems" (Morris 2005). Embedded within much of his work is a politics of resistance. The following piece shows a clear articulation of his revolutionary worldview as expressed through the prism of RastafarI and Afrocentrism.

> when you remember home say:
> ETHIOPIA
> when you remember slaves say:
> BLACK
> when you shout revolution say:
> FREEMAN
> when you shout Babylon say:
> DEATH
> when you speak of education say:
> GET IT
> when you speak of unity say:
> WADADA . . .
> when you think like i say:
> RASTAFARI
>
> (Morris 2005, 11)

The period within which Muta started to embrace RastafarI coincided with that point in which his work began to reflect his radical Afrocentric stance. Such a move toward a distinctly Afrocentric consciousness could undoubtedly be viewed as a risky one. This is particularly so because he was operating against the grain by writing and proudly claiming a worldview and identity deemed socially and culturally unacceptable at the time by the ruling elite in Jamaica. The established neoimperial order was of the view that Rastas were "communist inspired revolutionaries who threatened the sanctity of the democratic socio-political climate of the country" (Beckford 1980, qtd. in Lewis 1991, 76). It was also at this point that Rastas were subjected to heavy institutional policing (because of their association with marijuana smoking), and punitive sanctions were meted out by the neocolonial heads of state of whom Muta was critical throughout his work. Muta's choosing to center his work in the RastafarI worldview was indeed a revolutionary undertaking.

Muta's critique of the colonial education system is evinced in his art wherein he attempts to disrupt the teachings of dominant Eurocentric knowledge and to subvert Euro-American cultural imperialism, particularly as they were manifested in the classroom. Commenting on the inadequacies of the British colonial school system, he writes:

> shakespeare . . .
> still drenchin the souls of black folks
> tryin to integrate
> in my life your [British] life
>
> (Morris 2005, 2)

Here Muta raises awareness of the institutionalized colonial conditioning of the minds of Black/African youth who were taught to negate all things African and instead embrace all things European. In this piece in particular he is openly critical of the valorization and universalization of Shakespeare as pedagogy within the school system. For Muta, the problem that inheres in the centering of Eurocentric knowledge is that in this centering, there is no room for other ways of knowing. This ethnocentric logic imperils indigenous culture, moving African youth further away from their culture and themselves and more toward a Euro-Western experience and understanding of being in the world.

Throughout much of his work, Muta highlights the detrimental impact of placing emphasis on Eurocentric knowledge within the school system. In his critique of the educational system, Muta's discussion focuses on the ways in which Eurocentric approaches to education serve to perpetuate a one-sided view of the world, subsequently reinscribing the inferior versus superior dialectic. Within this framework, Europeans are presented as the sole producers of knowledge and possessors of culture and history, whereas the important contributions of indigenous groups, such as Africans, are devalued and rendered inferior. He is opposed to education through dominant Eurocentric lenses (particularly in social contexts where indigenous bodies dominate), arguing that such a process contributes to the erasure of culture and ultimately to the loss of cultural identity.

In a piece entitled "Nursery Rhyme Lament," Muta lashes out against the teaching of European nursery rhymes, arguing that they do not mirror the lived experiences of many Afro-Caribbean youth. Of this he writes:

> jack and jill use to run up di hill everyday
> now dem get pipe . . . an
> water rate increase
> everyday dem would reincarnate humpty dumpty
> fi fall off de wall . . .
> yet dem did ave di cat fi play fiddle
> so de cow coulda jump over it
> every full moon . . . an lite bill increase
>
> (Morris 2005, 12)

Clearly, as illustrated in the above words, Muta remains an ardent critique of classroom teachings that focus solely on subject matters that do not take into consideration the fact that children bring their harsh realities to bear on their learning experience. A student who comes to school unprepared may be mistakenly viewed by the teacher as a slacker when in actuality he or she may be facing serious economic hardships at home. Muta is critical of the teacher who emphasizes nursery rhyme drills, all the while losing sight of these difficult socioeconomic realities that some students face at home on a daily basis and that seriously impact their ability to fully engage in the learning process.

As was previously mentioned, one other important goal Muta tries to achieve through his work is that of highlighting the impending dangers of Euro-American cultural imperialism. Much of his pieces speak out against the excessive absorption of Euro-American culture. His vehement criticism regarding the usage of the colonizer language is but one example of his attack against linguistic imperialism. This position is made apparent in pieces like "Thievin Legacy" where he writes:

gimme mi language a know suh well
you mix up inglish confusin nah hell

(Morris 2005, 26)

This oppositional stance is also evidenced in works like "Miss Lou" where he calls for the celebration of Jamaican patois in mainstream schools and society:

Miss Lou yu mek dem know
dat is from de base tings jamaica grow
dem use fi she wi mus speak in twang
but yu mek wi proud seh wi a afrikan
now wi si dem a teach in school
dat jamaica patwa is not fi fool

(Morris 2005, 28)

Importantly, his work also cautions against the gradual encroachment of Western ideals on a global scale. Highlighting the impending dangers of capitalism, neocolonialism, and the like, he asks:

why are we measuring progress as determined by the west
why are we still saying yes to all their industrial mess
we have to understand the times we are living in
and remember where we have been
we have to remember what happened in slavery
so as to not repeat history

(Morris 2005, 20)

Here Muta puts forth a call for worldwide indigenous communities, encouraging them not to lose sight of their individual cultures and heritage. He inspires autonomy, emboldening us to assert our individual and collective agency, when he continues:

we have to live by our own spirituality
to determine our own destiny
to build our own economy

In this same piece he imparts lessons on the significance of remembrance:

we have to learn things from our ancient history
To help build a new society
We have to remember nkrumah and garvey

In "Thievin Legacy," he exposes the hypocrisy and contradictions inherent in Euro-American ideals, unearthing the various truths about legacies of Africa currently disguised by Eurocentrism as belonging to Europeans. He explains:

no spirtual concept originated here [in Europe]
suh wh I praise you shouldn't care
yu she steal not
yu tief mi lan
sex not
yu rape mi mada
keep de sabat
wi work seven days a week
you buil a nation from de sweat off mi back

(Morris 2005, 26–27)

In the same piece, Muta brings about awareness of important facts of which many today refuse to acknowledge or remain oblivious about. Contrary to the negative depictions presented through Eurocentric representations of history, Africa is the pillar of civilization where kings and queens and great scholars once dwelled. Much of the knowledge that Europe today claims as its own has been attained through the pillaging and exploitation of Africa and other indigenous spaces. Urging a radical reclamation of that which was stolen from Africa, he laments:

gimme mi dis
gimme mi dat
gimme back everything you got
gimme me philosophy yu carry to greece
tief homo and socrates . . .

gimme back mi name
gimme mi back mi kalinda
gimme mi books yu tief from alexandria
gimme mi queen like kleopatra
mi nuh wah ear bout queen Victoria . . .
gimme mi dis, gimme mid dat
gimme back mi every ting yu got . . .
gimme a space a can run mi own life
respect is due de time is now
no more tun cheek
dis time wi nah bow

(Morris 2005, 26–27)

Through his work Muta also imparts lessons on the importance of remembering. In "Revolt Ain't a Revolution," he recalls some great African men, teaching Africans to remember and celebrate our ancestors and to fashion our future moves based on ideas centered on African epistemologies. This he clearly sees as being crucial to our survival as a community as well as the continued development of our cultures. Contrastingly, works like "Dabaddabuninna" (they beat me) centers on remembering the suffering of Black/African people and punctuates the horrors of slavery:

never forgetting memories of yesterday's agonies
still lingering in my physicalness
bodies drained of their blood,
thunder sounds of whips
cracking against black flesh—I piss/I shit
"DABADDABUNINNA!"
bleed, bleed/bleeding
flesh separation
lips held together
salt in blood
agony cry souls dying . . .
never will I stop crying
yesterday's memories will always linger
i see it today in my black flesh

(Morris 2005, 27)

Here Muta speaks to the importance of blood and ancestral memory. It is through tapping into these memory banks that we as a people are able to recover bits and pieces of our selfhood and bond together to resist collectively neocolonial domination. Importantly, in this work he calls for Black/African people to resist neocolonial efforts to water down the horrors of slavery. He also cautions us against amputating ourselves from this important part of our history. Finally, Muta inspires African unity and communalism, summoning Black/Africans to

> unite . . . make one
> look to the east just once this time . . .
> for peace of mind
>
> (Morris 2005, 4)

Exploring RastafarI's Pedagogic, Communicative, and Instructional Relevance

There are certain benefits that can be garnered from incorporating some of the principles and philosophies of RastafarI into conventional schooling in the Caribbean. For starters, RastafarI imparts lessons about the importance of healing the self through recovering the past. To this end, Rastas continue to search through the pages of history to recover, rewrite, and resurrect the voices of the persecuted, marginalized, and silenced, irrespective of the consequences. There is a common consensus among Rastas that the truth must be published irrespective of the risks involved in doing so. Guided by Marcus Garvey's philosophy, RastafarI encourages the oppressed and marginalized people to read and research the truth, as it is only in doing this that Africans can begin to recover the untold stories of our past and become whole.

Muta's narrative illustrates that RastafarI does the work of resistance in the sense that its philosophies engineer decolonization on both a mental and spiritual level. This is exemplified in the fact that Rastas have engineered their own Black/African-centered theology of liberation based on their own interpretation of the Bible. This theology has functioned as the main corrective to the physical, mental, and spiritual injury Blacks/

Africans have endured for centuries. The RastafarI tradition of resisting the blind acceptance of Eurocentric epistemologies and narrations of history is of direct pedagogical relevance to those students who aspire to emulate the movement's teachings and who feel empowered enough to critically analyze and challenge what is being taught and presented in the materials in mainstream schools.

Also of pedagogic relevance is the emphasis within the RastafarI ontology placed on the inextricable link between humans and the environment. The RastafarI emphasize, through their way of life, an environmentally friendly ethos. There is a strong belief in the importance of preserving nature and the environment and the need to maintain a balance between what is taken from and given back to the earth. RastafarI philosophy teaches us that since the earth is a gift from our creator, it is incumbent on all of us to take care of its inhabitants. The principles of RastafarI imply a shift in current patterns of environmental degradation that will cause the ultimate destruction of the earth (Hill 2003). Land and nature are thus important because it is through communing with and respecting nature and the environment that humans are able to reap the necessary fruits the earth produces to sustain our bodies. Maintaining and encouraging a simpler, subsistence-based lifestyle is but one way in which Rastas lead by example in terms of trying to minimize some of the damage to the environment created through patterns of industrialism, overconsumption, and human materialism.

Connected to this idea is the emphasis placed on communal living. At the macro level, this communal living in the Rasta ontology reinstates the notion that we are all connected and dependent on each other by virtue of our common humanity (Hill 2003). This is of pedagogical relevance to youth as it moves them away from the "not in my backyard" mentality that often results in an attitude of complacency where global environmental issues are concerned. RastafarI communicates the message that individuals must always be mindful of how their destructive actions might leave a lasting imprint on the earth and impact the lives of others for generations to follow.

Dei talked about the adverse effects of this culture of individualism and competition fostered in conventional schools, particularly for students of Afro-Caribbean backgrounds whose culture, history, and ideologies are based on a spirit of collectivity and a communitarian ethos. At the micro level, the RastafarI emphasis on collectivity and community moves students away from the individualistic, competitive nature of dominant mainstream schooling (Dei 1996). The Rasta critique on international patterns of consumerism and consumption can help students develop critical awareness about global issues affecting them. In essence, the Rasta worldview helps to foster a greater sense of community and connectivity to the world around them. In this regard, RastafarI serves also to encourage youth to become "ethical leaders and responsible [global] citizens" (Hill 2003, 11).

Independent learning strategies used within Rasta communes are of direct pedagogical and instructional relevance and could thus be employed within Caribbean classroom settings. One example of such a learning strategy is the Rasta reasoning circle.[5] Reasoning circles are the main form of ritual activity within RastafarI. It is an event within which knowledge is produced and disseminated about historical and contemporary social situations. Within these ritual exercises, diverse sources of data such as historical and contemporary events, biblical prophecies, books, and newspapers, as well as oratorical performances (visions relayed by elders and chanting) are often used to formulate dialogue and critical reflection among those assembled within these circles (Homiak 1987).[6]

The above description positions Rasta reasoning circles as a useful pedagogical tool for engendering a nonbanking approach to education (Freire

5. It is important to note here that if the RastafarI reasoning circle is to become an effective anticolonial pedagogical tool worth emulating, there ought to be a critical interrogation of the attitudes, values, and beliefs that reproduce gender hierarchies. In this regard, the reasoning circle ought to be a revolutionary space where all participants can bring their diverse social locations to bear on the existing cultural definitions of gender as well as other socially constructed markers of difference, realizing that these social constituted differences reinscribe hierarchies of oppression and marginalization. Then and only then can the reasoning circle be effectively modeled within the context of Caribbean classroom.

6. It is important to note that there is "no set liturgical format, agenda, content, or length to a reasoning" (Homiak 1987, 224). The actual format of a Rasta reasoning circle challenges the current organizational structure of classrooms where the teacher is positioned both symbolically and literally as the head (absolute authority) of the class.

2003). Since as it has been noted that "teachers do not give knowledge" but are contributors, critics, and collaborators in the process of knowledge generation (Dei et al. 2000, 82), the reasoning circle could become a tool for challenging the power dynamic that positions the teacher as the all-knowing authority to be followed without question. In this way each learner becomes a teacher (and vice versa) and contributor to knowledge production as opposed to the linear pedagogical approach that mainstream schools embrace. Perhaps Caribbean teachers could model their pedagogy on the Rasta reasoning circles and in so doing facilitate "a more dialogical approach to learning" (Hill 2003, 10).

Conclusion, Limitations, and Future Implications

What I have tried to do in this chapter is illustrate how incorporating RastafarI into pedagogy can be useful for the transmittal and survival of Afro-Caribbean knowledge. For the most part, the works of Rasta artists such as Mutabaruka can be used to combat youth disengagement with the process of schooling. Artistic works like Muta's provide a personalized, subjective reading of reality, one that Afro-Caribbean youth can easily relate to. As illustrated, the content of Rasta poetry provides an oppositional narrative that differs from the mundane, nonpersonal narratives presented in dominant mainstream schooling. Indeed, the intellectual and critical tenor of RastafarI is evidenced in the body of orature, which aids in the transmittal of important information about the past and present experiences of particularly (but not exclusively) Afro-Caribbean youth.

RastafarI orature could become useful for resurrecting ancestral narratives, thus creating space for this marginalized knowledge within the classroom. Similar to hip-hop culture, RastafarI provides culturally grounded slang terms (such as blessed love, I-ley, and I-tes up) and symbols (such as the red, gold, and green banners; the lion of Judah; and locks) that instill in Afro-Caribbean youth a sense of collective identity based on the African-imbued spirit of resistance (Alim 2003; Dei 1996; Ibrahim 2003; Sackeyfio 2006).

It is critically important that Caribbean schools begin to recognize the profound effects that Afro-indigenous epistemologies have on student development, identity formation, and the process of learning. RastafarI provides an example of a cultural and spiritual expression that provides a strong African base from which Afro-Caribbean youth can make connections between themselves and others racialized as Black in the world. As Dei tells us, "A personalized subjective identification with the learning process makes it possible for the learner to be invested spiritually and emotionally in the cause of education and social change" (Dei et al. 2000, 86). Connected to this notion is the idea that youth learn better from those with whom they share a common history and culture and whose experiences mirror theirs. It is in this regard that music and musicians (Rasta artists are but one example) become important pedagogical mediums, because it is to them that students look for role models. More importantly, through them students are able to feel a sense of personal connection because of shared lived experiences.

In the final analysis, charting new trajectories of freedom begins with educating our youth and fostering within them the collective consciousness that we as Afro-Caribbean people need to rule our own destinies. To some extent school administrators, teachers, parents, and the larger community cannot remain blameless. We have to accept some responsibility for this cycle of Euro-American hegemony, because we wittingly or unwittingly acquiesce to the Eurocentric status quoism, privileging Eurocentric epistemologies and ontologies over indigenous knowledge, while relegating our own worldviews to the margins of schools and society. Challenging and transforming status quo approaches to education means promoting nonhegemonic indigenous epistemologies and ontologies to counter the Eurocentric ones. Though this may seem a daunting task, parents, teachers, administrators, and Afro-Caribbean youth will have to engage in collective efforts at challenging and transforming these systemic imbalances. Needless to say, RastafarI is but one means among the myriad oppositional narratives in our Caribbean community to achieve this end. The ultimate question is whether we as Afro-Caribbeans are willing to do so, instead of allowing Eurocentric epistemologies to maintain a privileged position within our educational system.

Rastafari as an Afrocentrically Based Discourse and Spiritual Expression

MICHAEL BARNETT
and ADWOA NTOZAKE ONUORA

In this chapter we suggest that the Rastafari religious and social movement is clearly Afrocentrically based, especially when compared to African indigenous religions that claim an Afrocentric orientation.[1] We argue this on the basis that Rastafari adherents worship a Black God and a Black Christ and celebrate their own African ancestry. Additionally, the Holy Land for Rastafari is in Africa (with the new Jerusalem clearly being

1. Molefi Kete Asante (2003) argues fervently that Islam and any of its offshoot movements, such as the Nation of Islam, are clearly non-Afrocentric because they do not put Africa at the center. One of the writers of this chapter makes a similar argument in his dissertation, "Rastafarianism and the Nation of Islam as Group-Identity Formation among Blacks in the United States" (Barnett 2000). According to Asante, Islam, which essentially starts with the Prophet Muhammad, originates in Arabia (somewhere between Mecca and Medina), not Africa. Additionally, the central language of Islam is Arabic, which is not an African language. Islam puts a great deal of weight on Prophet Muhammad and states that he is the last and most important prophet. But where was Prophet Muhammad born? It was not Africa, but Arabia. Therefore, Islam is Arabcentric as opposed to Afrocentric. According to Barnett the contrast with Rastafari theology and Islam could not be more stark. Rastafarianism originated with Haile Selassie I of Ethiopia; thus, the equivalent place of pilgrimage for Rastafari is Ethiopia specifically and Africa in general. Rastafari not only conceive of Ethiopia as their Holy Land, their Zion, but also the Garden of Eden, the birthplace of humanity that the Bible refers to in the book of Genesis. Rastafari also consider Ethiopia to be the cradle of human civilization as well as God's chosen place on Earth.

proclaimed to be in Ethiopia), and the origin of all humanity is seen to lie in Africa. Many Rastafari state that the Garden of Eden, which the Bible refers to, is essentially that expanse of land we now refer to as Ethiopia. Furthermore, Ethiopia is also heralded as the origin of all human civilization by many adherents of the movement. In this regard, the Rastafari movement is undoubtedly Afrocentrically based, arguably predating the Black Power and Afrocentric movements of the United States, which emerged in the 1960s.

To further investigate the implicit Afrocentricity of Rastafari, we begin this chapter with an outline of the foundational elements of the Afrocentric paradigm, according to the scholar Molefi Kete Asante (1991). We then continue our interrogation by focusing on Asante's five pillars of Afrocentricity and seeing whether there are any parallels between them and the Rastafari worldview. We hope to demonstrate that the Rastafari worldview and orientation, as articulated by lifestyle and ideology, has an Afrocentric leaning (tilt) and basis. We then conclude that it is indeed reasonable to propose that the Rastafari movement is an Afrocentrically based discourse as well as a spiritual expression.

Toward a Summary and Definition of Afrocentricity

The theory of Afrocentricity positions African ideals at the center of analyses involving African culture and behavior, traditions, and history (Asante 1998; Dei 1994). As a discursive framework, it problematizes the Eurocentric production of knowledge, empowering Africans to resist hegemonic views that extol Western European epistemology as superior and universal. Mazama sums it up well, describing it as a theory based on African "epistemological centeredness" (Mazama 2001, 388). Therefore, of major significance to the Afrocentric discursive framework is the notion of centeredness—a perspective that involves locating individuals within the context of their cultural references so that they can relate socially and psychologically to the myriad cultural perspectives in the world. This centeredness thus cannot be misconstrued as a mere reversal of white supremacist discourses. The reason being, inasmuch as Afrocentricity centers the experiences of Africans, it also makes space for the voices of other marginalized groups, viewing the European voice "as just one among many" voices (ibid.). In this regard, the notion of centricity is relevant not only to people of African descent but also to all peoples of varying cultural backgrounds. Afrocentricity thus differs from Eurocentricism in two fundamental ways. Although it places Africa at the center, it also emphasizes *all* peoples' entitlement to celebrate their own culture. Second, in contradistinction to Eurocentrism's domineering and imposing ideological stance, Afrocentricity is an antihegemonic, antiracist framework that seeks redress to the marginalization of alternative knowledge(s) (Asante 1991, 171).

One key aspect of Afrocentricity is that it moves Africans away from Eurocentric discourses of victimology. Importantly, it reinstalls the agency of Africans whereby they are no longer cast as "spectators of a show that defines [them] from without" (Mazama 2001, 387) but are rather "reinsert[ed] into the equation of social and political transformation" (Asante 1998, 20). Afrocentricity, Mazama tells us, aims "to give us our African victorious consciousness back" (Mazama 2001, 388). Ultimately, Afrocentricity aims to vindicate Africans from centuries of intellectual debasement, consequently breaking the shackles of mental colonization (Asante 1998; Dei 1994; Mazuma 2001).

In his book *Afrocentricity: The Theory of Social Change,* Asante defines Afrocentricity as

> a mode of thought and action in which the centrality of African interests, values and perspectives predominates . . . the idea that blackness itself is a trope of ethics. Thus to be black is to be against all forms of oppression . . . [especially] white racial domination). (2003, 2)

Additionally, Asante discusses five levels of transformation that come about through Afrocentricity (2003, 62). These levels are:

1. Skin recognition: a person realizes that his or her skin is Black.

2. Environmental recognition: a person perceives his or her environment as indicating their Blackness, through some form of discrimination or abuse.

3. Personality awareness: a person starts to discover his or her African self.

4. Interest concern: a person accepts the first three levels and expresses an interest and concern for Blacks the world over.

5. Afrocentric awareness: a person enacts the first four levels, but with the utilization of an Afrocentric cultural base and a conscious level of involvement in the struggle for the liberation of his or her own mind.

Once this transformation is complete, the individual develops his or her own distinctly African-centered outlook on the world, becoming largely impervious to the still dominant Eurocentric ideology. We argue that this is precisely the transformation that most Rastafari adherents undergo when they begin their spiritual and political journey (trod) of Rastafari.

The Afrocentric paradigm (as distinct from the Afrocentric idea or attitude) is framed by cosmological, epistemological, axiological, and aesthetic dimensions (Asante 1990). The cosmological dimension constitutes myths, folklore, legends, and oral storytelling traditions, encapsulated by a metaphysical perspective on life that emphasizes living in harmony with nature and the cosmos.[2] The epistemological dimension is concerned with the quest of knowledge and the production of knowledge in general. Asante (1990) argues that within the Afrocentric framework, language, mythology, ancestral memory, dance, music, art, and the physical sciences provide the basis for knowledge production. The axiological dimension pertains to the values and ethics that lie at the heart of the Afrocentric orientation. As Asante commendably notes, what is deemed good in a society depends on the historical conditions and cultural development of that particular society. By extension, what is deemed good or right conduct within an Afrocentric perspective can and does differ from that within a Eurocentric perspective. One of the distinctions made is that of individualism as a value as opposed to collectivism. A key argument made by Asante (1990) is that although individualism is a value greatly prized and even celebrated within the Eurocentric paradigm, collectivism is a value advanced and embraced within the

2. This is of course opposed to the dominantly materialistic outlook that predominates within Eurocentrism, which focuses on the exploitation and domination of nature and the cosmos.

Afrocentric paradigm. This perspective can quite easily be seen in the Rastafari movement and has been detailed by Barnett in a previous article (2002). In essence, we argue that the Rastafari movement by and large rejects the rugged individualism and crass materialism that are promoted and encouraged in Western capitalist societies in favor of more communal and collective ways of living (that is, Afrocentrically oriented lifestyles), such as living in communes or camps. The Bobo Shanti encampment based at Bull Bay, St. Andrew, is a classic example of this communal living.

The aesthetic dimension of Afrocentricity is concerned with the areas of art, dance, music, poetry, clothes, and architecture as produced by African people. In short, this dimension is concerned with the way Afrocentrists express themselves, visually and materially, as they live day-to-day and as they interact among themselves and with others in the wider world.[3] Rastafari is a movement that is arguably deeply grounded in the African aesthetic in terms of the art, music, and dance forms it produces as well as the clothes that many of the sistren and brethren wear.

Now that we have discussed the overarching theoretical concepts of the Afrocentric paradigm, as conceptualized by Asante, we are in a suitable position to consider what is arguably the precursor to this paradigm (namely, the Afrocentric idea or orientation) and more importantly, to show how the pillars of this *idea* are made manifest within the Rastafari movement, thereby affirming Rastafari as an Afrocentrically based conception and discourse.

Unfolding Rastafari's Afrocentrically Based Orientation

The Afrocentric idea or orientation has been distinguished by five definitive characteristics or pillars by Asante (1999, 4), the first of which is culturally oriented. It is essentially the firm establishment of one's particular cultural psychological location, through the use of symbols, motifs, rituals, and signs. The second pillar is a commitment by a person or group to finding the subject-place of Africans in any social, political, economic, architectural,

3. Asante (1990) draws heavily on Cheikh Anta Diop's arguments for a cultural unity and commonality among Black Africans in his work (see Diop 1978).

literary, or religious phenomenon. The third pillar is the defense of African cultural elements as historically valid in the context of music, education, science, and literature, by the person or group. The fourth pillar is a celebration of the notion of the centeredness and the agency of Africans as well as a commitment to a lexical refinement that eliminates any pejoratives about Africans. The fifth pillar refers to the powerful imperative to revise the collective text of Africans.

Pillar 1

So far as the Rastafari movement is concerned the fulfillment of the first criterion or characteristic is clearly evidenced with the wide use of cultural symbols as an expression of their Afrocentric ideological orientation.

Leonard Barrett Sr. once stated that "the symbol can . . . combine the most disparate elements into a unitary expression" (Barrett 1997, 137). Borrowing from this idea, we posit that Rastafari symbols are an articulation of a once shattered African identity now expressed in the form of a collective unit. At this juncture, it is important to note that these symbols are not just mere identity badges. Rather, as we contend, they give insight into the Afrocentric orientation of Rastas as a social group. Undoubtedly, a journey into the Afrocentric consciousness of Rastafari is one that begins with an interpretation of the meanings embedded within the many symbols used to recreate their connection to Africa.

Rasta identity symbols can be divided into two interrelated groups: literary and cultural (J. Hill 2003). Literary symbols, as described by Hill, are those that reveal the presence of unequal race or power relations, political oppression, and economic suffering or that evoke a distinctive mode of critical awareness. Cultural symbols are manifest or surface symbols that allow for easy identification of individuals belonging to a particular group. They can also be used as expressions of group bondedness. We opine that Rastafari cultural symbols allow for visible "separation and containment," while paradoxically affording persons who internalize Rastafari's Afrocentric orientation to organize as part of a collective. Within the Rastafari movement, the most notable and commonly used cultural symbols include diet, headdresses, locks or matted hair, ceremonial rituals and garbs, and props and banners. A summary and description of some of these symbols and their significance are presented below.[4]

HAIR. Rastas are highly visible because of their distinctive hairstyle. They do not cut their hair (except for when particular circumstances dictate) but allow it to grow naturally into long matted strands or "locks." Locks are symbolic of the lion's mane. As a result Rastas view the lion as a consummate African symbol of the freedom, power, and sovereignty that they, as Africans, inherently hold. Importantly, the locks evoke a conflict-ridden, multifaceted relation between Blacks/Africans and Western Europeans. The feared "dreadlocked" hair serves as a symbol of resistance against all forms of social, economic, racial, political, and spiritual oppression (J. Hill 2003). For Rastas in particular it signifies great spiritual and physical power, freedom and defiance of Eurocentric standards, and ideals of general deportment. This idea of defiance embodied through the hair is of major importance to Rastas, as it gestures toward a conscious effort to separate themselves from the Babylonian mentality (that is, dominant Eurocentrism) that dictates that a certain standard of beauty (short hair and little or no facial hair in the case of men and straight hair in the case of women) is universally desirable.[5]

The above ideals have since changed in the contemporary context. The once-feared dreadlocks have now been appropriated as part of a collective consciousness on the part of continental and Diasporic Africans alike (particularly those who grew up in societies where "kinky" "wool-like" hair had come to represent wildness, savagery, and degeneracy, the quintessential opposite of fine, straight, silky hair often indexed as "good" hair). For many individuals who identify themselves as Africans, the wearing of dreadlocks now signifies the articulation of pride and acceptance of their natural African beauty. Outside of the Rastafari movement, locks have

4. It should be noted that these symbols are not presented here in any ranked or hierarchical order. Other members of the Rastafari community may articulate alternative definitions into their meanings and significance.

5. This is particularly so when individuals seek economic mobility within dominant society. Punishments are often leveled at individuals who do not look or dress the part or do not conform to this Eurocentric standard of beauty.

taken on a new meaning so much so that wearing them is now viewed as a promotion of and appreciation of African physical attributes. To these ends, the wearing of locks conjures up sentiments of nationalism among Africans around the globe.

THE HOLY HERB. Rastas are commonly identified with smoking marijuana, also known as ganja or the "holy herb" or sacred weed when used in its ritual context. Rastas cite various scriptures (such as Genesis 1:12, Exodus 10:12, Proverbs 15:17, and Psalms 104:14) to verify its sacramental purpose. In keeping with the previously mentioned idea that Africans are the true Israelites spoken of in the Old Testament of the Bible, Rastas cite these same Biblical scriptures as direction for the usage of marijuana as a ceremonially sacred herb for meditative, sacramental, and medicinal purposes.[6] The holy herb has long been thought of by Rastas as a stimulant that aids the increase of spiritual insight. However, inasmuch as it gives Rastas a "special inner-connection to the Divine powers of Jah Rastafari" and facilitates the process of critical reflection on dominant Eurocentric ideologies, most noteworthy is its function as a catalyst for "heightening unity and communal feelings" so central to the African ontology (Barrett 1997; Davis 1994; J. Hill 2003).

THE LION OF JUDAH. The lion located on the Ethiopian flag is, arguably, one of the most prominent Rastafari symbols (Barrett 1997, 142). It represents Haile Selassie I, the conquering lion of the tribe of Judah whose "King of Kings" status implies an inversion of the colonial dependency syndrome and submissiveness Africans have been taught to accept. The lion is thus seen as a superior, all important, and powerful king of the jungle. This kingly character is of major significance, as it is through this

6. It is important to note that the use of marijuana for medicinal and curative purposes (though still heavily contested) is well researched, documented, and accepted in countries like the Netherlands and Canada and some parts of the United States. Moreover, we believe its use has been widely misappropriated among the wider non-Rastafari population, so much so that its sacramental purposes have been negated.

figure that Rastas are able to assert their African royal lineage. Moreover, the lion is symbolic of strength, thus leading to a rediscovery and reassertion of a sense of pride and dignity in one's Black or African selfhood. In historical and contemporary contexts, the jungle represents all nations and their leaders. In keeping with the notion that Africa is the cradle of civilization, this symbol thus ushers in a consciousness that positions Africa as the beginning and head of all other civilizations. This is, of course, in contrast to dominant Eurocentrism that promulgates a depiction of Africa as the tail (read: follower) of Europe and America.

OTHER PICTURES. Rastas are often seen proudly displaying pictures of His Imperial Majesty Haile Selassie, Marcus Garvey, Bob Marley, and other spiritual leaders, elders, or icons. These pictures can be found hanging in various spaces within Rasta homes and tabernacles and on clothing worn on a daily basis. The wearing of these symbols can be generally linked to the African tradition of the veneration of the ancestors as well as a general reverence for monumental personalities.

THE ETHIOPIAN, GHANAIAN, AND GARVEY FLAGS. Since the birth of the movement, Rastas have adopted the colors of the Garvey movement (red, black, and green) and the colors of the Ethiopian and Ghanaian flags (red, gold, and green) as unique colors that express their Pan-Africanist sentiments. Like the pictures, banners, and flags, these colors appear everywhere Rastafari go, and they are indicative of the impact of Garvey and Rastafari on the development of the formation of collective African identity.

Each color has its own unique symbolism. The red represents the blood of our African ancestors that was spilled to perpetuate the greatest crime against humanity, the Trans-Atlantic slave trade. In recent times, it has come to symbolize life as it runs through the veins of all people. The black represents the skin color of Africans, and the green, the lush vegetation of Africa. Last, the yellow is symbolic of the beautiful sunshine that allows for the springing of life from the soil. For some Rastas, however, the yellow also conjures up feelings of hope that a perpetual ray of light shines on the future of Africa and Ethiopia.

DIET. One less obvious but influential Afrocentric symbol of identification is that of the diet of Rastas, which consists mainly of vegetables, fruits, nuts, and ground provisions that are in most cases not grown under artificial or chemically induced conditions. The diet is largely vegetarian for many mansions of Rastafari, except for the Twelve Tribes of Israel Mansion, which allows meat, such as chicken and goat. Realizing that the body is the vehicle transporting the soul, Rastas are careful about taking care of themselves. As a consequence, Rastas try to limit their intake of excess sugar, artificial preservatives, and salts. They also make a concerted effort to give back to the earth and tend to the environment because it is through maintaining a balance in the earth that they are able to maintain this natural and earthly diet, the Ital diet.

Chevannes (1994), referencing Monica Schuler, discusses the significance of the salt taboo as it relates to the Rastafari spiritual journey. He notes that studies connect this salt taboo to the Bakongo tribe that came to Jamaica from West Africa after emancipation. The tradition held that the ingestion of salt prevented them from flying back to Africa. He continues by stating that many of their ancestors dreamed of a return to Africa but could not because they had found it impossible to abstain from eating the traditional salted fish and corned pork imported as food for the enslaved. In the Bakongo cosmology, the only way one could return to Africa was through a salt-free diet. Resisting salt is thus seen as a metaphor for resisting assimilation into European ways that were foreign to the African. In the Rasta ontology, excess salt is seen as debilitating to the individual's spiritual journey to Rastafari. Chevannes further notes that salt intake signals the loss of spiritual force. Hence, total avoidance of salt simultaneously meant the intake of the spirit. In essence, salt avoidance was a signpost of the individual's ability to tap into or become more in tune with one's greater spiritual self. The Rasta diet thus serves as another medium through which group social ideas and African ontological perspectives are animated.

Pillar 2

The second pillar of Asante's Afrocentric orientation is a commitment by a person or group to finding the subject-place of Africans in any social, political, economic, architectural, literary, or religious phenomenon. In terms of this second pillar, there are few occasions, if any, where Rastafari adherents fail to position Africa as the progenitor of civilization and science and as the source from which all other races and peoples came. Rastafari adherents have, since the inception of the movement (and up to the present day), described world events and world history as they directly pertain to and affect African people, whether on the Continent or within the Diaspora. In the Rastafari worldview, the first Egyptians and Israelites were irrefutably Black. Additionally, Egypt and Israel (to an extent) are considered to have been daughter civilizations to that of Ethiopia. Thus, the development of religious thought and religion as well as culture in general is ultimately reinscribed by Rastafari and positioned definitively as an African phenomenon.

Pillar 3

The third pillar is that of a defense of African cultural elements as historically valid in the context of music, education, science, and literature by the person or group. There is a clear expression of the third pillar of Asante's Afrocentric idea by the Rastafari movement, we argue, as it clearly defends and affirms the historical validity and importance of African cultural contributions to music, science, education, and literature. For the Rastaman and woman alike, the first civilizations were born on the continent of Africa. Thus, they believe that many key areas of culture and knowledge, which many assume were born out of the European Renaissance period, actually owe much to the groundwork laid by ancient African civilizations that grew up along the River Nile. Additionally, in the New World it is noted that many New World Africans continue to shape and produce culture as well as knowledge, even though their ancestors were forcibly displaced from Mother Africa centuries ago.

Pillar 4

The fourth pillar is a celebration of the notion of the centeredness (which was previously discussed) and agency of Africans as well as a commitment to lexical refinement that eliminates pejoratives about Africans. In terms of the fourth pillar, the Rastafari movement has historically placed the African and Africa at the center of its worldview. Largely inspired by Marcus Garvey's firm nationalism, its members have always aspired to self-reliant models for living and sustaining themselves. Thus, there is a strong emphasis on the potential agency of Africans to change their condition and to chart their own destinies through hard work and collective efforts. Much has been made of Marcus Garvey's achievements by the Rastafari movement, who through sheer hard work, determination, and the collective support of millions of Blacks, started and operated a plethora of businesses, including the multi-million-dollar (by today's standards) Black Star Line steamship company.

As far as lexical refinement is concerned, Rastafari have developed their own language (referred to as Rasta-talk by some) that has empowered a once disenfranchised and marginalized people, that affirms positivity over negativity, and that completely eliminates all pejoratives relating to Africans and Black people.

Pillar 5

The fifth pillar alludes to the powerful imperative, largely due to historical sources and forces, to revise the collective text of Africans. This final pillar of the Afrocentric idea or orientation is expressed by Rastafari through their collective desire to rewrite and correct a grossly misrepresented view of world history as seen from an extremely pervasive Eurocentric perspective. The goal that is sought after by brethren and sistren alike is to get to the narrative that is essentially *their story* and not *his-story.*

The overarching characteristic of this pillar is that the Afrocentrist strives for the liberation of his or her mind from any notion that Europe is the teacher and Africa is the pupil; in other words, the purging of one's mind of notions of European superiority and African inferiority. As Asante aptly points out, this is not a biologically determined position, but rather a culturally and theoretically determined one. Thus, it is possible for Europeans and Asians to be Afrocentrists, while simultaneously identifying Africans who are not. In the same regard, it is possible to find Europeans and Asians who have adopted a Rastafarian (and therefore Afrocentric) worldview, while there are many Africans who have a worldview that is opposed to the Rastafarian and Afrocentric one. In other words, we have a dynamic wherein one does not necessarily have to be Black to be Rasta, but one's mental frame of reference does have to be African. It is important to note that merely being Black is not enough to be regarded as Rastafari or an Afrocentrist. It has been shown historically on many occasions that having Black skin does not necessarily mean that one is African minded. Many Blacks do not relate to Africa and, even more significantly, do not *want* to relate to Africa.[7]

Nonetheless, Rastafarians, just as other Afrocentrists, do relate to Africa, so much so that many are seeking to repatriate there. Three notable Rastafari settler communities have sprung up on the continent thus far: in Ghana, Koforidua, and Accompong; Nigeria; and Ethiopia, Shashamane. These communities have originated from small remigrations of Rastafari who essentially have been sent through collective efforts of the various Rastafari Mansions, such as the Twelve Tribes of Israel, the Nyahbinghi Order, and the Ethiopia Africa Black International Congress, in preparation for the movement's planned mass exodus of Rastafari to the Motherland. The Rastafari movement is perhaps the most prolific and ardent advocate of repatriation of Black people to Africa, especially in the wake of the significant neocolonial attitudes that exist today in most predominantly Black Nations throughout the world.

Along with the political demand for repatriation comes the demand for reparations; that is, the demand for the West (the former European colonial powers as well as the United States) to provide the material means for Diaspora Africans to return to the Motherland. Ardent Jamaican Rastafari advocates for reparations include Ras Miguel Lorne, a Rastafari attorney, and the now-departed Junior Manning, who had the distinction of being

7. Upon reflection, this is not really surprising considering the prevailing and dominant hegemony of white supremacy. Additionally, Africa as a continent is often cast in a brutally negative light by much of the media, with its focus on the disease, wars, and famines that have ravaged it. Therefore, many Blacks are unlikely to be inspired to reconnect with it.

the founding chairperson of the Ethio-Africa Diaspora Union Millennium Council. They made strong arguments that the governments of Western countries that enslaved Africans and benefited (and continue to benefit) immensely from exploiting them have never compensated the enslaved or their descendants. Instead, in some specific cases (such as Jamaica), they chose to compensate the slave masters for their loss of free labor immediately after the abolition of slavery rather than compensate the slaves. Furthermore, many Rastafari leaders have noted that France, a former European colonial power, demanded and subsequently received significant financial compensation from Haiti for its argued loss of free labor, after the former slaves of Haiti fought for and won their freedom.[8]

The conception of repatriation (and reparations as a means of achieving this) is just one of the principles of Rastafari that reinforces the movement's Afrocentric orientation. The other is of course the movement's primary assertion that Haile Selassie, a Black African, is divine and descended from an ancestral lineage that links him to the first advent of Christ.[9] This implies that Jesus Christ of Nazareth was a Black African and thus that God himself is Black. This is implicitly Afrocentric.

Rastafari also acclaim Marcus Garvey as a prophet and highly influential Black leader for African people all over the world. The Rastafari movement, which emerged in Jamaica in the early 1930s, was undoubtedly

8. With regard to this discussion of reparations, it should be noted that it is a global political objective being pursued by people of African descent and not just exclusively by the Rastafari movement. Having said this, however, it should also be noted that the movement has been a significant force in championing this cause. Of significant note is the United Nations Conference on Racism that was held in 2001 in Durban, South Africa, in which reparations were discussed. The United States pulled out, and the former European colonial powers expressed their regrets concerning slavery, but they stopped short of making a full-fledged apology. In 2002, the Rastafari Legal Council, headed up by Ras Miguel Lorne, filed a lawsuit for reparations against the British Crown, which elicited a letter of profound regret from Buckingham Palace for the occurrence of slavery, but no formal apology.

9. In his treatise on Rastafari entitled "The Seven Principles of Rastafari," Ras Ishon Williams (2000) discusses in detail the seven foundational principles of Rastafari. The implicit Afrocentric nature of some of these principles is not made evident in his work and thus deserves some discussion here.

inspired both by the work and words of the Honorable Marcus Garvey. As such, the Rastafari movement is widely considered as the successor of Garvey's Universal Negro Improvement Association and Garvey's vision in general (Tafari 1996), in that it aspires to emulate many of Garvey's ideals. For instance, the Rastafari movement strives for African economic, educational, political, and cultural autonomy, in addition to its recognition of Africa as the base and center for African people (Garvey 1986). Rastas teach the importance of healing the self through recovering the past. To this end, Rastas continue to search through the pages of history to recover and to resurrect the voices of the persecuted, marginalized, and silenced. Guided by Marcus Garvey's philosophy, Rastafari encourages oppressed and marginalized people to read and research the truth, as it is only in doing this that they can recover the untold stories of their past and become whole.

Of noteworthy importance is that Marcus Garvey is considered by Asante (2003) to be an irrefutable Afrocentrist, which in effect places the Rastafari movement, a successor of Garvey's ideals and principles, squarely into the Afrocentric arena.

To date, Rastas have been ardent critics of the oppressive Euro-Western system of domination, a cause which Asante sees as pivotal in his definition of Afrocentricity (2003, 2). Asante also argues that the fight to liberate African people the world over from White racial domination is one that will ultimately liberate the oppressor as well as the oppressed, because systems of oppression ultimately constrain both the oppressor and the oppressed.

Concluding Thoughts

Being Rasta is a state of existence that does not lend itself to linear Eurocentric reasoning; rather, its phenomenological and ontological orientation lends itself to an Afrocentric existentialism. Through its continuous evolution and development of its own rituals, even while struggling constantly against the forces and agents of colonial and neocolonial oppression, the Rastafari movement has developed its own Njia (pathway), to which Asante refers throughout much of his work (2003, 30). Rastas have a collective African-centered (Afrocentric) spirit, an African essence that might lie dormant in many New World Africans. The Afrocentric spiritual epistemology, axiology, and ontology need only to be rekindled through a reimmersion in African cultural practices passed down through intergenerational African blood and collective memory.

With its deification of an African King (Haile Selassie I); its assertion that the Holy Land (Zion) is in Ethiopia or, by extension, Africa (Williams 2000); and its contention that Ethiopia is the birthplace of humanity and civilization, wherein Nubia and Egypt (Kemet) are considered the African daughters or inheritors of Ethiopian Civilization, we propose that the Rastafari ideology and world outlook are undoubtedly Afrocentric.

We hope that this chapter aids in the meaningful discussion of the proposition that the Rastafari movement is implicitly Afrocentric according to the highly theoretical and academic framework of Afrocentricity that has been postulated by the founder of the Afrocentric idea, Molefi Kete Asante.

Part 4 Gender Considerations in the Rastafari Movement

The Woman in RastafarI

MAUREEN ROWE

It is a well-known fact that little work has been done on the female in RastafarI. Nettleford (1970) and Kitzinger (1969, 252) suggest that this is because males more readily declare to be RastafarI. Kitzinger takes this point further and argues that RastafarI males do not consider females to be integral to the movement based on her observation that "leadership, status, prophecy and healing" rest with the male. She also suggests that RastafarI is a direct response to the matriarchal relations common to the Jamaican peasantry. Hence, she believes that RastafarI social structure is male dominated, and the dogma is mother denying (Kitzinger 1969, 260).

Although Kitzinger submits evidence for her observations, her conclusions are not generally acceptable to the RastafarI community. Her observations of RastafarI male and female relationships seem based on the Western theory of gender equality, which requires equal participation in the rituals of one's culture.

Perhaps it is the result of observations of the kind made by Kitzinger that has led to the growing view among RastafarI people that we ought to be examined from within. Stephen G. McDonald argues that this examination should be undertaken by those who have experienced the movement as a process (McDonald n.d.). Leahcim T. Semaj (1980), in setting out the

This chapter is a reprint, with light editorial changes and some explanatory notes by the editor, of an article first published in *Caribbean Quarterly* 26(4) in December 1980. Used by permission.

characteristic of cultural science, which is defined as the total study of a people, argues in favor of the following principles:

1. The primacy of self-knowledge.

2. No restrictions on issues and methodology.

3. No scientific colonization, that is, research of the people should also be for the people.

The importance of this view should not be underrated by scholars insensitive to the attempts of the observed to become their own observers. It is a development in the field of research that, if not articulated by traditional scholars, is recognized by them. Certainly, Owens's taped recordings of Rastafarians on RastafarI and Yawney's research methods, which were essentially to secure entry into RastafarI "livity" in order to experience the culture from within, are evidence enough (Owens 1976; Yawney 1978).

I subscribe to this school of thought. I am therefore writing from the base of a solid grounding into RastafarI and a continuous RastafarI livity.

Role of Females and the Bible

There can be no denying the fact that RastafarI is a patriarchal movement. The male is at the head, having responsibility for conducting rituals, for interpreting events of significance to the community, and for the care and protection of the family as well as the community. RastafarI is based on the Bible; it therefore follows that its structure in philosophy would pattern that which unfolds in the Bible.

The Bible is a sacred Book to most Rastafarians. It is an important source of guidance and inspiration (Yawney 1978, 99). To understand RastafarI attitudes toward females it is necessary to understand the role of females in the Bible.

The first female character is Eve, who when tempted by the devil in the Garden of Eden became Adam's temptress. Next is Sarai, who when asked by her husband to pose as his sister in order to safeguard his life did so unquestioningly. Following Sarai is Rebekal, who schemed against her husband to ensure that her favorite son would receive his blind father's blessing. Rachel and Leah, both sisters, vied with each other for their husband's affection, each relying on her fertility to win favor in his eyes. Potiphar's wife attempted to seduce Joseph; thwarted in her attempts to do so, she reported that he had attempted to rape her.

As the Bible stories unfold, a clear pattern for the role of the woman emerges. The stories are told primarily about the males, with females only being treated peripherally when they have relevance to a particular event. Even Miriam, recognized by scholars of the Bible as the first prophetess, is referred to in snatches as her actions gained significance to Moses. Perhaps Ruth, the ancestress of David and Jesus, and Esther, who directly affected the course of history for the Israelites, are the only exceptions in that entire books are devoted to them.

For the RastafarI male, it is significant that the first female mentioned in the Bible is unfavorably mentioned, which is interpreted as a clear warning against potential evil in the female. Though the interpretation is widely held by RastafarI males, their response differs. Some brethren are sympathetic in their response, arguing that the evil was in the devil and that Eve was the victim.

It was also natural for her to want to share with Adam. Adam is seen to have succumbed to weakness where he should have held fast to his knowledge of what was right. This interpretation is more protective of the female. The male is responsible for shielding and guiding the female away from sin. Gradually, with sufficient tutelage the female can be expected to distinguish the sinful from the righteous on her own.

The other attitude is more judgmental. It argues that the female is impure and must be kept from corrupting the male. It is also implied wherever this attitude is manifested that females should not get together because of the potential for sinful thinking and practices. The female then must be guided, instructed, and restricted by the male.

It is difficult to identify the strength of these beliefs from subgroup to subgroup. It is easier to identify as a characteristic of age groups. In general, the younger group of RastafarI males tend to be more understanding and manifest behaviors associated with the sympathetic interpretation. The elder brethren tend to manifest more of the attitudes associated with the judgmental interpretation. An interesting point to note is that some brethren articulate the protective interpretation but require behavior associated with the judgmental approach.

Other Factors Affecting the Role of Daughters

Although the Bible obviously played a large part in determining the attitude of male to female in RastafarI, other factors seemed to have had a reinforcing effect on attitudes and expectations of female behavior.[1] RastafarI, it must be noted, was first articulated by males. As it evolved, the movement was regarded as a cult of outcasts whose members bordered on the ridiculous, if not the insane. Females would, of necessity, be wary of involvement with a male without any obvious prospects. One of the reasons that females marry in the Jamaican culture is to advance socially and economically. A woman "advances" herself by choosing a mate who can move her up a rung or two on the social ladder. Both Dinah and Mabel[2] make their way out of the Dungle[3] (ghetto) through the establishment of relationships with males somewhat better off than themselves (Patterson 1971). This fact alone puts the RastafarI male at a disadvantage. RastafarI adherents were drawn from the lower socioeconomic group in the society and therefore had no significant prospects. This, coupled with the belief that individuals should work for themselves rather than others, made their income unstable. The unstable economics of the RastafarI male may well explain the temporary nature of relationships established in the early years. The fact that researchers have documented repeatedly the Rastaman's belief that a woman is not a Rasta "in heart" and comes and goes as she pleases (Kitzinger 1969, 252) is evidence enough.

1. In RastafarI circles, the term "daughter" is used to refer to a RastafarI woman. However, it should be noted that some Rastawomen protest the use of this term on the grounds that it is condescending to be referred to as daughters when they are in fact full-grown women.

2. Dinah and Mabel are two key female characters in Orlando Patterson's classic novel *The Children of Sisyphus*. Dinah, a prostitute, is one of the lead characters in the novel, and Mabel is one of her main rivals. Both originate from the Dungle.

3. The Dungle is a RastafarI term for a ghetto or slum or a depressed area of the inner city that at one time had (and may still have) a significant RastafarI presence.

The Doctrine on Females

RastafarI articulates specific views on females. These views have been translated into a code of behavior that governs all important group rituals. In general, RastafarI males accept that:

- Females are not called to RastafarI except through a male. Only a man can make a woman "sight" RastafarI. She therefore cannot be a leader in any RastafarI ritual.
- Males are the physical and spiritual head of the female as well as of the family. The female must seek the man's guidance in all things spiritual. He also accepts the responsibility for "balancing" her thoughts.
- A female cannot experience the "highest heights" of RastafarI if she is without a kingman or head.
- A woman is deemed unclean whenever she menstruates (that is, whenever she is having her period).

From these premises came certain behavioral restrictions or taboos:

- The female cannot share a chalice of the males. This excludes her from experiencing the communal nature of the culture in a direct way.
- The female should always have her head covered when praying (I Corinthians 115–6). Because she is always expected to be receptive to spiritual instruction, it follows that the head should always be covered.
- An "unclean" female cannot approach a ritual gathering of males (for example, at binghis) nor should she prepare meals for any males during any time she is designated "unclean."
- A woman is expected to be obedient and receptive to guidance as well as have a willingness to learn.

The male/female role in RastafarI is further strengthened by the fact that the "I" is seen to have come under the influence of Babylon and therefore stands in need of cleansing. The interaction between Jah and man cleanses the man and he in turn cleanses the female.

The RastafarI beliefs regarding the female are clearly based on the Bible and fall in line with the premise that RastafarI is a patriarchal movement. "Reasonings," the traditional way of sharing information, cementing views, or interpreting the Bible, take place primarily among the males. They take the responsibility for sharing relevant information with females. However, females are not restricted from reasoning together, particularly at important rituals or celebrations. In this way there is intellectual stimulation and the female is, through one means or another, every bit as informed as the male.

Not all of the doctrine regarding females is upheld by all the males. Furthermore, how a belief impacts on a particular family unit varies from household to household. Daughters (RastafarI women) have reported varying degrees of freedom based on the interpretation of the family head.

It is possible that the beliefs and practices common to RastafarI male/female relationships do not differ so drastically from that of the Jamaican peasantry. Further research may not only reveal this to be the case but, as Yawney suggests, may also reveal traditional West Indian standards in intrasex social relations (Yawney 1978, 120).

Females and the Doctrine

It should be noted that beliefs and their resulting taboos cannot be realized unless the females understand, accept, and practice them. With the exception of exclusion from the group, there are no ways of enforcing these practices. It is left to the individual to behave in accordance with his or her understandings. This last point is critical to the understandings of male/female relationships in RastafarI. The concept of male dominance can have no validity where the female understands, accepts, and operates within the parameters of a prescribed role. It is only when the female resists this role that the concept acquires significance.

For the female initiate to RastafarI, there has been a consistently clear pattern of acceptance of the behavior codes of RastafarI. A number of daughters have indicated an initial attraction to the way of life of RastafarI women. Only a few daughters seem to have queried beyond the obvious restrictions on dress, and the information they uncovered did not deter them. There seems to be a definite desire to function in that role and an attraction for this structured and disciplined way of life. This attraction may be a factor in the increased acceptance and popularity of RastafarI among Jamaican's female population. RastafarI also elevated the woman to a special place in her role as mother and wife. Contrary to certain suppositions, this is not a contradiction. The fact that the Black woman is regarded as a queen, madonna, or earth mother does not mean that she should not have a clear role in relation to the man and the culture.

It must be mentioned that not every female was interested in RastafarI despite an interest in the RastafarI male. The reasons are similar to what Dinah tells Cyrus, the Rastaman interested in her: "Just clear off you hear, ah not 'avin anything to do with you rastas, oonoo treat you ooman too bad, oonoo seem to think dat man only mek to serve an slave for you and dis is one ooman wha' nuh mek fo' dat" (Patterson 1971, 30). Despite her views, Dinah did eventually become Cyrus's woman for a while, before leaving to establish a union with another male. What is clear is the lack of interest in RastafarI philosophy. It seems that the females attracted to RastafarI share similar characteristics.

Elder daughters spoke of Alexander Bedward, Marcus Garvey, and Leonard Howell. It seems that these daughters were already "conscious" of Africa before their association with RastafarI, which made it easier to live up to RastafarI expectations. Some of these daughters had had a Christian upbringing, and a few had had associations with revivalist groups. Further research needs to be done in this area to identify the specific factors that brought these daughters to RastafarI. It seems to be the case that many of these daughters came to RastafarI through a specific male. It has already been observed that it was more common in the early years of RastafarI to have the female partner of a RastafarI male be identified as a Rastaman's woman rather than as a Rastawoman (Sister Ilaloo 1981, 7). This is consistent with the role that had been defined for females. If the female can only "sight" RastafarI through the male, it follows that her legitimacy within the movement would be dependent on him. Thus, a daughter would be known as Ras Meeshak's daughter. This identification also works in the reverse, and the brethren responsible for a daughter's place in the RastafarI community is known as "daughter Dinah's kingman." In this manner the claim that each has on the other in an established union is legitimized.

RastafarI in the Sixties

With the increased Black consciousness of the sixties, RastafarI was legitimized for young Jamaicans. The movement picked up support from middle-class youths in the civil service and on university campuses. Although the outward signs of the RastafarI lifestyle were not always evident, this new group of young people, because of their leanings, were termed "functional Rastafarians" (Nettleford 1970, 60).

This group of young people, again primarily males, made significant inroads where the interpretation of RastafarI doctrine was concerned. One of the most crucial areas was that of male/female relationships. It was difficult for the young males who had had formal schooling with females and had related to them as classmates, sharing thoughts and debating issues, to treat the women as secondary. Though this attitude may have reflected a general acceptance of RastafarI philosophy, the behavior was often less restrictive. Daughters became the recipient of reasonings as the younger males assumed the responsibility to explain and secure the females' acceptance of the faith. Many of these relationships were already long-standing and had evolved with the two individuals having more or less equal say in their decision-making process. In this atmosphere, where discussions of issues relevant to the Black cause were occurring with a certain amount of frequency, RastafarI seemed to have significant answers.

The females in this situation were likely to accept some of the thinking of RastafarI, most notably the thinking around Africa, politics, and economics. A number of daughters have indicated that they had problems accepting the divinity of the Emperor Haile Selassie. Rita Marley, in reasoning of her own experience, has said she had heard and reflected upon the seemingly valid arguments for the divinity of Haile Selassie, but she needed further proof. This proof finally came when she saw the black spot (nail print) in the middle of his hand (Marley 1979, 7). It is safe to assume that the visit of the emperor to Jamaica affected a number of individuals both male and female in this way. Among the Twelve Tribes, both male and female often recall this visit at meetings and share the impact it had on them personally and their resulting commitment to RastafarI. Because of the emphasis on political thinking in the sixties, however, a number of daughters had no problems identifying with RastafarI, because in certain circles it represented a level of political sophistication.

For these daughters, then, much of the experience of the elder daughters still applied, in that they were females relating to males who in turn were operating from a foundation that was RastafarI. Because it can be argued that these males were only marginally experiencing RastafarI, that is to say, their lifestyles allowed them easy access to RastafarI as well as to the Babylonian world, it can also be argued that the daughters relating to them were also experiencing a marginal RastafarI lifestyle.

RastafarI in the Seventies

With the recognition early in the seventies that revolutionary political thought alone could not liberate the minds of a people, the theorists for Black liberation argued for the inclusion of a religious component in the theory of Black liberation. As Haki Madhubuti (formerly Don L. Lee) argues, a Black value system should take into account the political, social, economic, spiritual, and emotional crises faced by Black peoples in the Western world (Madhubuti 1979, 79). With the shift in emphasis from revolutionary theory to an integrated approach, liberation movements such as the Nation of Islam came to the fore in the United States in the early seventies, and RastafarI continued to expand in Jamaica.

In 1972, the election campaigns were geared toward RastafarI. The People's National Party candidate campaigned around a rod that he claimed had been given to him by the emperor. The Jamaica Labour Party candidate claimed he had a better rod. That campaign stands as a clear indicator of the growth and entrenchment of RastafarI in the Jamaican society.

Among the younger Rastafarians there appeared to have been a firmer commitment made to RastafarI. More of these young people started to wear locks and to "trod RastafarI" in a more traditional way, which meant that more daughters were being required to observe the behavior codes as related to them by the brethren.

Daughters have indicated that they strictly observe the behavior codes because they desire to do so, but for some daughters it was especially difficult. Some were living with parents and others with friends. For those in the family home they had to cope with parental pressure as they tried to "live up." For those living with friends there was support as well as reprimands. One sister shared the fact that she lived with several other daughters and a few brethren and that the restrictions were trying; for example, she could not prepare herself a meal at certain times, but on the whole, the rules were willingly observed by all the daughters.

The mid-seventies were important for a number of daughters. Those women, in their mid- to late twenties, indicated that it was around this time that they first became aware of a need to commit themselves to RastafarI. Quite a number of these daughters also reported that there was no specific male involved in the process of them "sighting" RastafarI, but that it was the direct result of an attitude of searching. A number of these daughters were affiliated with the Twelve Tribes, which made it easy to manifest an affiliation to RastafarI by joining the organization. The Twelve Tribes of Israel allows daughters a certain amount of freedom in that they participate in the celebrations organized by the group. At official functions, twenty-four individuals are seated facing the audience, twelve males and twelve females, which signifies the importance attached to the female in this organization. It is more than likely that the Twelve Tribes organization played a significant part in the spread of RastafarI among daughters. Further research in this area may reveal this to be the case.[4]

By the latter part of the seventies more and more daughters were coming into prominence. They were easily recognized by the RastafarI colors, head wraps, long skirts, and often dreadlocks. Many of these daughters observed the belief that a daughter had to have a kingman and thus become a part of a family unit. Their roles for the most part remained unchanged.

4. As it is now more than thirty years ago that this article was written, it has become clearly apparent that the emergence of the Twelve Tribes of Israel Mansion not only attracted many middle-class youth of Jamaica to RastafarI but also many women, because it was perceived (and in fact still is today) as the relatively most egalitarian mansion of RastafarI as far as gender relations are concerned.

Daughters acknowledged the man as the head of the union and themselves as the supportive members.

At the very end of the seventies there was an increase in activities of RastafarI daughters. Daughters were beginning to assert themselves at RastafarI gatherings. They began to interpret the dress codes for themselves. The latter observation is particularly true of daughters who were salaried employees. Some argued that it was of necessity that they had to shorten their skirts; others indicated a preference for short skirts. Daughters also began to discriminate in terms of when and where to cover their hair, and some were seen in public with their locks partially exposed.

By the end of the seventies daughters had evolved into a new kind of awareness of self. It is important to note that this evolution, occurring as it had over time, did not create any disunity in RastafarI community. Rather, personal opinions were often expressed by observers of changing female behaviors by males at binghis and other gatherings, although some daughters reported receiving some hostility when they first attended a gathering without a head covering. For the most part, however, once a daughter's kingman overcame objections to her interpretation of the dress code, the hostility lessened as a more tolerant attitude evolved on the part of the males.

In addition to the changed appearance of RastafarI daughters, there was also an attitudinal change. Daughters were speaking out more often about their concerns and hopes. Even more important, daughters had begun to articulate their own perception of RastafarI. More daughters were beginning to reason together, and this created a solid base from which to approach the society in general and the RastafarI community in particular.

Daughters and the Golden Jubilee

November 2, 1980, was the fiftieth anniversary of the coronation of Haile Selassie. For all Rastafarians this was the golden jubilee year. Several activities were organized to mark this year, which turned out to be significant for daughters. During at least one binghi the issue of daughters and their abilities and place in RastafarI was raised. Although the issue was not resolved, it was at least raised. The brethren reiterated their love for the daughters and also that the man is the head.

While daughters are not challenging this reasoning, their behavior is more in keeping with the concept of interdependence. Daughters are manifesting more commitment to RastafarI. This was apparently strengthened in 1980 as daughters began asking more what they could do for RastafarI. This question was rooted in the awareness that male and female are equal partners in the liberation process and must therefore take full responsibilities for the tasks ahead. As Judy Mowatt[5] reasoned in an interview:

> We know as rasta queens and sisters that a woman is just as important as a man in the sight of God, and we live to please God and to live with man as brothers and sisters. . . . not for man as God, just sons of God. We are equal because, whatever is revealed to a man is revealed to a woman. It's not that a man has more knowledge, wisdom and understanding than a woman. It's the same mind that God has put in a man that a woman has, but it's the one who develops it more and uses it wisely. . . . And a woman must know what she is dealing with. (Yawney 1980, 3)

As confirmation that more and more daughters are becoming increasingly aware of what they are dealing with, three groups of daughters came into being in 1980: King Alpha and Queen Omega's Theocracy Daughters, a group of elder daughters from the theocracy; International Twelve, among the twelve tribes; and Dawtas United Working Towards Africa (DAWTAS).[6] This last group defined itself as a working group committed to addressing the educational needs of RastafarI youths, the need for social services within the RastafarI community, and self-development activities.

As these trends continue, we can expect significant changes in RastafarI. Already RastafarI males are defining positions in relation to the developments discussed here. For the most part, the brethren are supportive and

5. Judy Mowatt was one of the members of the I-Threes, who rose to prominence as Bob Marley's primary backing vocalists after he parted ways with original Wailers' members Peter Tosh and Bunny Wailer.

6. These three RastafarI female groups are no longer active but have since been effectively replaced by the Empress of Zion and the RastafarI Youth Initiative Council, which is primarily run by RastafarI females, although the membership includes RastafarI males.

lend whatever assistance the daughters have requested. This is most obvious among the younger males. Some males have taken observer positions and are watching from the sidelines. There has not been much resistance to this evolutionary trend among the brethren. With this kind of potential support, daughters may well begin to address themselves to some of the issues in RastafarI that directly affect their bodies and their lives. When we come to that point, the method of addressing the issues will be of far more significance perhaps than the issues themselves.

Editor's Closing Comments

More than thirty years after the writing of this article, RastafarI women are notably challenging some of the key dress codes and guidelines that have been laid down by the older RastafarI mansions, such as the Nyahbinghi Mansion and the Bobo Shanti Mansion. For instance, now many Rasta women are wearing their locks uncovered when out in public, and they are wearing trousers. This would be almost unthinkable thirty years ago. Additionally, many Rasta women remain active in the movement even after separating from their kingman (RastafarI male partner). This too would be almost unthinkable in 1980 and in the years prior.

Resistance Without and Within

Reasonings on Gender Relations in RastafarI

IMANI M. TAFARI-AMA

The Problematic

In an Internet survey conducted in 2010 with participants listed as attendees of the International Rastafari Studies Conference held at the University of the West Indies, Mona, in the same year, a RastafarI sistren in the 30–39 age category lamented that "many Rasta parents, because of the persecution for earlier times, seem not to reinforce Rasta as a livity for their children, oftentimes opting to leave the choice up to the children." She also noted that "there is also a lack of infrastructure to guide the youth towards RastafarI." She specified that the Rasta community had failed to provide its progeny with "schools, community centres [and] co-ops." Echoing the cry of many who are frustrated with gaps in Rasta achievements in this regard, she asked with anguish, "What do we own? Where is our empowerment?" In her vision:

> If RastafarI is the way, then our children shouldn't be left to make a choice; they should be raised in the way. If RastafarI is the way we the parents should ensure that by our works we construct the pertinent infrastructure needed to ensure the longevity and sustainability of what we believe in. Our lives should be the examples which they want to live. Furthermore, others outside of RastafarI should want to draw closer to our light. These things build confidence in our youth and when our youth are confident and are properly sustained and molded then our future is certain.

This chapter is a conversation piece to address some of the existential concerns that beset RastafarI sistren and brethren within the *livity,* or way of life. These concerns affect how they negotiate to produce identities of resistance while living in a cultural environment dominated by the Babylon system or societal apparatus to which they are essentially opposed but which defines the mainstream modes of thinking and behavior external to RastafarI. A principal node of anxiety is the paradox posed by some parents' failure to inculcate RastafarI values in their children as a preventative measure against the bombardment of Babylonian values; this outside influence hijacks the sensibilities of impressionable children, undermining the sustainability of the livity. The discussion to come wrestles with this contradiction and the consequent need for RastafarI to establish forms of social existence that do not capitulate to the dominant sociocultural discourses.

The chapter also addresses the fact that in Jamaica and, indeed, the world over, gender relations within RastafarI are eligible for debate because the patriarchal model that used to define how brethren and sistren relate to each other no longer pertains; this evolutionary ideological trend is also correlated with sistren raising children on their own and the implications of this independence for the maintenance of a patriarchal model of gender relations in RastafarI. As one brethren in the 40–49 age group who responded to the survey indicated in this regard:

> I initially thought that RastafarI was hyper-patriarchal in an unreformable way. Now with more experience and knowledge, I realise that actually there has always been significant progressive spaces (more than is provided in most western practices) for balance of values and self-determination of all. But my instinct is to say that these spaces can only be expanded and overstood when RastafarI is recognized to have emerged out of a whole constellation of practices and cosmologies many if not most of which do not have Christian roots. The Bible is *not* enough.

This comment questions the tendency of some adherents of RastafarI to confine their frame of religious reference to the Biblical interpretation of his/herstory rather than exploring the gamut of cosmological viewpoints and vistas available to children of the Diaspora, in their own terms of reference.

A gender and development framework therefore undergirds the discussion presented here. As I am using the concept, gender defines the socially constructed values ascribed to the roles that women and men should play in individual pursuits as well as in wider social contexts. Gender also provides a cross-cutting concept for analyzing power relations in both hierarchical and discursive applications. Gender is therefore an appropriate tool of analysis for understanding the contradictions inherent to a wide range of issues, including the political economy, class, race, color, sexuality, sexual preference, social geography, and the sexual division of labor, and as such it facilitates the development of a comprehensive analysis of a wide range of social phenomena.

It is therefore appropriate to use gender to unearth some of the prevailing paradoxes in relations between sistren and brethren in RastafarI, which are, in turn, addressed in the context of larger societal relations.[1] Therefore, though this article is concerned specifically with ideological and social codes that are used to prescribe for and proscribe against specific roles and responsibilities, it will also be necessary to focus on related issues such as performances of the body and the binary oppositions (Derrida associations) drawn between masculinity and domination and femininity and subordination (J. Butler 1999; Derrida 2001). Since these gendered interpretations of power are also related to social capabilities (Nussbaum 2000), it is also important to identify intersections of the political economy with definitions of gender norms in RastafarI as well as efforts advanced by both sistren and brethren to resist these stereotypes.

RastafarI Overview in Historical Context

For at least six decades, RastafarI have been a part of the Jamaican cultural landscape, and the internationalization of the *livity,* or way of life

1. In a discursive revision, RastafarI avoid the terms "men" and "women," seen as part of the contradictory identity apparatus inherited in the colonial tradition and opt instead to personify themselves as "brethren" and "sistren," respectively, which are also used interchangeably for singular and plural. Following Rowe (1998), I use the term RastafarI interchangeably in singular and plural; the capitalization of the I (also popularized by Rowe) at the end of the term denotes the emphasis placed by RastafarI on the indivisibility of the I, an enduring symbol of unity and strength.

through physical movement and technological dispersal, has reshaped the character of this social movement beyond the confines of its Caribbean genesis.[2] The RastafarI livity has popularized a reconstruction of fractured diasporan identities in an African mold. This renewal of self and perspective has been conveyed to the world through artistic media, particularly reggae music, accounting in large measure for Jamaica's current cultural superpower status.

RastafarI brethren and sistren alike refute the hegemony of mainstream identity discourses that regulate self concepts in the images of the colonizing regimes of White and Brown supremacy over Black, which set standards of racial, class, and gender hierarchies that are still influential despite the realization of the trappings of independence by countries like Jamaica.[3] RastafarI constructed the concept of Babylon as a metaphor of opposition to all forms of oppression and exploitation represented by the world economic system and its ideological and material apparatuses. RastafarI are arch resistors of the system of mental slavery referred to by Marcus Garvey and Bob Marley, which prevents oppressed peoples from thinking critically about their condition and consequently devising solutions.

Despite this radical insight and outlook, the ideology of RastafarI borrows heavily from Western liberalism, Christianity, and Judaism, all of which influence the popular belief in the livity that women have less authority than their male counterparts. This belief has been adapted to include the private domain of the household as well as public spaces, such as the congregation, work environments, or the wider society. Traditionally, the male leadership in RastafarI has portrayed the role of women as supportive and subordinate to the male. RastafarI sistren therefore find themselves at the nexus of race, color, gender, and class contradictions that

2. Many people who are not from Jamaica learn of RastafarI through reggae music, a subject considered in more depth in part 6 of this volume.

3. This denotation of race conflicts acknowledges the contradiction inherent in the assumption that such biological markers as skin color are indicators of inherent differences between peoples based on genetic makeup. However, one cannot also deny the reinscription of power and privilege with racial overtones explicit in design and construction of political economy superstructures that govern definitions of "haves" and "have nots."

make everyday life in Jamaica—and indeed, wherever in the world one lives—a knotty affair for those caught in the interstices of this conundrum. Filomina Steady argues in this regard that

> the experiences of the majority of Black women represent multiple forms of oppression rather than simple sexual oppression. Race and class are important variables in her experience and are significantly more important barriers to the acquisition of the basic needs for survival than sexism. (1981, 3)

Given that many sistren who "sight" RastafarI are from working-class backgrounds, it is also important to note that

> in Jamaica, females of working class backgrounds are caught in the triple jeopardy web of race, class and gender subordination . . . The RastafarI woman is in a super-exploited situation since she also has to grapple with gender subordination within her own cultural community, which is in turn, socially marginalised. (Tafari-Ama 1989, 42)

RastafarI and Patriarchy

There are strong parallels between practices of patriarchy in RastafarI ideology and those patriarchal practices that are prevalent in the wider Jamaican society. French and Ford-Smith (1986) critiqued the gender biases in the Moyne Commission Report, which was established after the 1938 labor rebellion. They noted that this paternalistic, colonial institution targeted women as the most accessible category to provide a scapegoat for prevailing social ills and tried to make grassroots women take responsibility (negatively) for the project of sociopolitical transformation.

> "The family" was to be the answer to the unemployment, the lack of wage work and the land hunger of the masses which the Moyne Commission identified as the main socioeconomic problems facing the island . . . If women were poor and families destitute, it was argued, it was because they did not have families with a man at the centre . . . The solution to female poverty, then, was not to pay women "proper" wages for the work they did, but to deprive them of what little wages they had through

> the establishment of "proper" families, and for the poor to establish the bourgeois family, without the bourgeois material base. (French and Ford-Smith 1986, 293–94)

The state agents wanted to maintain the status quo by institutionalizing the bourgeois family form at the grassroots level. Running parallel to this stream, RastafarI have appropriated the model of man as the head and breadwinner of the family. This can also be interpreted as an attempt to reclaim an idealized "African" organization of the household. Therefore, the ideology, language, and practices within the institution of RastafarI can be attributed to

> the African-style patriarchy among the RastafarI male. The man was the head of the house. He was the representative of His Imperial Majesty and therefore the "Kingman." The woman was his helpmate and, in the ideal family, occupied a place beside the Kingman in the same way that the empress remained beside His Majesty—silent and supportive in public but active, as we understood it, behind the scenes. This was not always the case in the movement. In some households . . . where the children were males, the women appeared to occupy a place below the children. However, this was not the rule. (Rowe 1998, 83)

This emphasis on male dominance at the household level has been an attempt to reinstate the authority that African men lost during enslavement. Nowadays, the classist and sexist construction of sex and gender role divisions in the household (hooks 1981) reinscribe the subordination of women across the board in the society and, therefore, within the livity of RastafarI. However, womanist resistance by sistren within the livity has also influenced significant changes in the patriarchal status quo.[4]

> Without a doubt, RastafarI is a patriarchal movement. However, as with all social movements, RastafarI have, over the years, experienced dynamic

4. Women of color coined this term to distinguish themselves from White women of privilege who they perceived had appropriated the term feminism as a means of speaking on behalf of and for all women and a strategy of maintaining racist and classist hierarchies in the women's movement. A womanist therefore uses difference as a site of struggle and resistance.

> shifts in gender power relations as a result of females revisiting their own self-definitions, juxtaposed against designations ascribed by males who created the movement. (Tafari-Ama 1998, 89)

RastafarI sistren have been primarily responsible for the persistence of the livity in the so-called private sphere, which also influences the public maintenance of RastafarI as a viable social entity. Yet, it is also important to acknowledge that man and woman are not always operating oppositionally. On the contrary, some brethren recognize the value of woman's liberation, not only as an inalienable human right but also in the interest of their own liberation, that of the family, the community, the nation-state, the world. In fact, the persistence of positive relations between self-conscious brethren and sistren has proved that gender relations provide a viable route for the manifestation of god and goddess indicators.

One cannot deny that (r)evolutions are taking place within the cultural psyche of RastafarI sistren and brethren—individually and as a collective. Intergenerational and international transitions and influences complicate this reality, resulting in a shift in paradigms and a change in the discourse of the ideology. In addition, no one house or individual speaks for all RastafarI. Gender relations surely provide an effective lens through which to view the contradictions not only of RastafarI livity but of life itself.

Spanning a Quarter Century

A Review of Gender Relations in RastafarI

In 1985, I facilitated the implementation of a research project in Jamaica that involved eighty-six participants and aimed at deconstructing notions of power espoused by RastafarI around issues of ideology, image, roles, and sexuality.[5] This island-wide exploratory exercise involved elders, youth,

5. The impetus to conduct this research emerged during my tenure on a bilateral UNESCO project between Jamaica and Belize, which sought to analyze what women define as obstacles to their cultural development. The RastafarI sistren who took part in this project identified their biggest challenge as the lack of space to discuss with the brethren the

male, and female participants from all houses of RastafarI as well as RastafarI not affiliated to a house and resulted in the changing of taken-for-granted relations of power within the livity. This study positioned the vexed issues relating to gender relations in RastafarI within the context of the class, race, and gender struggles of resistance waged in Jamaica over its turbulent colonial and postcolonial history; it also identified RastafarI in general as among the main agents of change within this panorama.

After the completion of that research, which was only published in thesis form (Tafari-Ama 1989),[6] it is clear that this inquiry is as relevant now as it was then, perhaps even more so. The power relations underpinning the concepts researched are as problematic as ever in the wider Jamaican society from which RastafarI derives as well as within the livity itself. This chapter therefore refers to some of the findings of this research with the aim of provoking critical reflection and discussion of these obstacles to the organic advancement of the livity. Additional data were also gathered recently through an online survey, mentioned in more detail in the methodology section.

Twenty-five years ago, it was unusual to implement a project to critique gender relations in RastafarI. I was twenty-five years old at the time and steeped in the womanist discourse that the personal is political. I was convinced that as Africans in the Diaspora, we should struggle to realize Africa for the Africans, at home and abroad. I straddled academic and activist worlds and definitionally was far removed from the "traditional" image of a RastafarI woman. Embracing modernity I indulged in artistic manicures, wore pants, and reserved the option to cover my locks or wear them loose. Does that make me less RastafarI than my sistren who faithfully cover their locks (in public at any rate), eschew pants as a public

---

things they found problematic in the livity, which when expressed were categorized into these four areas.

6. Many people who have trod this route know that one of the most difficult things to do is to translate one's thesis into a publishable book or article. Although it has taken this long for me to revisit this work, I am grateful that this publication stirred me into action on this long outstanding project.

garment, and take being natural to its logical conclusion? Should I prepare meals when I am menstruating? If I am a single empress with no law of the brethren to adhere to (by choice), do I have advantage over my sistren who daily negotiate such a power arrangement, or am I woefully lacking in natural yin-yang balance?

These kinds of questions about embodied representations that were considered in the past project need revisiting because we have never defined a "book of rules" for RastafarI but, rather, have adopted and adapted writs and rites from the sources mentioned earlier (Western Liberalism, Christianity, and Judaism), while constantly trying to reinscribe notions of African identity into our existential package. We have therefore never really arrived at consensus about images of collective representation that apply to all our aspirations for ourselves and our progeny. Although some know a smattering of what His Majesty (or Empress Menen for that matter) might consider appropriate for social-self definition, to a great extent we have not internalized the specifics of such teachings or made them guiding lights for epistemological development. Sanctions and allowances about body image have mostly come from our interpretations of the Bible. It is the Bible that admonishes the woman to cover her head while praying or prophesying as an indicator that as woman, she is subordinate to her head (whether a kingman is actually in the picture or not). These embodied rules are based on the Pauline Doctrine, which has seeped into the ideology of the sacred and profane in the livity of RastafarI.[7]

So here we are, catapulted into the technologically advanced twenty-first century, and I personally feel as if I am in somewhat of a time warp.[8] Is the Morgan Heritage sentiment that "you don't have to be dread to be Rasta" correct, or is the more Orthodox stance that "by their fruits you shall know them" the correct perspective? Or should one sidestep the

7. Religious doctrine that is based on the writings of St. Paul in the Bible is referred to in religious circles as Pauline Doctrine.

8. It is amazing to me that twenty-five years ago, I sent telegrams to brethren and sistren across Jamaica to alert them about the workshop details, whereas while conducting the online survey, I was in touch with brethren and sistren not only in Jamaica but as far afield as Mexico, New Zealand, South Africa, Anguilla, Great Britain, and the United States.

confusion of appropriation of embodied space by dogma? Can RastafarI once again—as it did in the 1970s when it influenced raging gunmen to sign a peace treaty—exert the influence that will help to influence sociopolitical transformation in Jamaica?

These are the kinds of questions underpinning this renewal of the gender analysis of the philosophy and praxis in the livity, from a position of critical commitment. Maureen Rowe, affectionately known as Sista P, was a pioneer of this cause of interrogating gender relations in RastafarI (see Rowe 1980, 1989; see also chapter 9). She participated in the gender relations in RastafarI project but, sadly, is unable to respond to the reader's comments since she has joined our ancestors. This consideration makes the catalyzing of more critical discussion on the gender politics of the RastafarI livity even more urgent.

It is ironic for me, too, that Junior Manning, the RastafarI youth leader in the Nyahbinghi house who gave wholehearted support to the project of interrogating the patriarchal tendencies in the livity, has made his transition and joined the ancestors. As the transitioning generation we need to refresh our memories about some of the observations made a quarter of a century ago and buffer these analyses with emerging discourses about gender relations in RastafarI.[9] At the time of the initial project in 1985, Junior Manning led the charge to encourage brethren to break ranks with then accepted traditions and listen to the sistren's insistent voicing of their discomfort with obstacles hindering gender equality in the livity, including ideology, roles, image, and sexuality. It was Junior Manning who objected to some elder brethren objecting to the ensuing island-wide conversations, which encouraged irreversible changes to the ways females were perceived and relationships constructed. The legitimacy of his endorsement encouraged brethren who wanted to maintain dogmatic stances on the gender equity question to engage in productive revisions with brethren who

9. I am currently pursuing research on the taboo subject of death among the other neglected rituals in the livity, which results in moral confusion as to which institution should perform marriages, burials, and so on. It is a contradiction in terms that Christian churches are usually brought in when RastafarI are to be buried, for example.

maintained more openness to the notion that females should not be suppressed simply because of perceptions about masculinity and femininity and attendant power positionalities of women and men, in the society generally and in the RastafarI livity in particular.

Impact of the World Recession

As the economic times have become more challenging and relationships have changed, resulting in a trend toward single-parent households superseding the nuclear household or extended family networks, previously held beliefs and practices about gender relations in RastafarI have also adjusted. Concurrent with increased independence of RastafarI females, there has been a decline of patriarchal opportunities; consequently, increasing efforts have been made on the part of some brethren to reinstate the old order. However, as happened a quarter of a century ago, there is a current trend among brethren, especially the youth, to question old adages that served the patriarchal order well but repressed feminine power. Nowadays, more lip service is also being paid by several brethren (joining sistren) to the need to encourage the Empress Menen principle, previously ignored in the concentration of His Imperial Majesty I only. In other words, some brethren acknowledge the validity of woman power rather than previous practices of silencing, which have, traditionally, been a dominant trend within the livity.

Undoubtedly, the womanist critique within RastafarI has also been influenced by the Caribbean women's movement generally and by efforts to encourage empowerment of women and girls in Jamaica specifically. However, this interrogation has its own legitimacy since a revolutionary movement (which the livity is, culturally at any rate) deserves internal interrogation especially in terms of its organization and deployment of gender power. It would be a tragedy if we as elders all made our transition without arriving at some form of resolution.[10] Of course this constitutes merely a

10. This is another area which needs elaboration: we have not defined appropriate rituals of birth, death, marriage, divorce, communal living, and care for the elderly, sick, and destitute in order to enable us to be faithful to the livity at these significant moments.

minor component of the larger discussions that have, obviously, been taking place in different quarters; I am honored to be the griot for this episode of ongoing critical reflection.

Research Methodology

This paper represents a dialogue between the past and the present. Twenty-five years ago, I conducted research on gender relations in RastafarI, and although some of the findings were published (Tafari-Ama 1998), most of the data remained hidden in my unpublished master's thesis (Tafari-Ama 1989), which looked at RastafarI as a component of a resistance continuum in Jamaica and the evolving discourse on gender relations in RastafarI as an indicator of resistance from within. The issues that were raised in that investigation were never resolved, mainly because there was no follow-up to the island-wide outpourings that characterized that initiative.

In view of the internationalization of RastafarI over the period since that research was conducted and the technological leaps that have also changed the landscape of communication, updating the data on gender relations in RastafarI also required a change of mobilization methodology. Instead of mobilizing participants into workshops, which was the approach used to invite brethren and sistren to the discussion table back in the day, I administered an online survey in January 2011 to gauge the current temperature of gender relations in the livity, so to speak.

Although the issues addressed in past and present research episodes are not perfectly aligned, emerging themes nevertheless offer some scope for comparative analysis. Revisiting this problematic is also timely; without the input of critical reflection and discussion the obdurate obstacles to the organic advancement of the livity will remain intact.

To test whether these impressions are supported by experiential evidence, I administered an online survey to participants who attended the 2010 International RastafarI Studies Conference held at the University of the West Indies, Mona, as well as to a cohort of purposively selected participants from my own mailing list. Although this population is skewed toward the socially privileged, who have access to the Internet and who constitute an intelligentsia rather than being representative of the diverse socioeconomic classes occupied by RastafarI, the results are nevertheless significant for the international perspectives offered as well as for the sentiments expressed about social, economic, and political trends within the livity and the gender relationship adjustments denoted by these shifts.

Of the sample of 122 persons, 23 (18.8 percent) responded; 18 indicated their geographical location. Participants indicated that they were introduced to RastafarI through various media, mostly through associating with ones who had sighted the livity previously, acknowledging the inborn concept and a pathway to Black Power through Afrocentric consciousness.

Strengths of RastafarI

Participants were in agreement that despite challenges RastafarI have encountered as a result of their separation from Babylon, the livity embodies significant strengths, including political consciousness, which manifests, as far as the research participants expressed it, as race pride, spirituality, and organized action. The first of these, race pride, was represented by one participant as RastafarI's embodiment of "a great step forward from mental slavery" in the Jamaican context as well as internationally. By defining all forms of domination and oppression as Babylon and providing knowledge about Africa for thirsty diasporans, RastafarI have infused a perspective on identity, a principal indicator of transformational politics. Second, participants indicated that RastafarI has been responsible for elaborating on the teachings of His Imperial Majesty Emperor Haile Selassie I and operationalizing a discourse on peace and love, which has revolutionary potential in the face of the pervasive fear that currently characterizes culture reproduced by Africans and their progeny in the Diaspora. Third, RastafarI, inspired by Marcus Garvey's admonition to "get organized, and you will compel the world to respect you" have formed various mansions to regulate worship and social affairs (Garvey 1986). Unfortunately, however, these institutions have served to divide RastafarI adherents along institutional lines. Most useful has been RastafarI's elaboration of the oppressive role played by the embeddedness of European ideology in prevailing institutions in postcolonial societies like Jamaica.

RastafarI have also been forerunners in the promotion of health consciousness as a form of resistance against mainstream unconsciousness in Babylon. By advocating the indivisibility of healthy lifestyles and harmony with the universe, RastafarI demonstrated the universal good to be realized through the fusion of the material and the spiritual. In addition, through the pursuit of alternative forms of education to curricula that is acknowledged to be inimical to the interest of African liberation, RastafarI have been responsible for the development of a psychosocial aesthetic, which has also positively contributed to the process of raising consciousness about the need for alternative paradigms of identity construction to those still reproduced through the institutional framework of the state and its apparatuses.

The fact that RastafarI share these perspectives, gender notwithstanding, is an indicator of the basis for a politicospiritual and psychosocial revolution to take place in the livity. However, the fact that RastafarI have not been able to galvanize the political energy that resulted in the cessation of hostilities among warring factions in Western Kingston in 1978 (Tafari-Ama 2006) also suggests that efforts devoted to salvaging troubled gender relations may have siphoned off vital energy from the livity. Needless to say, this is an unproductive use of vital resources and strengthens the impetus to use these critical reflections as an opportunity to rationalize all relationships, within and without the livity, and ensure that outcomes are anticipated and positive.

On Gender Relations in RastafarI

As with all other spheres of life, gender—and the identities socially constructed around this concept—determines the way one experiences RastafarI, as the majority of the 23 respondents to the online survey on this issue indicated. Looking through the lens of gender has made sistren question patriarchal precedents, and brethren also acknowledged that shifts need to be made from domination to equality in respect to gender relations in RastafarI. One sistren observed candidly that "being female has made [her] aware of the patriarchal system that is Rasta," and another admitted that she adjusts her behavior depending on the level of liberation of those with whom she interacts. This process of selection was echoed by a sistren who does not feel it is productive to confront patriarchy. Instead, she indicated that by choice she is

> closer with brethren who define themselves more as "new age Rastas" in terms of how they think about the relationships between men and women and the roles each play, both with each other and in the greater world.

The critical reflection included an acknowledgment by a brethren who noted that because of the pioneering publication of a critique of the role of the woman in RastafarI by Maureen (Sista P) (Rowe 2008; see chapter 9) more and more sistren had been inspired to voice their own concerns about gender inequities in the livity. Another brethren in the 30–39 age set concurred and echoed the critical turn of the younger brethren (like Junior Manning did twenty-five years ago) when he explained:

> Sistren have been downpressed and their voices not respected. I know a lot of brethren that have treated sistren awful to the extent they leave the livity due to his misrepresentation.

While the reproduction of patriarchal perspectives in the ideology and practice of gender relations in the RastafarI livity has totally escaped the attention of some brethren, others have been consistent in expressing concern for the plight of sistren as a whole. This consciousness about sexism among some brethren, which was evident twenty-five years ago, was endorsed in the online survey by another brethren in the 40–49 age group who said in this regard:

> As a *man* I am impelled to redress the imbalances and short-sighted practices within the "Order" as they relate to women and to fullcourage[11] the

11. The doublespeak evident in expressions such as this denotes RastafarI critique on the ways in which language reinforces negative connotations. The phonetic implication of "en(d)courage" is here revised and represented as "fullcourage."

> inclusion of our sisters, mothers and daughters in the glorification of Our Majesty, Emperor Haile Selassie I, Jah Ras Tafari.

Inevitably, ideological and religious references are used to rationalize sistren's subordination, in terms of their public participation in the livity as well as in the private spaces of embodiment and sexual relations. Since many of the attitudes evident in the past research project have persisted to this day, it is important to revisit this study, since the body is the slate onto which everyday scripts of domination and resistance are inscribed (Tafari-Ama 2006).

RastafarI Attitudes Toward Sexuality

Results from a Previous Study

In summarizing the data that emerged from the participatory action research on gender relations in RastafarI for one component of my master's thesis, I combined responses from groups of Sistren; the quotations used here should therefore be read as the choruses from the litany of differentiated responses produced in the extended sessions.[12]

A quarter century ago, sistren defining matriculation criteria for intimate gender relations responded:

> A sexual relationship involves both procreation and recreation. Both partners should discuss these areas and their differences because their enjoyment of sex for its own sake should not be affected by the fact that they also bear children. Before embarking on a sexual relationship one should be sure that it can last because of the amount of energy that it takes to work to both partners' satisfaction. Many sistren struggle with their lack of autonomy in choosing the terms of the sexual relationship. Because many brethren don't like to use birth control many sistren bear too many

12. The second component of that paper was using the case study of resistance within the livity to dominant patriarchal ideas and practices as a model for analyzing the continuum of resistance in Jamaica, which has, for obvious reasons, featured the African majority as protagonists.

> children at a fast rate and their bodies deteriorate and this is very bad when the brethren are not around to provide the necessary support. Sometimes, even the use of the rhythm method, which is a natural form of birth control, is a problem because the man usually demands sex when the sistren should abstain. A woman should not have sex while breastfeeding so that she can rest and have a safe period from getting pregnant. But some brethren don't see that. (Tafari-Ama 1989, 104–5)

Referring to the issue of birth control, there was general agreement among the sistren:

> [We are against] most of the available methods but the rhythm method is the best. If a woman's life is in danger if she is to have a youth it is better to tie off her tubes. Sometimes the condom is also good. Birth control methods should not be decided on alone but a sistren should discuss it with her Kingman. But since it is the woman's body that has to carry the youth she should have a strong say if not the final word because she is the one who also has to take care of the youths when they are growing up. (ibid., 105)

On the question of how much sex should be indulged in for the pleasure of it and the extent to which it should be for reproduction there were various responses:

> Once a woman has sex without applying any protection against pregnancy, she may get pregnant and end up with a lot of babies. Because of this, it is sometimes better not to have sex at all. Since sex involves so much pleasure, it is better for the woman to make sure that the man uses a condom if she doesn't want to become pregnant. Sistren should realise that they have a choice and not just have sex to fulfill their brethren's desire to father children. When the relationship has been good for many years a woman can afford to have sex without protection because by then she will lose the fear that the man will not support the child, if the relationship is not steady before the woman becomes pregnant there is a big chance that it won't last. (ibid., 105)

A direct connection was also drawn between brethren's attempts to control women's sexuality and restrictions on how a woman's hair (locks) were to be treated. The livity stipulates that in the tradition of the Pauline Doctrine, a woman should have her head covered when praying or prophesying; by extrapolation, this includes public appearances. Her "beauty" should only be seen in private by her kingman. This can be read as a restriction at not only an ideological level but one that has implications of control of women's sexuality as well. However, this perspective, which is maintained by those seen as more traditional (that is, old fashioned), was contradicted by those with a more contemporary standpoint. According to the youth, for example:

> The natural beauty of locks should shine forth and not be covered at all times especially in public as the doctrine demands. Like all growing things, locks need air and light. Only when a woman is praying should her locks have to be covered. Brethren say that a woman should keep her hair covered to maintain her spirituality but he can have a choice to have his locks covered or not. (ibid., 105)

In response to this radical discourse, some elders maintained:

> Sistren should cover their locks at all times because the Rasta woman will not be able to present herself as being different from the Babylonian woman if she has her locks uncovered in the presence of heathens. The practice of uncovering the locks is being used to take the seriousness out of one of the highest principles cherished by RastafarI. (ibid. 105)

The reinscription of the practice of female head covering into the ideology of RastafarI may be an attempt, on one hand, to retain a practice seen as "African" in the face of the erosion of many such identity markers during the centuries of enslavement. The head covering is associated with spiritual functions, and it is a fashion statement as well, since a headpiece is taken for granted as part of typically elaborate African dress.[13] On the other hand, the Bible generally, and St. Paul's teachings in particular, were cited

13. This generalization may be excused since the practice is observed in different countries on the Continent and reproduced in diasporan contexts.

as responsible for that "cherished" principle that RastafarI hold most dear, in the parlance of the elder quoted earlier. This influential instrument of socialization was further accused of reinforcing the taboos that surround women's sexuality. As some of the sistren concluded:

> Although INI respect the teachings of the Bible, it is used extensively to impose inferiority complexes on many sistren. Sections of the Bible are quoted especially by males to show that women are like Eve and evil and responsible for the corruption of mankind. They use the teachings of St. Paul and some of the Old Testament to show that woman is unclean during her period. This was how the Bible was used by translators and slave masters. His Majesty said the Bible is the rallying point for all humanity so it should not be used to deliberately mislead but should be used as a historical document for spiritual reinforcement. It is important to be aware of the conflict of some sections. For instance, in one passage of the Bible it says that husbands should love their wives and wives should be obedient to their husbands. This means for the wife to be obedient she has to be inferior. (ibid., 106)

From these responses, it was clear that there was a general desire on the part of the sistren to be in control of their sexuality in general and reproductive capacities in particular. Some sistren pointed out that sex can result in short-term pleasure, but if it results in unwanted pregnancy, it may have dire implications for both partners. And while some sistren have internalized the dominant patriarchal tenets, others have opted for celibacy rather than succumb to that form of male domination. Of course, this reticence could also be interpreted as an avoidance of confrontation of sexual control mechanisms that they may experience in their relationships. Furthermore, there was some tension between elder and younger sistren around the issue of hair covering, a proxy for sexuality. The former concurred with continuously covering the locks, whereas the latter protested that releasing locks to the public view was also a political statement. The attempt by the former to impose their opinions on the latter also indicates the power of age in this discourse.

As far as some of the brethren were concerned, the subjects of sex and sexuality should not be discussed in an open forum. After this was debated for some time they conceded to proceed.

The first debate concerned whether RastafarI believe in casual sex, and a collectively negative (if idealistic) response was applied to this inquiry. The brethren elaborated:

> RastafarI should not support casual sex in any way. The terms of a sexual relationship should be based on honesty and fidelity. Although there is much temptation to stray from this ideal, to do so is harmful and brings negative results and should therefore be avoided. An African woman is the ideal partner to have a relationship with. But a relationship should not be based on sex but it is best if the woman is flexible and agile in bed. Since the sexual relationship should be with a long term partner it is also best if the woman is able to cook, be faithful, conservative, truthful and *with a consenting and submissive attitude.* (ibid., 106; emphasis added)

This response reinforced the hierarchical perspective that is ingrained in some brethren's responses to sistren, particularly around issues of sexuality. Following up the discussion with response to birth control, some brethren were emphatic in their negative responses to this option, whereas others were more compliant. Those taking the latter position suggested:

> Natural methods of self control like rhythm and withdrawal should be used to limit the number of pregnancies. Since sex for pleasure can easily lead to pregnancy a great deal of restraint on the part of the man is necessary and he should not be demanding during the woman's cycle when it is necessary for her to abstain. (ibid., 107)

Those supporting this view elaborated that "when a man uses a condom, he is throwing away his seed" and that "sex should be free from all restrictions." By implication, the many seed and their human potential should have equal opportunity for life; since the dominant voice in the sex act in many cases is that of the male, the ontological implications for sistren's control of their sexuality are ominous. When this issue was again raised in the final workshop, some sistren countered that the sentiment of the sacredness of all seed is spurious, since menstruation is not equally regarded as a discarding of a child.

On the questions of whether sex should be indulged in for the pleasure of it and whether this objective should be separated from the reproductive function, brethren replied:

> Sex is an extremely pleasurable activity and this is the main reason for indulging in it. It is also for reproduction but reproduction should also be pleasurable. RastafarI should not deal with sex merely for pleasure but should incorporate it into their divine communication and cause a union which should produce children. A man should be aware of a woman's cycle to know when to abstain from having sex with her[14] in cases where children are not immediately desired. Couples should try to avoid conflicts that are bound to arise if the man wants to have sex all the time to make the woman pregnant—while she wants to abstain from sex. His pleasure would be at the expense of her pain. (ibid., 108)

The power drama being alluded to here is a familiar one; many otherwise beautiful RastafarI relationships may end up on (or off?) the rocks due to unresolved discontent around just how embodied transactions should be negotiated and who should have the "final" say in issues about having sex. When children are included in the relationship, it becomes even more difficult to untangle the intertwining strands of masculinity and femininity and their apparatuses of gender, sex, sexuality, culture, and power; in a word, identity tropes of (dis)content.

Turning to the topic of how locks should be treated brethren responded:

> The RastafarI man covers his locks primarily for health reasons, to maintain cleanliness. It should therefore not be compulsory for the man's head to be uncovered when praying, as the Bible says, but it is better to be uncovered in the congregation and when spiritual matters are being discussed. It should be a matter of free personal choice. The true answer lies in the Bible but the Bible should be challenged. Not all interpretations of the Bible should be accepted. (ibid.)

14. See Tafari-Ama 1998, 98–106, for elaboration on gendered issues of menstruation.

Referring specifically to the extent to which the Bible should be used by brethren to determine the course of their relationships with RastafarI sistren, the brethren agreed that the Bible is used extensively to regulate these relationships; they suggested that the Bible is authoritative because it says that Jah is the head of man and man is the head of woman. However, it was also suggested that "being the head does not mean that the man should exercise spiritual dominion over sistren but he should act as a spiritual channel."

By attaching taboos to natural processes like menstruation, some brethren have reinforced ideological systems of controlling sistren's sexuality. They also control women's reproduction by stipulating what kind of birth control methods if any, may be "allowed." However, some brethren objected to this position, supporting female autonomy within the livity. Many brethren object to methods of family planning as they see them as part of the overarching plot to "kill out black people." However, the fact that some brethren and sistren support the need for sistren to have more control over their sexuality suggest that this is a potential site of solidarity for realizing transformation of hierarchical gender relations in RastafarI. This emerging theme of gender solidarity acknowledges the strength of unity, or inity in RastafarI parlance, and the modus operandi for the sustainable development of the livity. As one brethren reiterated, "Unless the brethren acknowledge the power and authority of the livity, the RastafarI movement will always be stagnant." Therefore, at both ideological and practical levels, a revisionist approach to the livity of RastafarI suggests that rejection of traditional role stereotypes is essential because they do not promote gender equality or the harmonious advancement of the livity as a whole.

Gender (In)Equality

Summarized below are the responses by sistren in the earlier research to two questions: Do RastafarI women feel inferior to kingmen? To what extent does gender equality exist in the livity?

- Generally speaking, the Rastaman is superior to the woman, because in the livity the woman is often denied equal opportunities to develop as the man does due largely to domestic responsibilities.

- The Rastawomen who live in the hills (rural areas) usually feel inferior to their men, whom they regard as almost if not equal to Jah. The behavior of these brethren usually does not reflect the superiority they claim to have, though. Sistren who live in less rural areas find it easier to be independent because they get more support from their families.
- Brethren impose inferiority complexes on sistren to hide their own weaknesses and when Jah becomes the woman's first love.
- Much of the doctrine of RastafarI is based on negative interpretations of Bible teachings. The language and content of these teachings encourage images of the woman as being responsible for lust and corruption, which contributes to sistren's inferiority complexes. These doctrines started with the elder brethren and have been accepted ever since.
- The strength of character and discipline necessary to run a home are proof of the woman's ability to manage and be creative, but she could be more powerful if these abilities were utilized in other areas than that of a domestic. A man's only area of real superiority over a woman is physical strength.
- Sometimes the man feels superior if he does not take part in domestic work. (Tafari-Ama 1989, 89)

These propositions epitomize the gender power tension that is inherent to relations between women and men, not only in RastafarI but worldwide. Patriarchy manifests through hegemonic discourses about how women and men should relate, which have been reproduced through ideology and practices propagated by RastafarI. By reinscribing these Babylonian perspectives into the livity, brethren exacerbate the oppressions that all RastafarI face in the wider society, because family relations suffer from the failure to even recognize this contradiction. The resulting communication stresses provide indicators of the need to deconstruct this power mechanism. As Leary (2005) argues, Africans in the Diaspora are parodying Western notions of gender relations that are based on the racist and sexist myth of man as the breadwinner (a central tenet of capitalism) and, by extension, head of the household. When this presumption fails to materialize, the authority that that positionality should have provided the man is contrived by assuming psychological and emotional control, which may result in abuse and its discontents. Leary argues further that the intergenerational defects and distortion of cultural identity that endure among Africans are attributed to a failure to problematize the damaging effects of racism and a failure to see both its structural reinforcement and the effect that individual internalization has had on self-perceptions.

> Post Traumatic Slave Syndrome (P.T.S.S.) is a condition that exists as a consequence of multigenerational oppression of Africans and their descendants resulting from centuries of chattel slavery. [This] form of slavery which was predicated on the belief that African Americans were inherently/genetically inferior to whites . . . was then followed by institutionalized racism which continues to perpetuate injury.[15]

The culturally normalized so-called beauty practices of hair straightening and skin bleaching are indicators of this intergenerational syndrome of identity trauma (Tafari-Ama 2006). The production of paternalism in RastafarI also fits into this scenario of how hegemony (Gramsci 1957) works: the dominated perform the dominant discourse as if it were their own. This pattern of uncritical acceptance of even discourses that are damaging to personal happiness and social harmony is a manifestation of internalized racism. You can tell that the post-traumatic slave syndrome (PTSS) so eloquently mapped by Leary is present because, as is readily observed in African communities (on the Continent and in the Diaspora), "People begin to doubt themselves, their experiences, and their worth in society because they have been so invalidated their whole lives, in so many ways."[16] RastafarI communities, like other communities, need to acknowledge this

15. See http://www.Joydegruy.com/ptss/index.html. See also Leary 2005 for the thorough discussion on the entrenched dysfunctions that comprise routine reality for those whose ancestors endured enslavement. Therefore, whether one identifies with this past or not, or politicizes it or not, this past is a haunting feature of the psychosocial deficits that contribute to the chronic underdevelopment at individual and collective levels of the dispersed and dispossessed progeny of the enslaved.

16. From an interview published March 10, 2006. Available at http://www.inthesetimes.com/article/2523.

contradiction and develop mechanisms for healing this breach rather than perpetuating it through dogmatic interpretations of gender roles, responsibilities, and relations.

As with the findings emerging from the online survey, the brethren responding twenty-five years ago were as vocal as the sistren on this subject. Even more remarkable were the debates that ensued between elder and younger brethren about how sistren should be regarded. These ideological challenges provided an important space for articulating contradictions that are inherent to the livity of RastafarI and that have become more pronounced over the years, resulting in disaffection among the youth with some of the traditions set by the elders. However, the inevitable outcome of the patriarchal tenets in the livity of RastafarI has been

> the cultural and self-awareness of the Rasta woman [which] has forced many brethren to adjust their attitudes towards relating to her. Other brethren need to follow this trend. But there are established principles and guidelines for behaviour in RastafarI, which should not change. What needs to change is the economic situation. Brethren have to earn more to maintain their responsibility as head of the household. (Tafari-Ama 1989)

This response contains a number of contradictions. Though acknowledging the consciousness of sistren and their resistance to domination and adjusting their responses accordingly regarding females in the livity, (some) brethren insist on reinforcing the very tenets regarded as problematic. At the same time, there is a shift in emphasis from the site of gender relations to the economic, which, although undoubtedly important, might also represent a rationalization about what actually constitutes the primary area of tension. The perceived need to improve the economic situation is, paradoxically, a strategy to reinforce male domination (that is, as the head of the household). This is evidently overcompensation for male powerlessness and yet another manifestation of PTSS.

Emerging trends from responses in the online survey to the query "How do you see gender relations in RastafarI today?" revealed a general impetus to transform unequal gender relations. As noted by one female participant, one has to place gender relations in RastafarI in the context of social relations in the wider society. As she elaborated, "Gender relations in RastafarI are no different from that of any other group in the society; we come together as man and wife, we have children, some of us get divorced, some just walk away. Many of the men have multiple women and thus children." This pragmatic perspective suggests that we should not treat problems evident in relations between brethren and sistren as exceptional but strive for the course of gendered cultural evolution. Sharing this general view, another sistren suggested that attempts to generalize about gender relations in RastafarI are futile because individuals and couples differ. However, she fails to acknowledge that such an atomized approach does not provide formulas for treating dysfunctional unions. She suggested that "the respect given to [her] as a woman by male RastafarI practitioners should be commended" and that male RastafarI practitioners are more respectful of women than the "other" males in the society. Respect here needs some interrogation; if unpacking this concept reveals tendencies to treat women as cultural and sexual objects, then more efforts need to be made to reconcile this dissonance and promote substantive practices of gender equity as a human rights obligation.

Another respondent acknowledged the revisionist approach adopted by brethren and sistren alike, which is inclusive of Empress Menen and therefore blunts the patriarchal thrust of dominant RastafarI discourse. As a result of such signs of evolution, she does "not retreat from Rasta for its patriarchal tendencies" but instead forms her own livity where the gaps exist. On the other hand, another sistren observed that "gender relations in general within those who call themselves RastafarI are very confused and undefined." Finally, another sistren concluded that "some elders (and particular houses) maintain a more antiquated vision of women's complementarity, and younger men (and women) feel less threatened about transforming their ideas about women's roles."

These contrasting views all concur with the general thesis of this chapter, which is that RastafarI could benefit from sophisticated strategies of communication and analysis of the problems of gender inequalities in the livity, resulting in the potential for improved harmony between genders and the ultimate improvement of the livity as a whole.

Brethren responding to the survey questions also offered a sharp critique of patriarchal precedents that have characterized RastafarI to date.

As one participant observed in this regard, "We need to change gender relations, [since] . . . there is a distance between males and females" as far as the deployment of power in the livity is concerned. This view, influenced by changing economic roles, was reflected in another brethren's observation that changes in the livity are inevitable "with women becoming more independent and less willing to be led by a man." In the same vein, another masculine opinion expressed was that changes in relationships between sistren and brethren have been significant but still have room for improvement to "update or advance the overstanding of the 21st century role changes." He proposed further that "the female must get her due respect as the centre of the family, community and nation especially with the role change in the providership function [since] the woman today finds a job or means of earning a livelihood," which has released her from dependence on men.

On the other hand, eight brethren suggested that they feel things have improved significantly with "Empress Menen more acknowledged [and] the Sisters of the RYIC (RastafarI Youth Initiative Council) playing a leading role" in the institutional development process. This progress is unmistakable but contradicted by lingering patriarchal tendencies. As a participant from New Zealand noted, "The self-determining divinity and politics of sistren [seem] to be more accepted now, if still grudgingly in some quarters. [However], amongst Maori Rasta I have not come across the same force of patriarchy as I have amongst the ones living in the West. I believe that this is due to a living tradition in indigenous culture, that even if patriarchal in many ways, nevertheless has always provided for women a public purpose/responsibility for particular culture or social practices." When all is said and done, despite undoubted advances, such shifts need to be formally articulated through ideology and praxis in order for the ideal of gender equity, a fundamental human right, to be acknowledged as an inevitable feature of the sustainable development of RastafarI as a whole.

Twelve of the 20 persons (60 percent) who responded on this item were male, and 8 (40 percent) were female. Perspectives offered on current views of gender relations are therefore skewed in favor of this gender distribution. In several of the responses, the brethren acknowledged that there have been improvements in gender relations, attributed to increasing liberation of women from male (socioeconomic) control. Although their views coincided with what some females had to say, this impression might also differ from reality. In addition, the theme of RastafarI brethren being more respectful than "other" men presumably results from their elevation of women to statuses of empress, queen, and princess, which some in the livity have argued, is more de facto than de jure acknowledgment of gender equity with a kingman. This area deserves further research to probe the tenor of cynicism and acceptance of the status quo evident in responses from females. Until the convergence among racism, classism, and sexism (hooks 1989) is acknowledged and treated, resulting in systematic healing of engendered wounds, then the gender power conundrum and the promise of revolution that RastafarI embody will not be realized.

Participants were also asked who provides for the household, another indicator of gender power. Improvements in sistren's socioeconomic status may be having an impact on the shift in gender relations in RastafarI. The responses suggest that brethren and sistren are equally responsible for the division of responsibility for the household. This concurs with the impression indicated in the research project twenty-five years ago that unlike their counterparts in the wider society, RastafarI brethren are active participants in domestic labor as well as being regular contributors to the maintenance of the household. However, I would argue that the active involvement in the domestic space is informed not by an effort to move toward gender equity, but rather as a compensatory mechanism to maintain male dominance in the absence of the man being the breadwinner in the household. In fact, the data from twenty-five years ago reveal that in respect to the role they should play in the household, brethren were already uncomfortable with emerging trends of shifting gender roles. Responses from that encounter on this issue included:

- The man is the head of the household. He should accept and not shirk this responsibility. If this basic requirement were met it would naturally follow that all patterns of behavior would be above board.
- The man should demonstrate to the woman those qualities he expects of her. In other words, he should show love and cooperation; be courteous, humble, and tolerant; follow the teachings of Haile Selassie I; demonstrate integrity, discipline, and righteousness; be gentle yet possessing and utilizing leadership qualities.

- If the man performs his *natural leadership role,* there would be less incidence of family dislocation. (Tafari-Ama, 1989, 92; emphasis added)

Taking it for granted that he is the head of the household demonstrates the ways in which RastafarI brethren internalize a viewpoint that not only derives from the Bible but also informs bourgeois notions of Western liberalism (based on capitalism) that man is head of a nuclear family and that "his" woman and children should be dependent on his "living wage." The housewifization ideology developed out of this assumption and is, to a great extent, responsible for the inequalities that exist not only within the household but also in the area of waged work (Mies 1986).

The attempt by some RastafarI brethren to install a power hierarchy within the space of gender relations is an attempt to compensate for the loss of power they experience at the hands of Babylon. Then again, sistren also experience socioeconomic exclusions, hence their multiple experiences of domination. As the research findings noted, within RastafarI, the control that is exercised is manifested particularly in the area of ideology and sexuality, which are related to several social practices such as food preparation, mode of dress, self-presentation, perception of the genders, and domestic roles. The avoidance of birth control, for example, is one indication of the ways in which hierarchical relations are played out; it is contradictory that this emphasis on women as reproducers is reproduced in RastafarI, ostensibly for the purpose of strengthening the potential of the livity, and by extension Africans, to resist domination (Tafari-Ama 1989, 42).

The development of a feminist or womanist consciousness in Jamaica impacted gender relations in RastafarI as a matter of course. On the other hand, as the participant in the online survey from New Zealand explained, indigenous performances of gender (J. Butler 1999) result in pragmatic gender equity, in contradistinction to the relations displayed in the West, which denote a heavy influence of Western liberalism on even resistance discourses like RastafarI.

The plates have shifted, however, as a result of sistren's self-conscious expressions of agency. Instead of an attack on brethren (who are instead encouraged to participate honestly in the critical reflection), the impetus to generate a discourse of woman's liberation within the livity of RastafarI indicate the Rasta sistren's commitment to the livity itself and not just to the kingmen with whom they might have been affiliated. It also represents an invocation of the tradition of resistance by African women in the Diaspora (and indeed, on the Continent) in the face of any form of domination and exploitation.

Recommendations

From past and present research it is evident that the recurring themes of political, spiritual, psychosocial, and socioeconomic strengths and weaknesses of RastafarI present a paradox to the livity's longevity. For RastafarI to collectively maintain its cultural and political influence and solve its socioeconomic problems, its housekeeping concerns will have to be addressed. Addressing this objective, the participants in the online survey made the insightful recommendations, categorized in Table 10.1.

RastafarI have always articulated an apolitical stance, so it is interesting to note that one of the recommendations calls for greater partisan political involvement. This is not rocket science, however; beyond cultural impact, it is inevitable that in order to generate structural changes RastafarI is well advised to organize the international network suggested and generate the accelerated critical evaluations that will make operationalizing these recommendations possible.

To reiterate, the personal is political, and the envisaged changes are dependent on a partnership approach to personal and community relationships. The socioeconomic and psychosocial concerns expressed also have to be integrated with the political agenda in order for anticipated renewal of the livity to be realized. At the bottom line, the Judeo-Christian ethic that forms the spine of the prevailing ideological framework of RastafarI should be replaced, once and for all, by an African orientation, geared toward the emancipation from mental slavery that Bob Marley, following Marcus Garvey, advocated.

Since gender provides a cross-cutting tool for analyzing a wide range of social concerns, additional participatory action research should be pursued on gender relations within RastafarI, which incorporates current perspectives. This reconsideration is relevant for updating the conversations

Table 10.1.
Recommendations from Respondents

Political	*Psychosocial*	*Socioeconomic*
• If we are followers of Haile Selassie I then we ought to start with His Imperial Majesty. • A New Testament has been written; let us practice it and see where it leads. • The saddest aspect of the Rastafari movement is the fact that the messages, ideas, programs, and prayers have been there for at least 80 years. [As Bob Marley sang], "Just give us the teachings of His Majesty. For we nuh wann nuh devil philosophy." A it dat! • The sistren will be pursuing the struggle whatever happens. But for bredren, especially those of standing and influence, they must (and I include myself humbly in this challenge) try and find the strength to call out the wrong attitudes of fellow bredren. That is hard. • Become more involved directly in the political process.	• Take a perspective of self-analysis, and understand the weaknesses that have stymied the Rastafari movement. • Practice discipline of the mind, which will transfer to the temple. • Be guided by the good examples of our elders. • Make education the main focus. • We need a Council of Elders and a "Rasta think tank" to provide guidance through these uncharted waters. This will provide the framework to harness the socioeconomic potential and political power that are possible. • Education on Rastafari and of Rastafari. • A united front for all the houses and individuals involved.	• Build an all-media, coordinated Rastafari information network. • Form inclusive Rastafari associations around actionable objectives. • Rastafari should speak out more about things affecting Rasta as they happen in communities and countries. • Rastafari should work with other Rastas around the globe on matters of mutual interest. The message has reached the globe now so we need to take up the challenge to use our numbers to our benefit. • We need to use the law and courts to vindicate our rights vigorously. We have lots of Rastas in the legal fraternity.

concerning how sistren and brethren within RastafarI relate to each other both within and outside of the household.

Utilizing tools like the Web, it is possible to bridge some of the gaps that currently yawn between and among various groups and individuals. One participant recoiled from a twenty-year visioning of the way forward for RastafarI, suggesting that more strategic planning is required for generations to come, incorporating lessons learned, critical self-analysis, and impetus to transform inappropriate politics into sustained and sustaining life skills and behaviors.

I concur with Leary's treatise on the vagaries of institutionalized and internalized racism and its enduring psychosocial impact, in which she calls for cleansing and healing processes that should not accommodate the damaging patterns reproduced in many episodes of gender relations in RastafarI (Leary 2005). The mirroring of dysfunctions inherent to the wider societies in which RastafarI are located proclaim the need for an alternative model that eschews sexist discourse and praxis and instead promotes, as several participants said, a holistic paradigm that is self and other reinforcing.

11

Cultural Ideology and RastafarI Women

OBIAGELE LAKE

Generally speaking, Rastafarians engage in many practices that set them apart from the rest of the Jamaican populace. For instance, many Rastafarians abstain from eating meat and subject themselves to other dietary restrictions. These constraints have been motivated by a belief in natural foodways and are supported by Biblical scriptures. In addition to food differences, Rastas have also developed a language in which they integrate normal Jamaican speech with one they believe better accommodates their belief systems. In many cases Rastas are also physically distinguishable from other Jamaicans based on their dress and hair.

Rasta Language (I-Man)

Rastafarians add new prefixes to words, wholly create new words, and give different meanings to the existing lexicon. Rastas are sensitive to English words and sounds that have negative connotations: for example, the "sin" in "sincerely" is changed to "incerely" or "icerely." Similarly "ded" in "dedicate" is redolent of "dead," and is changed to "levicate." Other words in this category include "downpressor" for "oppressor," and "downstroy" for "destroy."

Rastas habitually use the "I" (from Haile Selassie "I") and pronounce it the way North Americans would pronounce the first person singular "I."

This chapter is a reprint and has been lightly revised for this publication. It originally appeared as a chapter in Obiagele Lake's *RastafarI Women: Subordination in the Midst of Liberation Theology*, published in 1998 by Carolina Academic Press. Used by permission.

Often they replace the first letter or syllable of words using "I." A few examples are "Ital," meaning vital (or natural); it usually refers to natural food. "Irie" is another Rasta term meaning "cool" or "alright," and it has been adopted by many other Jamaicans and non-Jamaicans.

The term "I and I" or, more accurately "I n I," is used to refer to the first person singular or in place of "you." One "I" represents the person speaking and the other "I" refers to the god that lives within the self. Dennis Forsythe, a Rastafarian writer, discusses the meaning of "I n I," and states:

> The little I or me refers to the lower self of man, to his body and its ego, that part of him which is born and will die . . . The Big I is the everlasting, immortal or "true" self that was never born and can never die. It is the spirit of divinity and holiness residing in the depth of each. (1983, 85)

As indicated by Pollard, scholars have differed on their understanding of the meaning of "I n I" (1994, 6). These different views notwithstanding, what is more important is the perceived need on the part of Rastafarians to create a language that reflects their own vision of reality. The term "I-man" is particularly interesting for our purposes here since it is a term meaning "I," but one that can only be used to refer to men.

Other words in the Rasta Iyaric glossary include:

Irate: Create
Icall: Recall
Iceive: Receive
Iclare: Declare
Iditate: Meditate
Itation: Meditation

Rasta also have a lexicon of other words that are created from existing usage such as "livity" (way of life), "livit" (diet), and "overstand" (understand). Such conversions factor out the negative connotations ostensibly implicit in their original form. This conversion of the standard language is typical of groups who seek to set themselves apart from the rest of society. As indicated above, Rastas have organized themselves in such a way that would preclude their alliance with the masses of African people. Creating a specific language that is based on the divinity of Selassie I widens this chasm.

Ital Food

Food beliefs and practices also distinguish Rastafarians from the larger population (Lake 1985). In general, they advocate a philosophy that repudiates processed foods. Their focus on natural foods emanates from their emphasis on living according to African tradition and from a strict interpretation of the Bible. Although some Rastas have a great deal of flexibility in their diet, some adhere strictly to food rules.

Rastas emphasize eating food that is in its natural, unprocessed state. Some are vegetarians and practice all types of vegetarianism from vegan to lacto-ovo.[1] Others do not consume milk because they incorrectly believe that it is not consumed in Africa (Landman-Bogues 1976). Other foods and beverages that some Rastas avoid, at least theoretically, include cheese, white flour products, and alcoholic beverages. Some Rastas also believe that they should only consume "air foods," that is, foods that are not grown underground. The origin of this belief is not clear, but it does not appear to be one that will endanger their health status since the carbohydrates and vitamins A and C found in most root foods are readily available from other sources. Other foods that are forbidden by some members who follow strict dietary guidelines are shown in Table 11.1.

While Rasta proscriptions around food are discussed in much of the literature (Nicholas 1979, 61; Landman-Bogues 1976), I want to emphasize that food rules are often relaxed. The majority of Rastas may not deal with alcohol, pork, or beef, but many members will eat all manner of other foods, even if the food is processed. Necessity often takes precedence over dietary proscriptions.

1. A segment of the Rastafarian population is vegetarian and may observe any one of the following vegetarian regimes: Lacto-ovo, consumes no animal flesh but includes eggs and dairy products; ovo, consumes no animal flesh and no dairy products, but does consume eggs; vegan, consumes no animal flesh and no eggs or other dairy products; fruitarian, consumes no animal flesh, eggs, or dairy and also excludes grains and vegetables.

Table 11.1.
Foods Forbidden by Some RastafarI

Animal Protein	*White Flour Products and Salt*	*Alcoholic Beverages*	*Processed Beverages*
Meat	Salt	Rum	Milk
Fish	Buns	Beer	Horlicks
Eggs	Bread	Stout	Ovaltine
Sardines	Cake	Wine	Milo
Bully beef	Dumplings	Brandy	Cocoa
Ham	Gravy	Gin	Coffee
Bacon			Soda
Chicken			
Cheese			
Patties*			

*Patties are meat and pastry pies, most often filled with ground or minced beef. Vegetarian patties have recently entered the market in Jamaica, wherein the filling consists of cooked vegetables such as cabbage and carrots, a type of cooked greens (callaloo), or veggie or soy mince.

Some Rastafarians go through a fasting period that lasts from March 1 through Good Friday. The Bobo Shanti in Bull Bay indicated that they did not impose this restriction on children. Studies concerning child nutrition in Jamaica have not found that malnutrition is more prevalent among Rastas than in the Jamaican child population in general. Rastafarian infant feeding practices may even be superior.

My fieldwork, as published in my book (1985), revealed that Rastafarian women are more likely to breastfeed their children and do so for a longer period of time than other women in Kingston. These findings were based on a small sample of thirty Rasta women and thirty non-Rasta women who were used as controls. Fifty percent of the Rastafarian mothers breastfed their children for four or more months, compared to 43 percent of the non-Rasta mothers. This difference is not statistically significant; however, it was significant that more Rastafarian mothers were committed to breastfeeding their infants with the addition of supplements than members of the control group. This is even more remarkable given that Rasta mothers in this sample were better educated and more likely to be employed than non-Rastas. Although the sample size in this study was too small to suggest that cultural identity was the cause of breastfeeding practices, there was a strong indication that Afrocentric orientation had a positive effect on attitudes about and the duration of breastfeeding.

Hair and Headdress

Just as Europeans exploited African land and labor, they also undermined their cultural economies. During the period of enslavement, Africans in the West were forbidden from speaking their own languages, playing their own music, and continuing their kinship patterns. These proscriptions created a deep chasm between Africa and the Diaspora, but none as deep as the self-hate created by the idea that African physical bodies were somehow less worthy than that of Europeans. Europeans vilified African skin color, physiognomy, and hair.

The most devastating aspect regarding the derogation of the African body is that a large percentage of Africans themselves have internalized these views. As discussed in a number of works (for example, Isaacs 1964; Jones 1994; Lorde 1986; White and White 1995), negative values placed on the African body were introduced and proliferated during the slave era. These ideas continue into the present. That Diaspora Africans have a negative attitude toward natural African hair texture is witnessed by the large percentage of people who have straightened or otherwise processed their hair. The negative language used to describe natural hair and negative attitudes directed toward women with natural hair is also evidence that African hair texture is devalued.

Almost all Diaspora Africans beyond the age of five (perhaps even younger) understand the concept of "good" hair and "bad" hair. Hair is thought to be good if it approximates European hair in straightness (grade) or curliness. If a person has kinky African hair, many people of African descent refer to it as "bad" hair. Along with negative views regarding hair, dark skin is also considered by many to be a badge of inferiority (Russell, Wilson, and Hall 1992; Rushing 1988). I have written more extensively on these issues elsewhere (see Lake 1998, 2003).

In spite of ample evidence to the contrary, many people contend that Caribbean peoples are free from the problems of racism and color stratification that exist in the United States. In fact, colonialism and capitalism have had the same effect all over the Diaspora, differing from place to place only in particulars. Just as they did in the United States, European slave owners in Jamaica gave freedom and other privileges to their mulatto offspring. Darker skinned Caribbeans internalized the European value that "lighter was somehow better." "Good" hair was also at a premium.

Although this cultural and racial hierarchy was true for women and men, women were more closely compared to and evaluated in terms of European beauty standards. Still today, in order for African-descended women to be considered feminine and beautiful, they are encouraged to straighten their hair in order to approximate European models. For women especially, by maintaining their natural hair texture, they are exhibiting their Africanness, which for centuries has been devalued based on European standards of beauty.

African men, whether their hair is straightened or not, are stereotyped as super virile. Thus, women and men of African descent are derogated based on their *being* African. Women bear a double burden since many men of African descent have also internalized the notion of superior European female beauty and expect women of African descent to follow this model.

Most people of African descent around the world, including in Africa, are straightening, Jheri curling, or otherwise transforming their hair. As a group, Rastas are exceptional in this regard since they revel in the glory of their natural African crown. From their own accounts, they let their hair grow long and do not comb it, preferring to leave it totally in its natural state.

Although this may be true for some Rastas, it is clear that others, even though they let their hair lock and maintain its natural African texture, regularly groom their hair in a variety of lengths and styles. According to a report by Smith, Nettleford, and Augier, hair treatment falls within three categories. "Locksmen" refers to those

> whose hair is matted and plaited and never cut, neither their beards; the Beardmen, who wear their hair and beards but may trim them occasionally and do not plait the hair. . . . Both these groups wear moustaches. Thirdly there is the Baldhead or "cleanfaced" man who is not obviously distinguishable from the ordinary Jamaican except by some article such

> as the yellow, green and red pompon or scarf. Cleanfaced men are mostly employed. (1960, 25)

It is interesting to note that this passage describes dreadlocks in terms of men. The original impetus for Rastafarians to lock their hair has been a matter of much debate. Some Rastas have reported that they began to grow dreadlocks in the fashion of Masai warriors. Mansingh and Mansingh suggest that Rastafarians began wearing dreadlocks as a result of seeing East Indian indentured servants and holy men in Jamaica who wore their hair in this fashion (1985, 109). They also assert that Joseph Hibbert, one of the original Rasta leaders, referred to locks as Jagavi or Jatavi, which are Hindi terms. While it is possible that Rastas may have borrowed from Hindi aesthetics, it is also likely that they fashioned their hair after African styles. The origin is less important than their impetus to follow the dictates of the Bible (discussed below) and to set themselves apart from the rest of Jamaican society. Their attribution of this practice to ancient Africa is telling.

Chevannes (1998b, 1998c) suggests that the first group of Rastafarians to wear dreadlocks was a group of young dissident Rastas known as the Youth Black Faith (YBF), which emerged in 1949. According to Chevannes, this group consisted of younger Rastafarian converts who were interested in changing the revivalist practices within the organization. It is Chevannes's contention that the YBF's impetus for wearing dreads did not emerge from East Indian prototypes or, as suggested by Campbell (2007), from images of Masai warriors, but from a desire to be viewed as deviants.

Before Rastas emerged on the scene there were homeless men who roamed the streets with long, unkempt hair that was essentially the same as dreadlocks worn today. They were unkempt in hair, dress, and cleanliness and were regarded as outcasts by the rest of Jamaican society. The YBF adopted this shocking style in order to similarly and intentionally distance themselves from the rest of Jamaican society. This practice is similar to that adopted in the early 1930s when Rastafarian men wore beards to more closely associate themselves with Haile Selassie and to distinguish themselves from the general populace. Even though there have been women RastafarI since the beginning of the organization, the group was often referred to as "bearded men, the beards or beardmen" (Chevannes 1998c, 98)

Homiak differs in his account of the origins of dreadlocks and asserts that the YBF kept their hair cut and groomed and did not wear beards. He put the date of wearing dreadlocks in the 1950s when young males came into the organization after the YBF. He suggests that "the prior generation (exemplified by the YBF) entered Rasta as Combsomes and later became Dreadlocks" (1998, 133). Homiak recounts portions of an interview with Sister Merriam Lennox, an elder Rastafarian woman, who describes the splits over hair culture that took place in the 1950s.

> At dat time in Abacka [Back-a-Wall] man spring up dem own different kinda Rasta . . . different Rasta was still existing . . . [but] is only after de [1958] Convention close date we have the springing up of de Nyabinghi Order. Dis is when de Locks-Dread . . . come right up. We [older Rastas] were talking of de Coptic House when dem man come and "low-rate" Coptic. . . .
>
> Those ancient bredrin [from before the Convention], some a dem "fall dong" [leave Rasta], some a dem pass off, some still ina demself. Still, plenty of de old time Rastaman couldn't tek de message of de Locks-Dread Nyahman . . . couldn't tek de message! (Homiak 1998, 133, 134)

Whatever the origins of this practice, it is clear that it fits well within Rasta's African cosmology. The fact that there are Africans who wear their hair in dreads was enough to validate the practice.

Even though Rasta women and men wear dreadlocks it is only women who are admonished to cover their hair. This practice is partially based on Christian dogma that admonishes women to wear a head covering to hide their beauty, which is also seen as their shame. The shame, of course, emanates from them being a woman.

> Wives, submit yourselves unto your husbands, as unto the Lord. For the husband is the head of the wife, even as Christ is the head of the church: and he is the saviour of the body. Therefore as the church is subject unto Christ, so let the wives be to their own husbands in every thing. (Ephesians 5:22–24)

> But I would have you know, that the head of every man is Christ; and the head of the woman is the man; and the head of Christ is God. Every man

> praying or prophesying, having his head covered, dishonoureth his head. But every woman that prayeth or prophesieth with her head uncovered dishonoureth her head: for that is even all one as if she were shaven. For if the woman be not covered, let her be also shorn: but if it be a shame for a woman to be shorn or shaven, let her be covered. For a man indeed ought not to cover his head, forasmuch as he is the image and glory of God: but the woman is the glory of the man. For the man is not of the woman; but the woman of the man. Neither was the man created for the woman; but the woman for the man. (I Corinthians 11:3–9)

The vast majority of Rasta women take these passages seriously and routinely cover their hair in public.

The Bobo Shanti men are distinguishable mainly by their turbans, which are often colored red, black, green, and yellow. However, men can choose whether to cover their hair or to go bare headed, but women are expected to always cover their hair in public. Even though most Rasta women accept these proscriptions, there are a few who move to a different drummer. One of the most outspoken and independent Rastafarian women that I know offered the following:

> If I feel like wearing my locks out, I wear them out. But if I feel like wearing a head thing I wear it. When I feel like wearing European clothes I wear it. At the end of the day, I'm not fighting for equal opportunity with nobody. Equal to who? I'm fighting for my freedom. And the first step to freedom is freedom of choice.[2]

Cross-Cultural Markers of Inferiority

In all societies clothes are used as markers that connote economic status, gender, and sexuality (among others). For example, in *Veiled Sentiments*

2. In the course of my research, beginning in 1983, I have formally interviewed more than one hundred women and have engaged in informal conversations with many more. It is important to note that not all RastafarI women that I approached were willing to talk with me, and a few thought that only Rasta should study Rasta. These few exceptions notwithstanding, I collected information from women in all of the fourteen regions (parishes) of Jamaica.

Abu-Lughod focuses on ways that Bedouin women communicate their social and sexual availability with various articles of clothing. Indeed, the transition from being single to being married is marked by a change of clothing. After the marriage is consummated, the woman's apparel includes "two critical pieces: the black headcloth that doubles as a veil and the red woolen belt" (1986, 134). The red belt symbolizes her femaleness and fertility.

The black veil always accompanies the red belt in this society. Bedouin men wear head coverings, but they are not obliged to wear a belt that would symbolize their fertility. Bedouin women do not cover their entire faces with their veils, but wear it in a variety of ways and circumstances to communicate respect and sexuality.

Abu-Lughod argues that veiling is not done to prevent sexual interest, but to indicate "shame of sexuality." The veil represents a woman's distance from sexuality in general and, concomitantly, her respect for social order. It is also important to emphasize that these women do not wear the veil out of respect for other women, but in deference to men whom they consider to be higher in the social hierarchy. Essentially, women wear the veil for those who have power over them (ibid., 163). In so doing, they pay homage to and perpetuate their own subordination. Arlene Macleod suggests that the ankle-length skirts and veils worn by Bedouin women demonstrate that they are righteous and deserving of respect (1991, 125–41). This view raises the obvious question: Why are women not deserving of respect without these accouterments?

In spite of the fact that men require no such symbols as markers of their status, several contemporary scholars claim that this garb gives women power (ibid., 125–36). Such views lead one to believe that some women have accepted oppression as a given and are helpless to change the structure that confines them. Macleod contradicts her own assertion when she states that "*hijab* [veils] can protest and ameliorate women's situation . . . by . . . encompassing traditional values of honor, virtue, and dignity. . . . Veiling, however, . . . [conveys] protest but also symboliz[es] women's need to acquiesce and accommodate to the existing structure of power relations" (1991, 133, 137).

A return to "tradition" does not empower women, but further submerges them to the will of men. By covering their bodies in extreme ways, women are seen as adhering to two basic principles. The first is that women's dress is controlled by men. It is interesting that in Muslims, Rastas, and other societies there is little discussion about controlling men's behavior or their dress (Watson 1973). Second, if women do not wear the veil, then, according to advocates of this practice, it is *they* who are the instigators of sexual harassment. Last, it is clear that women are not viewed as dignified and virtuous in and of themselves. This is the underlying issue, which, if placed on the table, would upset the panoply of myths and attitudes about women that relegate them to a polluted status.

Physical markers are necessary codes that inscribe social messages across women's bodies. As Mary Douglas states:

> Bodily control is an expression of social control. . . . There is little prospect of successfully imposing bodily control without the corresponding social forms. And lastly, the same drive that seeks harmoniously to relate the experience of physical and social, must affect ideology. (1970, 71)

Indeed, one of the essential characteristics of oppression is that the oppressed population must be easily identifiable (Turner, Singleton, and Musick 1984). Although women would in any case fit this criteria, the clothes they wear and how they wear them are used as badges that stamp their inferiority in very specific ways. Prescriptions for women's clothing do not end with head coverings but extend to their entire bodies.

With the exception of Bobo Shanti men, who sometimes wear a long robe-like covering over their pants, most Rastafarian men dress the same way as other Jamaican men. Almost all Rasta women wear long skirts or dresses and head coverings. Some of the women wear pants but stipulate that they must not be tight fitting, must be made out of African print, and must be cut in an African style. All Rasta women stated that their dress is symbolic of their difference from other women.

Rasta women's dress, like other aspects of their belief system, is predicated on Biblical interpretations.

> The woman shall not wear that which pertains to a man, neither shall a man put on a woman's garment: for all that do so *are* abomination unto the Lord thy God. (Deuteronomy 22:5)

Given the internalization of Biblical rhetoric most Rasta women spoke positively about their dress code.

> When you see a Rasta dawta come, you know she's a Rasta because of the way she adorns herself. We no wear pants, we no wear shorts, you know. In the good old ancient way, that's the way we dress.

Another Rasta woman has similar opinions about the meaning of Rasta women's dress.

> People look up to you for certain things. Like in my community, everybody looks up to me. They wouldn't expect me to walk around bare headed or without sleeves.

Another informant asserts that long dresses are the mark of morality, which gains them respect.

> Rasta women have a certain dignity, the way they dress and the way they speak and the way they walk in such a dignified way. You'd never see a Rasta woman dye her hair six different colors and wearing some little thing. It's a total consciousness. So we are seen as more of a moral people in terms of keeping the sanity of the flesh on a low profile. Yes. That is how we as a people gain respect from society.

While this woman lauded the dress ethic of Rastafarian women, she also thought that some of the proscriptions were unnecessarily restrictive.

> I'm one of the women who likes to wear my hair without a tie and you might find that the [Rasta] sisters have a problem with that. So others who are radical like me might defend it and say, "No, she's a Rasta because she do this and she do that. Just what Rasta is about." Because we are about development and progress, yes. And being a Rasta is one of the highest forms that you should definitely try to promote in terms of His Majesty [Haile Selassie] because he's a progressive man. He speaks of development, that we should develop ourselves so that our race can be strong. So I might put beads in my hair and somebody might have problems with that. A Rasta woman might say that I shouldn't decorate my hair, but

> that's just her concept. Because whether you wear it on your hair or on your neck or ankle, it's no different because each part of you is important. My hair is as important as my neck. So you get different people's views. You just have to live and be satisfied deep down within yourself and know what you want.

This passage is indicative of the fact that Rasta culture, like all cultures, is not static, but in a constant state of dynamic change. This more radical stance might indicate that changes are occurring among Rasta women, but I suggest that these changes may not outpace gender-based codes in the rest of Jamaican society.

The Linguistic Containment of Women

Language is the symbolic purveyor of culture. It not only allows us to express ideas and values, but is the foundation upon which they are built. Ways in which language, as part of a panoply of other symbols, has sustained male privilege and the derogation of women in all societies points to the pivotal position of this medium. The language of sexism, much like the language of racism, relegates women to the status of children or second-class citizens. Because this language is so regularized in our everyday speech, we hardly notice how it "reflects the 'superiority' of the male and the 'inferiority' of the female, resulting in a master-subject relationship" (Bosmajian 1992, 341). Examples of this hierarchal use of language is replete in all societies. Let me suggest a few examples.

In many African societies there is no word for she, he being the pronoun that represents all human beings. While there is a pronoun that represents females in European societies, often the male pronoun is used to represent both sexes. Likewise, "mankind" represents humankind, "man" represents women and men. Moreover, the ordering of words, such as men and women, boys and girls, he and she, gives primacy to males. The commonality of this usage has had the effect of institutionalizing images of women as secondary or nonexistent. Although many people hasten to suggest that this "generic" language does not have any deleterious effects or malintent, reactions to biased language when it is inverted tells another story. If, for example, "womankind" replaced "mankind," I suggest that many people would have to rethink the "generic" argument.

Another way that men advance their own image and their credibility is by exercising their privilege of using language more often in public spaces. Looking at the entire span of African and Diaspora African movements, including civil rights movements (Burks 1993, 71–83), it has been men who have assumed the roles of spokespersons, even though women serve as the foot soldiers in these organizations. Among Jamaican Rastafarians, in all but a few arenas, men are the spokespeople for the entire group. They reinforce their privilege by exploiting the performative aspect of language while silencing women.

Rastafarians also have a unique way of referring to females and males. Among the Bobo Shanti men are often referred to as "priests" or "prophets." Girls may be referred to as "princesses" and boys are called "princes." Adult women can be referred to as "empresses." Rastafarians as a whole sometimes use the term "queen" to refer to women and "king" or "kingman" for men. Although "queen" is a term that is available, it is rarely used in everyday exchanges, which is not the case for "kingman." Moreover, to the degree that it is used, it exemplifies how women are deified in the abstract and derogated in reality.

Several of my informants remarked that the term most often used to refer to women is "daughter" (or "dawta"). Using the term "daughter" to refer to women relegates them to the status of children, subordinated, once again, to the adult male "kingman." Ironically, the language of RastafarI is considered by some to be a language of resistance. In order to arrive at such a conclusion, the status of women must be factored out of the picture.

Part 5 Religious Considerations in the Rastafari Movement

12

The Wages of (Sin) Is Babylon

Rastafari Versus Christian Religious Perspectives of Sin

ANNA KASAFI PERKINS

> Hear the words of the Rastaman say:
> "Babylon, you throne gone down, gone down."
> —THE WAILERS, "Rasta Man Chant"[1]

Rastafari constitutes an oral culture, with no written constitution or book of rules. The richness, variety, and complexity of its theological perspectives are often obscured by scholarly attempts to treat Rasta in a generic fashion. Nonetheless, it is possible to argue that there are several core beliefs held by the various Rasta mansions, beginning with their belief in the divinity of Haile Selassie I. Rastafarian beliefs are reflected in and given expression in their use of language. In fact, they have developed language into a keen instrument for defining reality and stating the distinctive Rasta worldview. Word is power. For Rastas the spoken word as a manifestation of the divine presence and power can be creative or destructive, kill or cure. Words are an ontological phenomenon, which have the power to manifest what they really are and must therefore be used precisely and judiciously (Homiak 1998, 175). Rastafarians therefore examine the word and

1. This is a line from the song by the Wailers, "Rasta Man Chant," which appears on the album *Burnin'* (1973). This was a traditional chant arranged by Bob Marley, Peter Tosh, and Bunny Livingstone.

sound structure of standard Jamaican English for negative connotations in both the spelling and pronunciation of certain words and transform these in the development of their distinctive Iyaric language. For most Rastafari, for example, "dedicate," which emphasizes the word "dead," becomes the positive word "livicate." "Appreciate" becomes "apprecilove" to remove the hate sound and to speak love into being. The effects of this belief on the wider Jamaican society can be witnessed in the refusal of many to say 2008; rather "2000 and love" is a more common phrase to be heard on the lips of many Jamaicans.[2] For some Rastas, even the word sincere is problematic because it includes the syllable "sin"; therefore to express positive livity it becomes "incerely" or "icerely" (Simpson 1985, 288).

This rejection of the power of sin, even at the level of language, points to profound reflections on the matter. Rastafari has a deep theology of sin that has been somewhat neglected and begs for a fulsome exploration. As Christian theologian Noel Erskine details it:

> Sin [for Rastas] is not merely an individual or personal matter, but also a structural matter. Because of this Rastafarians attack nations, corporations, empires, and races, applying the teachings of the Ten Commandments to them as well as to individuals. (1981, 113)

The nations, corporations, races, and empires "attacked" by Rasta are captured in the biblical referent of "Babylon." This chapter is a first step at exploring one dimension of Rasta theology, the idea of sin. Special attention will be given to the notion of structural sin, that is, the failure to obey Jah's will, which is embodied in nations, corporations, empires, and even races. It can be argued therefore that the embodiment of structural sin is Babylon, the epitome of all that goes against Jah's will and oppresses Jah's people.

Caribbean philosopher Paget Henry captures well the connection between oppression and sin and moral evil, Babylon and living in sin, in the theology of Rasta:

2. The Rastafarian movement builds on the tradition of Jamaican fascination with words: puns, proverbs, pithy sayings, etc. See Chevannes 1994, 159f.

> The present period is seen as the last decade of a two-thousand-year cycle of oppression in which the downpressors of the Rastafarians have been the imperial countries of the West, their local political supporters, the police, and the established Christian Churches. Ironically, this constellation of oppressive forces has been given the biblical representation Babylon. Thus the actions of these "Babylonians" are not only politically oppressive but also morally evil. Consequently to be oppressed in Jamaica is not only to be in captivity but also to be *living in sin*. Hence both redemption and liberation are on the Rastafarian agenda. (2000, 211–12; emphasis mine)

Some Rastas believe that God allowed Blacks to be exiled to Jamaica as slaves because of their past sins and those of their ancestors. However, the advent of the invincible emperor was a sign that their sins had been expiated and the end of their suffering was near (Desmangles, Glazier, and Murphy 2003, 288).

The response to sin in all its dimensions is both particular and temporal, hence the Rasta call for liberation, which gets expressed in a desire for repatriation and a destruction of the Babylon system; but it also has a prior cosmic-moral dimension that requires redemption through the work of a divine man, Je-sus. Most Rastas reject the notion of Jesus Christ, who is either considered to be a false God of the White man used to oppress Black people or a demon. To that end, they will not speak of the Messiah in the anglicized form of his name, Jesus, but rather refer to him as Iyesus or Je-sus (Jeh-sus). Ras Dermot explains that the pronunciation comes from the name Jesse who is an ancestor of King David, the ancestor of Je-sus. (The importance of the Rastafarian use of words should not mask the fetish that is sometimes made of the power of the word.)

The foregrounding of a Rasta theology of sin surfaces points of contact and disconnect with Christian theologies of sin, which will also be investigated. A note of caution even as some first steps are taken in this exploration: the orality and the often individual pursuance of truth that marks Rastafari impacts any attempt at a systematic presentation of key elements of doctrine that is "true" for all mansions. So in the attempt to surface some understanding of sin in the Rasta worldview, I engaged in some reasoning with Priest Dermot Fagan, the founder of the Emperor Haile Selassie I

School of Vision Bible Study, Prophecies and Sabbath Worship. He considers his mansion to be a member of the long-established Nyahbinghi Mansion. The members of this Nyahbinghi House can often be found at worship in the park in Papine, St. Andrew, Jamaica, on Saturdays. They live the life of a Nyahbinghi man who, as Priest Dermot describes it, "must keep the Ten fingers and the Ten toes—the Ten Commandments."[3]

Christ in Rasta Theology

> I'll show you mystery.
>
> —RAS DERMOT

According to Ras Dermot Fagan, the Bible is a key, compass, and bridge for the Rasta community. Through the process of inspiration, a Rastaman can be enlightened to overstand (understand) what God wants to say to the world through those words. "Each Rasta is divinely guided by Jah" (Erskine 2007, 189). Indeed, many Rastas believe that the Bible refers primarily to Africa (Sankeralli 1995, 126). Every key doctrine that the community lives by is to be found within the pages of the Bible, particularly the idiosyncratic King James version. Many of the key interpretations turn on the presence or absence of individual words. The most important belief of Rasta is the divinity of Haile Selassie. Most Rastas regard the Emperor as the Christ, the Black Messiah, who came to save them:

> To speak of Rastafari without acknowledging the centrality of H.I.M. to the faith is like propounding a Christianity stripped of Christology. Rastas cannot explain human failing without accepting Christian teaching that "Iyesus Christus" came on earth to help humanity recover from its critical fall from grace. This viewpoint springs from a faith that acknowledges that only God—not humans—can forgive sins. For the Rastafarians after Leonard Howell, Iyesus Christus, the one whom the world calls

3. Special thanks to Priest Dermot Fagan, Imhotep and Sevens of the His Imperial Majesty Haile Selassie I School of Vision Bible Study, Prophecy and Sabbath Worship for many of the reasonings and insights that ground this discussion.

> Jesus Christ, has returned a second time in H.I.M. of Ethiopia, Haile Selassie. (Wint 1998, 161)

Rastas engage in an anthropological reversal; by seeing Haile Selassie, a Black man, as god, they reversed the anthropological poverty of Blackness and revalued themselves by seeing themselves created in the divine image (Erskine 2007, 34). The main question that arises in the face of the divinity of Haile Selassie is his relationship to the Christ of the scriptures. Ras Dermot argues that Christ is the perfect lamb, who was offered up as the perfect sin offering. Quoting from Hebrews 9:26b–28, he presents an interpretation that Christ was *once* offered up to bear the sins of many. The word "once" is key—it is interpreted to mean only one time. No further sacrifice is necessary, so all the sacrifice that is being offered now is being offered to demons.

> Psalm 40 verse 6: before Christ born, Moses offered a temporal offering, the sheep, goat, oblations . . . Christ took upon himself the work of redeeming the whole mankind not only Black people . . . Redeem us from the penalty of death brought upon us by Satan because the first man never obey according to [the book of] Genesis. Ezekiel 28, Lucifer was created. Christ as God come into planet earth to take us from under the bondage of Satan who has deceived us. Disobedience meant a death of the spirit, a separation from God. (Ras Dermot Fagan, in interview with author)

However, Christ shall come again "and unto them who look for him shall he appear." The second time he shall be without sin and unto salvation. Christ will come again a second time to offer salvation. Christ must be born twice for humanity to get salvation. God seeks to give people today another chance before "him come to bun this place wid fire." Ras Dermot charges that church people were not looking for a second birth: "What the theologians have not seen is that Paul [in Hebrews] is teaching that Christ must appear the second time without sin unto salvation." The Messiah has already come in the person of Emperor Haile Selassie I.

It is noteworthy that in the same breath Ras Dermot claims that when he [Je-sus] comes the second time he will not come to offer salvation but judgment. Redemption and judgment are clearly features of the Second Coming that shade into and reinforce each other in Rasta theology.

The true nature of this Second Coming (Parousia), Priest Dermot claims, is explained in Isaiah 9.6–7:

> Unto us a child is born and the government shall be upon his shoulder. This is not a reference to Jesus, for Christ must be born. [Be]cau[se] Haile Selassie is the one that carry a government right from the age of 12 right through his persecution to constitution one and two [of Ethiopia] until they declared him dead 1975 without a speck of evidence for a man like I. . . . Yuh have man se God kyaan bawn but ah nuh dat de Bible se. The Bible speak of a child that shall be born an him describe this child as mighty (capital G not common g) God. . . . We go further to verse 7 to show you the authority of Rastafari; the increase of his government. . . . Je-sus god is God born in a stable, run gaw ah Egypt, come back a Galilee, work miracles. Nuh throne, nuh crown, nuh sceptre, nuh subject dat man show authority over more dan a few apostles that love him an si di works and want to help him. Dat is the limitation of Je-sus Christ work. (Ras Dermot Fagan, in interview with author)

Any reference to the kingly nature of Jesus is interpreted as a reference to the imperial power of the Emperor Haile Selassie. He argues further from the Book of Revelation that the reference to Jesus as King of Kings and Lord of Lords was not referring to Je-sus but rather Selassie, since the book was written after Je-sus had come and gone. More interestingly, Ras Dermot refers to the expectation of a Third Coming:

> Christ must come a second time for salvation and we know him in our day as Haile Selassie. There will be a third coming—"a galactical advent," which mean not by birth but sudden appearance, Acts chapter 1. The way him went, an him se so shall he appear but the world was looking for an immediate return for judgment not a second coming to grant us the privilege that were given to the people before us. King Selassie I nevah dead him went up with a shout!

Ras Dermot affirms his belief in the living emperor and rejects any notion that Selassie I died or was assassinated. The three appearances of the

Messiah are linked: Je-sus Christ the first was sacrificed for the redemption of sinful humanity. His Imperial Majesty was the second Christ whose being born again was not expected by Christians because they are blind. This is perhaps the same blindness from which Jesus accuses his opponents of suffering in John's Gospel (9.39–41). The importance of sight-knowledge in the Rasta worldview is reflected in this charge of blindness. Similarly, the notion of being born again has a different referent in Rastafari than it does in Christianity, where it is understood as what happens to the individual believer in Christ (Jn. 3.3).

Haile Selassie's coming was akin to Je-sus descending into hell to free the captives who had not known about him. The coming of the emperor was to give people in the present age a chance to know the truth. Unlike Je-sus, Selassie did not die, but rather was taken up into the heavens as is described of Je-sus in Luke-Acts (Lk. 24.50–53; Acts 1.7–11). So there is a Third Coming to be expected of a galactic, cosmic nature that will bring everything to fulfillment. Perhaps this Third Coming is simply Judgment! This Third Coming is to be paralleled to the expectations that many Christians have of a Second Coming of the Messiah at the end of time.

Of course, not every Rasta mansion would hold to Ras Dermot's interpretation. The prophet Gad of the Twelve Tribes of Israel said in an interview in 1997, in response to a question about the difference in doctrine between Twelve Tribes and other Rasta groups, "Yes, there is a basic difference because we see Christ, that die and rose again, and that die for sin, we see that person. So that is, you know, a different teaching, because is not many see this teaching, that Christ is the person" (Bedasse 2006, 49). The Prophet Gad taught that a person can be saved by no other name but that of Jesus Christ, recognizing that though Haile Selassie is indeed divine, he is really only the custodian of the Davidic throne on earth (ibid., 51). Ras Dermot and the members of his school would certainly reject this position. In the same way, Ras Dermot rejects the Ethiopian Orthodox Church as being a "goat among sheep"—not true Rasta because they do not revere the divinity of the emperor whom they crowned. It is for these and other reasons that Ras Dermot laments "[Rastas] don't express or speak with the same voice and dat is the main problem among us today. And we seek to have Rastafari express itself with a singular voice."

Sin in Christian Theology

> They need to be more aware today of the social face of sin—the inequalities at the social level. They think of sin too much on an individual level.
>
> —FR. GERALD O'COLLINS, former professor of moral theology at the Papal University in Rome

Sin has always been a significant category in Christian theology. In the last fifteen hundred years, Christian theologians have discussed this topic more than any other topic, including Jesus (Dear 1994, 59). Sin has been described in a variety of ways: missing the mark (harmatia), offending God, disobeying God's command, a selfish turning away from God, pride.

> Contemporary theology defines sin as "any thought, word or deed that deliberately disobeys God's will and in some way rejects the divine goodness and love." Sin includes any deviation from God and God's way of non-violent love. Sin is not just passive; it is deliberate infidelity to the will of God. (Dear 1994, 60–61)

Dear argues that until the past few decades Christian tradition has relied on the teachings of Augustine and focused almost completely on sin as an individual, personal matter. Nowadays, however, Christians are beginning to examine the social dimensions of sin and to speak of systemic and institutionalized sin. He claims that the way to understand the human community's deviation from its relationship with God is found in the way individuals relate to one another as peoples and nations (61). Perhaps the best-known recognition of this move to focus on social as well as individual sins is the recent updating by the Roman Catholic Church of the traditional seven deadly or mortal sins, that is, sins the result of which is that "immediately after death the souls of those who die in a state of mortal sin descend into Hell." (The original seven deadly sins are lust, gluttony, greed, sloth, wrath, envy, and pride.) We can make the argument that now in these modern times, the traditional deadly sins have morphed into modern deadly sins, sins that have become prevalent in a modern era of "unstoppable globalization." The Roman Catholic Church now includes as mortal sins environmental pollution, genetic manipulation, accumulating excessive wealth, inflicting poverty, drug trafficking and consumption, morally debatable experiments, and violation of fundamental rights of human nature (Willey 2008).

Notions of Personal and Inherited (Original) Sin in Rasta and Christian Theology

Personal Sin

For Ras Dermot, sin is "actions that are contrary to the Lord's will." He also notes that:

> In the scriptures, ignorance to a certain extent is defined as sin. And not only defined but get judgement to[o]. Hosea 4, verse 6, my people are destroyed for lack of knowledge, so lack of knowledge would be equal to ignorance . . . Because thou has rejected knowledge. So god not looking on a man total ignorance . . . he looks upon you in your ignorance as having gotten knowledge now to move ignorance with proper knowledge an you reject it. (Interview with author)

This lack of knowledge is about the real Je-sus as opposed to the Jesus that many Christians accept. By implication, Ras Dermot and other Rastas are able to charge that many now know about the real Je-sus through the preaching of Rasta and so have no excuse. He is especially wrathful against the pastors of Christian churches:

> Jeremiah 10 . . . Show you that the pastor is responsible for all that is happening in Jamaica today doh he may not want to hold himself responsible . . . Him nuh speak about Je-sus, is him tell you bout Jesus and moreover put up dat White man dat doan fit the scriptures either by name or race . . . The leader gwine get a greater punishment than di people cause is dem cause de people to err. Deeper than dat, the pastors are held captive by Lucifer the fallen angel . . . They are deceived.

Joseph Owens (1976) concurs that most Rastafarians believe that the major sin of the churches is their refusal to acknowledge the divinity of Selassie publicly and their blinding of the people to the truth (81).

The consequences of this sin are dire indeed. As Ras Dermot states forcefully:

> The wages of sin is death . . . spiritually meaning that you spirit is far from God cause man is a spirit to[o] yuh nuh. Man is not only flesh . . . The spiritual death you soul is not in the special prerogative with Christ anymore because you become an enemy. Especially if yoh nuh repent and are stubborn still. "When you call I will answer you not" . . . Why the people are still bound is not their fault. (Interview with author)

The fault for human sinfulness lies with pastors who mislead and are themselves mislead by Satan. This raises the question of where "fault" can really be found. Can sinners be blamed if in truth the devil made them do it? A similar question could be posed around the notion of structural sin, which will be explored later.

> On the question of death, many Rastafarians will have nothing to do with anything dead—bodies, funerals, meat ("deaders"), etc. Joseph Owens's research in the 1970s surfaced that the strictest Rastafarians allow no exceptions to the doctrine that a person's death is always punishment for sin and could have been avoided by living faithfully. Owens claims that despite various attempts to soften this doctrine, there are still many Rastas who accept it in all its starkness and insist that death is always the wages of personal sin. "If a person dies, it is because he has been unfaithful; there can be no other explanation" (Owens 1976, 137). Ras Dermot and members of his mansion would certainly not hold this extreme view. Death is seen as a natural part of living, and there is no expectation of the immortality implied by the Rastafarians Owens identifies in his study as being particularly strict.

Inherited (Original) Sin

> Born in sin and shaped in iniquity and you the person who practice sin; both of dem is sin. You that is grown is more aware.
>
> —RAS DERMOT

In Catholic theology much is made of the concept of original sin, which is the state or condition in which, because of the sin of Adam and Eve, all human beings are born (McBrien 1994, 184). The term has two references, as outlined by theologian Richard P. McBrien: (1) the initial, "originating" sin of Adam and Eve (*peccatum originale originans*); and (2) the subsequent "originated" universality of human sin (*peccatum originale originatum*). The first dimension focuses on the source of sin, its historical roots, that original event in the mythic past. It points to the fact that the source of our sinful human condition resides in the choices of humanity. The second dimension focuses on the consequences of turning away from the divine, for all who enter human history after the original event occurred (Hanigan 1986, 112). The consequences are both personal and social, affecting everyone in their mutually reciprocal interaction. As was demonstrated previously, it is easy enough to see how individuals are affected by the sin of others; how the social environment can have a harmful influence on the individual. It is more difficult, however, to understand how or why we are socially affected by someone else's sin to the degree that we are born in original sin and are in fact sinners from birth. What the doctrine of original sin explains is that "each one of us is unable to say yes to God without the healing, liberating gift of God's grace, a gift which is symbolized and effected in baptism" (ibid., 113).

Original sin remains a particularly powerful religious symbol even in today's world. It was Protestant theologian Reinhold Niebuhr who stated that original sin is the one empirically verifiable Christian tenet (Himes and Himes 1993, 29). All that is necessary is the observation of one's neighbor, Niebuhr claimed. Niebuhr cited original sin as the religious symbol to best explain and justify the issue of self-interest in politics. In 2008, in a response to the stirring speech by Barack Obama (the Democratic presidential candidate at the time) on race relations in the United States, South African–born, New York–dwelling writer Roger Cohen declared that "There are things you come to believe and things you carry in your blood" (Cohen 2008). The thing that Cohen believes Americans carry in their blood is racism, which "dwells in the deepest parts of the [American] psyche." At the same time, he pronounces that "Slavery was indeed America's 'original sin'" and admits that "'the brutal legacy of slavery and Jim Crow' lives on in forms of African-American humiliation and anger that smolder in ways incommunicable to whites" (ibid.). By identifying original sin as something passed on in the blood from generation to generation, literally and figuratively, Cohen unwittingly presents an updated perspective on an old theme. In so doing, he, like others before him, struggles to capture the elusive notion in modern form.

Ras Dermot for his part prefers to speak of inherited sin rather than the more traditional original sin. He too roots his belief in the story of the Fall in Genesis. He refutes any misunderstanding of the notion of original sin that occurs because some persons equate original sin with personal sin—a personal sin that has been imposed on our innocent shoulders. Similarly, like most modern Christian theologians, he would reject any notion that original sin is passed on in the blood from generation to generation. For Ras Dermot each person is born as a sinner due to their relationship with Adam, the forefather in sin.

> "All have sinned and come short." Child just born, innocent. Came out of the womb out of the father and the mother . . . Their father inherited sin through the act of Adam; Adam sin replaced by Christ the last Adam who is sinless. We who are born out of Adam cannot put out Adam; only free through your confession; born with the sin, born a sinner but not by *yuh* act. [You] have no power over dat because you are a descendant of the first sinner; that is why Christ came to give you and I an opportunity. The Bible se if thou confess Christ, plus you be baptised, thou shall be saved. Sin is a spirit is not something yuh can demonstrate. It is something that you born with it. The one that is developed is more cognisant . . . Ah inherited sin that I child cannot get away from until the time the child baptize. (Interview with author)

His mention of baptism implies that this is the ritual that removes original sin—pretty much in line with current Roman Catholic teaching. In his attempt to pin down the elusive notion of original sin he ventures into the language of the spirit to describe that which cannot be seen with physical eyes. Yet the demonstration of inherited sin is structural, social, Babylonian. He returns to the notion that with knowledge of the truth comes deeper responsibility and offers advice for human beings as they continue to live: "Still have to acknowledge on a daily basis you are a sinner. How can a child be born in sin? No one can get up and say I am without sin. If you are smart any at all you must always see yourself as vulnerable or that you might be doing something that err."

The Wages of Sin

> Babylon being a structure of sin. How do we define Babylon as sin? Babylon is emanating out of humanity; ah nuh spook a do it.
>
> —RAS DERMOT

In Rasta the term Babylon includes both the Church and State structures in the West (Owens 1976, 69). The continuity in the succession of forces arrayed against God's people was easily discernible to the author of Revelation. "In the Rasta's eyes, the same Babylonian-Roman empire exerts continuing dominion over the elect even to this day in the form of the British and American empires. The prophecies of Revelation concerning the downfall of the ancient empires apply as well to those modern successors" (81–82). "Babylon is, in sum, the whole complex of institutions which conspire to keep the Black man enslaved in the western world and which attempt to subjugate coloured peoples throughout the world. Against this power the Rastafarians fight continually and trust in the help of the Almighty to fell this ancient enemy once and for all" (70).

Examining Babylon with enlightened eyes shows that it represents, as portrayed in the Book of Revelation, the fullness of all the powers that are arrayed against Jah and disobedient to Jah's will. The Babylonian system that exists is the creation of sinful human beings, not "spooks." Yet, there is no suggestion that the destruction of Babylon, which has been created by human beings, can be destroyed by human beings. The expectation is that divine intervention in the Third Coming will bring about Babylon's destruction: "Fallen, fallen is the great Whore!"(Rev. 18.2).

Babylon Throne Gone Down

In conclusion, Rastafari has a rich and complex theology of sin, particularly as seen from the perspective of the Nyahbinghi mansion of HIM School of

Vision Bible Study, Prophecy and Sabbath Worship. For many Rastafari sin is not simply an individual moral problem but also has political and social dimensions. The Rastaman has been enlightened with knowledge to recognize the true nature of reality. Human beings live in a world of sin—personal, inherited, and corporate sin. Perhaps the key sin is corporate sin that is reflected in a Babylon system that practices racial, economic, and cultural domination, particularly against the African. To overcome the Babylon system requires not just individual redemption and liberation but also social redemption and liberation. The key of the scripture assures Rastafari that this liberation is certain:

> Four hundred years inna Babylon
> Four hard hundred years (a Nyabinghi)
> Bynghi man, four hundred years
> Four hundred years inna Baby-ram
> Four hard hundred years (Slavery)
> But I an I nevah yet ease a fire till
> Baby-ram wall burn dung
> Bongo man se four . . .
>
> The words of a Nyabinghi chant by Ras Dermot Fagan

Part 6 Rastafari and Reggae

13

Kumina, the Howellite Church, and the Emergence of Rastafarian Traditional Music in Jamaica

KENNETH BILBY *and* ELLIOT LEIB

Music history tends to be bound to the ebb and flow of current tastes, often catering to trends of the moment. Once called "the Caribbean's only entirely new musical form in this century" (Roberts 1972, 132), reggae music was spawned in the ghetto of West Kingston in the early 1960s. It overcame its humble origins and has emerged as a major current in international popular music. Now that reggae has won eager audiences on every continent (not to mention massive borrowing and co-optation by American and British top 40 pop) and has risen to become "a prime world-pop music" (Bergman 1985, 18), its history is considered worthy of serious study.

It has become standard practice for popular treatments of reggae to include a brief section on the traditional Rastafarian music that contributed to the development of the style. Owing to the popularity of reggae, the religious music of Rastafari, particularly the drum ensemble form known as Nyahbinghi, has begun to receive wider recognition. Commentators on the reggae phenomenon, wishing to point out the music's "deeper" African roots, have tended to represent the Rastafari Nyahbinghi music as merely

This chapter is a reprint and has been lightly revised for this publication. It originally appeared in an article by Bilby and Elliot entitled "Kumina, the Howellite Church and the Emergence of Rastafarian Traditional Music in Jamaica," published in 1986 in *Jamaica Journal* 19(3): 22–29. Used by permission.

a modified version of an older recreational African-based drumming form known as *Buru*.[1] This, however, is but a part of the story, an oversimplification that neglects the importance of early cross-fertilization between various styles. Growing popular interest in reggae and Rastafari and the rush for simplistic answers to questions about origins have led to hasty and incomplete conclusions.

This chapter takes as its point of departure not reggae, but traditional Rastafari music itself; it presents recent evidence of an important historical connection between the Rastafari Nyahbinghi tradition and the musical practices of the religious cult known as Kumina.

Kumina is an African-derived religion that originated among post-emancipation African contract laborers sent to Jamaica during the late nineteenth century. Today it is practiced primarily in the eastern parish of St. Thomas and centers on possession by and communication with ancestral spirits.

Many aspects of the Kumina tradition, including the ritual language, music, and dance through which contact with the ancestors is maintained and fostered, are derived primarily from Central African (particularly Kongo) cultural traditions (see Moore 1953; Warner-Lewis 1977; Brathwaite 1978; Schuler 1980; Bilby and Fu-Kiau 1983; Ryman 1984).

The Debate on Origins

Since the earliest days of the movement, Rastafari attitudes toward traditional Afro-Jamaican religious expressions such as Kumina and Revivalism have been ambivalent, and this attitude has been carried over to associated musical styles. Writing in the early 1950s, George Eaton Simpson noted:

> Despite the fact that they have the same general socio-economic status, Revivalists and Ras Tafarians are enemies. Revivalists often take an interest, outside their church meetings, in Cumina drumming and John Canoe

1. Although the word is often spelled "burru," we have chosen to render it throughout this article as "Buru," in accordance with the systematized orthography for Jamaican Creole used in Cassidy and LePage 1984.

> music. Members of the Ras Tafari cult spurn both of these activities, as well as Revivalism, and regard them all as "backward." (1955, 170)

Ambivalence toward certain African-derived folk traditions continues. The position that Rastafari Nyahbinghi music is partly derived from Kumina remains unpopular with many present-day Rastafari who, in spite of a respect for the "Africanity" of Kumina drumming, disapprove of certain fundamental aspects of the Kumina religious experience, such as ancestral spirit possession and the emphasis placed on the continuing participation of the dead in the affairs of the living. Many younger Rastafari today as well as some elders categorically reject the idea that Nyahbinghi music has roots in Kumina.[2]

The scholarly literature on Rastafari music, however, has not been so quick to dismiss the possibility of Kumina influence. Although researchers often mention Kumina as an influential source in addition to Buru, the nature of their mutual influences remains ill-defined. Count Ossie, a towering figure in the development of Rastafari drumming, is said to have been steeped in Kumina and Buru music (Reckord 1977, 6–8; White 1980, 7, 1984).[3] Still others, perhaps influenced by the oft-expressed Rastafari distaste for Kumina "duppy (ghost) worship," have argued that Kumina played no role in the development of Rastafari music. Yoshiko S. Nagashima sums up the current state of the debate in her recent monograph on Rastafari music:

> There is controversy . . . about the local origins of Rastafarian music. Two different opinions exist among the authorities. One is that Rastafarian

2. One of the authors (Bilby) has several times heard young Rastafarians looking on (but not participating) at Kumina dances, and they assert that Kumina is derived from Nyahbinghi, not the other way around, and is therefore less authentically "African" than the latter. Interestingly, some of the Howellites discussed in this study make a similar ideological reversal, claiming that the St. Thomas Kumina practitioners got Kumina from them. What in fact occurred, as shown in this chapter, is clearly the opposite.

3. Mortimer Planno, a Rastafari elder who became active in West Kingston in the late 1950s, is also known as Bro. Cummie, a reference to his skill as a kete man. Note here the creolizing merger of Kumina and Rastafari referenced in the role of the "African" master drummer.

> music links with Kumina and Burru with respect to the instruments used, the rhythmic patterns followed, and, to a certain degree, the participants' backgrounds. This opinion seems to be shared by some of the staff of the (Jamaica) School of Music and others including the art researcher, Verena Reckord. The other opinion, which is supported by the excellent folk singer-folklorist, Olive Lewin, relates Rastafarian music to Burru only and recognises no significant connection with Kumina. In short, the Burru-Rasta linkage is generally accepted, while the Rasta-Kumina connection is controversial. (1984, 72)

Disentangling the Historical Threads

More than twenty years ago, Count Ossie and others helped to re-Africanize Jamaican popular song with the introduction of the Rastafari drum ensemble into the then emerging ska form. Less than a decade before the Folkes Brothers teamed up with Ossie to record "Oh Carolina," there was a marked absence of drumming in Rastafari music in West Kingston (Simpson 1955, 170). In the urban Rastafari gatherings of this early period, music was characterized by hymns and choral chants, sometimes accompanied by a shaka (rattle), rhumba box, and scraper (ibid.).

The introduction of drumming into Rastafari music came from the "camp" and "yard" experience of Black shantytown life in the ghettos of West Kingston.[4] An urbanized version of Buru drumming was in vogue at a time when the nascent Rastafari movement was still without drums of its own. Taking the three-part drum ensemble of Buru (consisting of the bass, runde, and repeater drums) and freely adapting it to the musical needs of the cult groups, the Rastafari helped to create a new style of African inspired dance-drumming known today as Nyahbinghi.[5] The three drums used in Nyahbinghi today are also referred to as kete or akete drums.

4. In a 1983 interview with one of the oldest living Rastafari women active in Kingston at the time of Simpson's fieldwork, one of the authors (Leib) was informed that the type of instrumental group described by Simpson was associated with the "yard" of a Bro. Miles.

5. For a background on Nyahbinghi music and dance, see Smith, Nettleford, and Augier 1960, 13–14; Reckord 1977; Nagashima 1984; Leib 1983. The ethnographic film *Rastafari*

This process of musical genesis cannot be reduced to a simple wholesale adoption and incorporation of the Buru tradition into Rastafari worship. What actually occurred was a good deal more complicated than this. Nyahbinghi drumming was born in West Kingston in the 1940s and 1950s, when the area was a cauldron of competing cultural and musical styles, with each style interacting and influencing the others. The rural migrants who were flowing into Kingston from all over the island in search of opportunities gravitated mainly to West Kingston, bringing with them their varied musical traditions. Along with Buru and Kumina, other rural African-based forms (and certainly Revival) were present. As the styles began to overlap, a confusion of terms and labels resulted in some fluidity in their application.

The flexibility in the application of names or terms to different folk musical styles is nothing new, making the task of pinning down specific origins much more difficult and hazardous (see Ryman 1980). The potential for confusion is exemplified by the term "Buru." This term refers not only to a specific dance-drumming tradition found today in St. Catherine and Clarendon, the form discussed above as having contributed to the Nyahbinghi tradition, but has also been used in many other areas of Jamaica as a sort of generic label covering a wide variety of African-derived dance and drumming styles (sometimes with pejorative connotations) (Cassidy and LePage 1984, 83; White 1984, 78). It is still used in St. Thomas, where the traditional religious form of Kumina is centered, to refer to secularized Kumina dances held for mere entertainment rather than to invoke the ancestors. Kumina practitioners sometimes use the term "Buru" to denote the "bailo" segment of religious ceremonies, such as the early "warming up" part of the dance, which serves a primarily recreational rather than religious purpose (Ryman 1984, 121). It is easy to see how in the urban context where traditional musical forms such as Buru and Kumina met and mingled, any number of terms might have been used,

---

Voices (1979) includes footage of Nyahbinghi dance-drumming recorded at the 1978 Nyahbinghi meeting held at National Heroes Park, Kingston (available on request from Eye in I Filmworks, 1919 Fern Street, San Diego, CA 92012).

possibly interchangeably, to connote the resultant African-derived and oriented fusions.

This seems to be precisely what was happening in the shanty towns of the Jamaican capital as the stage was being set for the development of a new style of music to serve the religious needs of urban Rastafari. It is well known that Buru, in the strict sense of the term, existed in Kingston as early as the 1930s. In the urban setting it had become secularized, losing whatever religious vestiges it might have once had, and was danced mainly on holidays and to celebrate the return of discharged prisoners to their communities in the slums. This urban tradition is said to have later merged with Rastafari ceremonial observances to create the new Nyahbinghi form. When George Eaton Simpson was undertaking research in West Kingston in 1953, he found that a secular drumming style known as "Cumina" was also in use there. According to Simpson, during that time Rastafari music in West Kingston was still performed without drums. Simpson's description of this style provides us with valuable evidence of ongoing cross-fertilization between Buru and Kumina at a crucial period in the history of Rastafari music, a historical moment almost coincident with the first appearance of the Nyahbinghi form:

> Cumina drumming is seldom used in the religious ceremonies of Revivalist groups. Informants refer to this drumming as "African" and this appears to be an accurate characterization. . . .
>
> Usually the members of a Cumina band sing as they play, and hand clapping and body swaying, as well as drumming, accompany the singing. . . . The rituals associated with Cumina drumming in some of Jamaica's country areas seem to have disappeared in the urban fringe. . . . In West Kingston, the occasions for Cumina drumming are: the celebration of some one's release from prison, a "day of sport" in the country, Emancipation Day (August 1), a big gambling game, and rites marking recovery from a serious illness. Since it is regarded as "rejoicing" music, it is not used in ceremonies connected with the dead (wakes, funerals, Nine Nights, Forty Day services, or memorial services). (Simpson 1955, 170)

Simpson's statement that this "Cumina" drumming was associated with "the celebration of someone's release from prison" shows that its functions overlapped with those of the urban "Buru" tradition that eventually fed into Nyahbinghi. Moreover, this urban form of "Cumina," like Buru and unlike the rural religious Kumina tradition, had no association with ceremonies connected with the dead. Thus, its stigma would be reduced for Rastafari musicians seeking inspiration from African-derived drum-related musical forms. Even more interesting than the above description was the photograph of "Cumina" drums that accompanied Simpson's notes, illustrating that the drums used in West Kingston were a modified three-drum ensemble, which was similar to the traditional Buru set. The photo showed a large double-headed bass drum, played with a beater, and two smaller drums that, according to Simpson, were held between the knees and played with the hands. (In the rural religious Kumina tradition, the smaller drums are turned on their sides and mounted by the player.) The smaller drums that were depicted in the photo were of a design that combined features of the Kumina playing cyas as well as the Buru funde and repeater. Although they were somewhat similar in shape and length to traditional Kumina drums, their skins were attached to the bodies and tightened with iron clamps and bolts, as is usually the case with both types of Buru hand drums. This contrasts significantly with the two drums associated with traditional Kumina, where the heads are normally fastened by nails driven in to increase tension.

Simpson's field recordings of this urban "Cumina" music present the listener with a drumming style that is clearly related to and essentially indistinguishable from present-day variants of the Nyahbinghi style used by Rastafari worshippers. It certainly would not be recognized by contemporary rural Kumina devotees as Kumina drumming.[6] Like modern Nyahbinghi drumming, with which it shares all the essential features: the heartbeat double-pulse of the funde (here shifted to the off-beat as sometimes also occurs in Nyahbinghi); the thunder clap of the bass drum, which is free occasionally to vary and set up complex cross-play against the patterns of

6. Simpson 1954, side 2, band 7. Interestingly enough, these field recordings were made in Trench Town, a section of the West Kingston ghetto especially noted for its musical activity and the large number of reggae musicians it has produced.

the other drums; and the rolling syncopations, high-pitched rim tones and pops, and strongly accented cuts or slaps of the repeater. The drumming on this recording combines elements of both Buru and Kumina but is recognizable as neither.[7] Like most successful musical fusions, it is more than the sum of its parts.

An important conclusion to be drawn from all of this is that the fundamentals of the style that has come to be known as Nyahbinghi were already present in West Kingston by 1953 and had already been fused into a Nyahbinghi-like hybrid, although this had not yet been claimed by Rastafari. That this new style bore the name "Cumina"—even if it might also have been called "Buru" at the same time—would seem to be more than fortuitous.

There is no reason to believe that cross-fertilization between Buru and Kumina was limited to the urban context or the period of time when Simpson happened to make his field recordings. On the contrary, indications are that representatives of the two styles have long been in contact in a variety of settings. As Cheryl Ryman points out, traditional Buru performers in Clarendon and St. Catherine see Buru drumming as being related to Kumina, and some of them possess, in addition to the three-part Buru set, traditional Kumina drums, which they also play in the Kumina mode (1984, 121).

7. For notated examples of the fundamental rhythmic patterns belonging to Kumina, Buru, and Nyahbinghi and more detailed comparative descriptions of these drumming styles, see Reckord 1977, 8; Nagashima 1984, 77–78. Recorded examples of traditional Kumina music may be heard on the following recordings on vinyl: *From the Grass Roots of Jamaica* (Dynamic Sounds, n.d.); *Folk Music of Jamaica* (Folkways Records, 1956); *More from the Grass Roots of Jamaica* (Jamaica Information Service, n.d.); *Bongo, Backra, and Coolie: Jamaican Roots, Volume 1* (Folkways Records, 1975); *From Kongo to Zion: Black Music Traditions from Jamaica* (Heartbeat Records, 1983); *Jamaican Ritual Music from the Mountains and Coast* (Lyrichord Records, 1985). Examples of Buru drumming may be heard on a cassette tape entitled *Rhythm Kit No. 1* (Jamaica School of Music, 1981). Examples of Nyahbinghi drumming may be heard on the following: The Mystic Revelation of Rastafari's *Grounation* (Dynamic Sounds, n.d); *From the Grass Roots of Jamaica* (Dynamic Sounds, n.d.); *Churchical Chants of the Nyabingi* (Heartbeat Records, 1983).

The Howellite Connection

It has only recently come to light that Leonard P. Howell (alias "Gong" or "Gangunguru Maragh"), a tremendously influential figure in the early Rastafari movement, used and sanctioned Kumina drumming and other aspects of the Kumina tradition in his ceremonies. Howell is widely acknowledged as being among the first to preach the doctrine and creed of Rastafari in Jamaica.[8] He is also famous, or perhaps infamous, as the founder and leader of one of the first and most important Rastafari communes, called Pinnacle, in the parish of St. Catherine. He started by preaching the divinity of Haile Selassie I at street meetings in various parts of metropolitan Kingston and parts of St. Thomas during the 1930s. Howell suffered repeated persecution by the police. By 1940 or so, he had moved his operations to St. Catherine and founded Pinnacle. When Pinnacle was raided by police and finally broken up in 1954, several hundred members dispersed into West Kingston, contributing to the urban spread of the movement. Several important features of modern Rastafari religious practice, such as the wearing of dreadlocks and the sacramental use of ganja, are thought to have been evolved by the Howellites before or during the Pinnacle era. Barry Chevannes, in his historical study on the origins of Rastafari, writes:

> On Sundays it was customary for Howellites who owned Goats to slaughter and sell them to members who did not. And after the Sunday dinner they would gather in the Parade, dancing and singing to the rhythm of the baandu and funde, the two Kumina drums. (1979, 151)[9]

8. For background on Howell and his role in the development of the Rastafari movement, see Smith, Nettleford, and Augier 1960 and Barrett 1977a. For an appraisal of Howell's contribution to early Rastafari in Jamaica, see R. Hill 1981. An abridged version of Hill's article, with photographs, can be found in R. Hill 1983.

9. The use of the term "funde" here is interesting; in the St. Thomas Kumina tradition, the lead drum that plays alongside the bandu is always referred to as the "playing cyas," never as "funde," which is associated in the minds of Kumina people (those who have heard it) with Rastafari Nyahbinghi music.

This was confirmed by the present authors first in 1982, when we visited a small community of Howell's remaining followers in Tredegar Park, St. Catherine, and again in 1983 and 1984, when one of us (Leib) carried out further research among this group. (Tredegar Park is located on the outskirts of Spanish Town, a few miles from the original site of Pinnacle, which was in the vicinity of Sligoville.) The Tredegar Park Howellites, consisting of twenty or so individuals, several of whose association with Howell goes back to the early days, were residents of Pinnacle during its heyday in the 1940s and 1950s. Today they continue to observe practices that formed part of the daily life at Pinnacle.[10]

The oral testimonies and reminiscences of these Howellites allow us to reconstruct, to some extent, particular links with Kumina. What appears to have happened is as follows: originally in St. Thomas during the mid-1930s and later at Pinnacle, after 1940, a core of Howell's followers integrated Kumina dance-drumming with their seminal practice of Rastafari ritual. A number of informants state that the original group at Pinnacle was composed primarily of persons originally from St. Thomas, the parish where Kumina is most strongly represented.[11]

One younger Howellite, born at Pinnacle in 1945, indicated that Kumina figures prominently in his earliest memories:

10. Yoshiko S. Nagashima briefly visited and talked with Leonard Howell at Tredegar Park in July 1980, but she apparently did not learn of the Howellites' use of Kumina drumming because she does not mention it in her monograph (1984, 39–40). Cheryl Ryman also visited Tredegar Park and presents some data she collected there, but she does not make it clear whether or not her Tredegar Park informants were Howellites. She speaks of a strong Rastafari influence on the Tredegar Park Kumina group she writes about, implying that they were originally a traditional Kumina group without Rastafari connections who have recently been absorbing influences (including elements of drumming) from Rastafari. We wish to emphasize—so as to avoid confusion—that those Tredegar Park Howellites we interviewed claimed to have been playing Kumina since the earliest days of Pinnacle or before; they are Howellite Rastafari who long ago integrated Kumina into their worship and are not traditional Kumina players recently coming under the influence of Rastafari. See Ryman 1980.

11. One Howellite informant stated that some of the earliest and most important Kumina drummers at Pinnacle were associated with Duckenfield, a sugar-producing area in the eastern part of St. Thomas that is still known as an important center for Kumina.

> I remember when I was a kid in Pinnacle, in the early days in Pinnacle, I remember we have a parade (square). Every six o'clock that (Kumina) drum play and everybody got to come, because it is a gathering, like what we annually keeping on here now. And we learn our language there, and learn our descendence (i.e. descent) there, so we can get along. He (Howell) teach us a lot of discipline, and a lot of ways of going on about life.[12]

The language and music referred to in this passage, taught by Leonard Howell and his St. Thomas associates, was largely the language and music of Kumina. This cultural heritage has been retained, if in somewhat fragmentary form, by the present-day Tredegar Park Howellites, who still know and use a large number of standard Kumina songs. They also possess a limited vocabulary of Kumina "African Country" or "Bongo" words, derived from Kikongo. In interviews, for example, Howellites used and provided accurate glosses for the words *malembe* (a greeting), *kento* (a woman), *Zambi* (God), *langu* (water), *kwenda* (to go), *matato* (earth), and a number of other words and stock expressions from the Kumina "Country" lexicon. One informant pointed out a connection between this language and a number of African tribes, which he referred to as Muyanji, Mumbaka, and Mumbundu; all of these are among the tribes most commonly cited by Kumina people as having contributed to their own tradition.[13]

Likewise, the drum-based music of the Tredegar Park Howellites (called "Kumina" or "Kumeka") evidences the Kumina heritage.[14] It does not make use of the akete drums—the three-part set derived from Buru—that have become standard in Nyahbinghi. Rather, it is still played, as it has been since the Pinnacle days, on the traditional Kumina drums, the bandu and the playing cyas, referred to as such by the Howellites. These drums, as in St. Thomas, are turned on their sides and mounted by the players. The

12. Tape recorded interview conducted by Elliot Leib, Tredegar Park, July 23, 1983.

13. See the "Kumina Lexicon" in Bilby and Fu-Kiau 1983, 65–97, 9–10. For a more detailed discussion of Kumina influence among the Howellites, treating other aspects as well as music, see Leib 1984.

14. In the African Country language of Kumina in St. Thomas, *Kumeka* (or *Kumeika*) is also used to refer to ceremonial music and dance; see Bilby and Fu-Kiau 1983, 76.

drumming itself is essentially the same as the St. Thomas variety, although slight modifications and an overall simplification can be heard in the style of some cyas players (the bandu pattern remaining unchanged), giving it what seems to be a distinctive St. Catherine flavor.

Many of the songs used by the Howellites in their present-day services and recreational performances are well-known Kumina songs that form an integral part of traditional cult ceremonies in St. Thomas. Among these are both "bailo" (recreational) and "Country" (sacred, African language) songs, some of which are specific to St. Thomas Kumina and not found elsewhere. A Kumina song sung by present-day Howellites that shows as much as any other connection with the St. Thomas religious tradition is "Kongo Man, Delay You Know de Law," recorded by one of the authors during a Howellite performance at Tredegar Park in 1983.[15] This is the same song cited by Ryman, who interprets it as an exhortation to participants in Kumina to heed the "Bongo law"—the Kumina canons for proper living (1984, 10). Other common Kumina songs recorded among the Howellites are "Tan to You War," "Tambu lele," "Nki balongo," "King Zambi," and "Malembe mbem, soso water."[16] In addition, the female leader among the present-day Howellites refers to herself as a "Kumina Queen," and is often invited to attend government-sponsored Kumina functions.[17]

Clearly, if it were culturally significant at that time, the Rastafari aversion to ancestral spirit possession or rituals having to do with death did not prevent the early Howellites from adopting and reinterpreting those elements of the Kumina tradition that appealed to them. In learning and passing on the Kongo language or Bongo language of Kumina as well as other aspects of the tradition, the Howellites had only to make the necessary

15. Tape made by Elliot Leib, July 1983.

16. All these songs are on a tape made in Tredegar Park by Elliot Leib, July 1983. For a version of "Nki balongo" from St. Thomas, in Kikongo/African Country and with an English translation, see Bilby and Fu-Kiau 1983, 55–59).

17. "Kumina Queen" is the title given to a female spiritual and organizational leader in traditional Kumina; one of her several important functions is the "raising of songs" or the invocation of ancestors. See Ryman 1980, 91–97.

ideological adjustments to bring this body of cultural knowledge into line with emerging Rastafari tenets and doctrines, as preached by Howell. The possessing spirits of Kumina, for example, seem to have been abolished, whereas the omnipotent deity of Kumina, Zambi, or Kinzambi became identified with Haile Selassie I, Jah Rastafari. (The Howellites continue to state that "King Zambi" and "His Imperial Majesty, Earth's Rightful Ruler" are identical.)[18] The Kumina dance-drumming tradition, with some modifications, was also allowed to make the transition from one religious form to the other. After the necessary reinterpretations it prevailed as the key drum-based liturgical music among the Howellites.[19]

In 1954, only a matter of months after Simpson made his observations and recordings in West Kingston, Pinnacle was broken up by the police. Howell's followers dispersed, and many of them headed for the city. Whether some of the Howellites brought Kumina drums of their own to the urban ghettos is unknown, but their mass exodus to Kingston coincided with and appears to have been directly related to the merging of Buru (or a hybridized form carrying this or other names) with Rastafari worship. Consequently, Nyahbinghi emerged as the leading Rastafari

18. Leonard Howell eventually proclaimed his own divinity, and now he also is identified by his remaining followers with both "King Zambi" and "His Imperial Majesty, Earth's Rightful Ruler." In his early manifesto, *The Promised Key*, an important literary document of early Rastafari theology, Howell admonishes "revivalists" against practices associated with Obeah (Howell 1997, 12). There is, however, no clear indication that the early Howellite church in any way linked the possession rituals of Kumina religion with the practice of Obeah. As indicated above, among traditional Rastafari of the Nyahbinghi Order, Obeah and spirit possession are both identified with death and the works of duppies and are therefore considered to be satanic.

19. In 1980, CBS News correspondent Dan Rather visited Leonard Howell and his congregation in St. Catherine, in the company of Jamaican journalist Arthur Kitchin. At this time, a CBS film crew shot footage of a ceremony held by Howell's followers in which traditional Kumina drums were used, played in the traditional manner (turned on their sides and mounted, with the heel of the foot used to change pitch). Some of this footage was incorporated in the CBS news program *60 Minutes* (vol. 13, no. 12, broadcast on Sunday, December 7, 1980); the segment in which it was included was entitled "The Rastafarians," Jeanne Solomon, producer. Howell died a few months after Rather's visit, in February 1981.

dance-drumming form (Smith, Nettleford, and Augier 1960, 11).[20] It seems more than probable that some of the Pinnacle Kumina drummers, recently displaced to West Kingston, were among those who helped to forge and embellish the nascent Nyahbinghi tradition being nurtured by their urban Rastafari brethren. Even before the mass migration to Kingston, throughout the Pinnacle period Kumina-steeped Howellite musicians were probably contributing to the West Kingston musical brew, because Howell's operations were not limited to his St. Catherine settlement. Frequent traffic between the rural commune and the capital ensured a flow of ideas, probably including musical ideas, back and forth.[21]

The precise weight of the Howellite contribution to the Nyahbinghi musical tradition has yet to be established. Further research, drawing on the recollections of some of the remaining musician elders, may eventually help to settle the question. It seems certain, in any case, that the Howellites and their brand of Kumina did play a part.

Conclusion

A major conclusion to be drawn from this brief study is that the origins of the Nyahbinghi drumming style cannot be traced back along a simple unilinear path. A careful search reveals an interconnecting web of influences

20. The influence of Kumina on the urban dance-drumming styles of Rastafari should also be related to the ganja trade associated with Pinnacle. Ganja grown at Pinnacle was marketed in Kingston and elsewhere, along with bread baked at the commune. The illegality of ganja subjected the early Rastafari to criminal prosecution and harsh penalties for its possession and use. The linkages between Buru, which was often performed on the occasion of a prisoner's release, and Kumina in Rastafari dance-drumming are best appreciated with this sociological background in mind.

21. It should be remembered that both the St. Catherine and Clarendon Buru traditions (which differ in several ways)—the best documented examples of Buru to date—are located in the same general area as the former site of Pinnacle. It is likely, therefore, that at least some contact occurred between the Howellites at Pinnacle and the Buru people at both Spring Village in St. Catherine and Lionel Town and Hayes in Clarendon. Rural Buru influences could have also been operating among the Kumina-playing Howellites at Pinnacle. This deserves to be researched further. See Nagashima 1980, 73–77.

spanning several parishes and decades, several strands of which have yet to be explored by researchers. Like most Jamaican folk musical traditions, the Nyahbinghi style must be seen as the product of a complex and gradual process of adaptation and blending of a variety of earlier Creole traditions. There remains no room for doubt that Kumina was among these.

This sort of ready borrowing between different traditions is still common in Jamaica. In 1974, for instance, one of us (Bilby) attended a Kumina ceremony on the urban fringe of Spanish Town, St. Catherine, in which a Nyahbinghi repeater drum (painted in the Rastafari colors red, gold, and green, and with a metal tuning apparatus) was used, turned on its side and mounted, in place of the traditional Kumina playing cyas. In fact, this penchant for blending is central to the vitality and creativity so evident in African Jamaican folk and popular music. Through such interchange, the invigorating rhythms of Kumina, meshed with those of Buru and perhaps others, have indirectly been able, via Nyahbinghi, to enter the Jamaican musical mainstream and travel throughout the world. Time and distance, in such cases, tend to obscure origins. As it turns out, the Rastafari insistence on the African roots of Nyahbinghi may be historically accurate in ways that even many Rastafari brethren themselves, not to mention others, do not realize.[22]

22. The original article contained a short acknowledgment section thanking George Eaton Simpson for providing essential data for the study and Marjorie Whylie of the Jamaica School of Music for providing information that helped to make the connection between Pinnacle and the Kumina tradition. The original article was expanded and updated from the liner notes to *From Kongo to Zion: Three Black Musical Traditions* (Heartbeat Records, 1983), written by Bilby and Leib.

From Wareika Hill to Zimbabwe

Exploring the Role of Rastafari in Popularizing Reggae Music

MICHAEL BARNETT

In exploring the role of the Rastafari movement in the popularization of Jamaican music, we first need to go back to the days of the emergence of ska, which is widely heralded as the first musical genre uniquely indigenous to Jamaica. There are several theories in regard to how ska was created. One of the theories holds that the world-famous producer Clement Dodd (Coxsone) called a meeting with two members of his backing band (the Blues Blasters) in 1959 (specifically Cluett Johnson, the bass player, and Ernie Ranglin, the guitarist). He told them that he wanted to change the sound of the then immensely popular American R&B, just slightly, to give it a more original sound. He wanted there to be an emphasized offbeat in the music that would serve to distinguish it from the run-of-the-mill R&B music of that period. So, the next day Ranglin and Johnson and other members of the Blues Blasters band went to the newly built JBC Studios in Half Way Tree to start experimenting and to get something new on wax. Cluett Johnson was on bass, Ernie Ranglin on guitar, Arkland (Drumbago) Parkes on drums, Theophilus Beckford on piano and vocals, and Rico Rodriguez on brass. The end result was "Easy Snappin'," which contained a distinct boogie bassline and is still widely considered the seminal ska tune because of the distinct offbeat sound given by the piano and guitar. The first recording of this song was used exclusively for the purpose of dub-plates to be played on Coxsone's Downbeat Sound System. That tune was so popular with the crowds, however, that Coxsone decided to re-record the track so that it could be released for commercial sales. Subsequently, "Easy Snappin'" was re-recorded at Federal Studios, with all of the same musicians, except for Ernie Ranglin (who was replaced by Ken Richards on guitar) and Arkland Parkes (who was replaced by Ian Pearson on drums).

This perspective on the origin of ska has been heavily advanced by Coxsone and his admirers, but it does not allow for another perspective, that of the likely influence of Roscoe Gordon, a popular African American R&B artist from Memphis. He had perfected the offbeat style (emphasis on the second and fourth beats of a bar instead of on the first and third beats) years before the recording of "Easy Snappin'" (Barnett 2007). Gordon's tune "No More Doggin'" (which came out in 1951) is a classic example of the offbeat style that he had perfected. When we consider also that Roscoe frequently performed in Kingston in the 1950s (because of the popularity of his music among Jamaicans), it is quite reasonable to assume that this musical style strongly influenced Coxsone, who then went on to create the musical arrangement for "Easy Snappin'."

Two more perspectives on the origin of ska involve the indomitable Prince Buster. When Buster (who used to work for Coxsone as his bodyguard), left Coxsone in early 1959 and branched out on his own, he was determined to mount a serious challenge to both of the major players in the music industry, Duke Reid and Coxsone. He craved a new sound that he could play on his sound system that would distinguish him from them. He wanted to go beyond the R&B boogie music that Coxsone and Reid greatly depended on at their dances (whether the records were recorded by Jamaican musicians or were the original American versions). Buster was inspired to seek out the veritable Count Ossie at Wareika Hill. He knew that the Rastafari sound carried the pulse of the Jamaican people, and he had proclaimed himself to be a man of the people, so it seemed like a natural progression to attempt to capture the raw undiluted African essence of Rastafari on wax. Prince Buster spent days grounding with Count Ossie at Wareika Hill trying to persuade him to do the record. He was finally able to convince him that such an endeavor would prove to be worthwhile. A few weeks after the recording of Coxsone's "Easy Snappin'" came the recording of the seminal Jamaican classic "Oh Carolina," a collaborative work that married the percussive contributions of Count Ossie and his Mystic Revelation of Rastafari with the vocals of the Folkes Brothers (ironically enough at the same JBC studios). "Oh Carolina" eventually became a huge commercial success, which was somewhat surprising at the time considering that it was so rootsy and so obviously far removed from the popular R&B sounds of that time. Not only did "Oh Carolina" have a distinctive African percussive underlayer, but it also had a strong offbeat, especially in the chords played by Prince Buster's pianist, Owen Gray, and the guitarist, Jerome Hines (Jah Jerry) which gave it a distinctive ska feel.[1]

Because the "Oh Carolina" track chops up the boogie bassline that is so clearly present in "Easy Snappin'," in addition to adopting a percussive feel that emphasizes the offbeat, a case can be made for the former being more authentically ska than the latter.

Prince Buster has long maintained that his attention to the percussive elements of his ska productions is what qualifies them as more distinctly ska than much of the earlier material that contains the offbeat (Bradley 2000a). In fact, in his personal account of the development of ska, Buster says that ska music became fully formed when he incorporated the marching band drum style into the music. After this, ska came into its own, so to speak. In Prince Buster's own words, "The belly of the Ska sound is the marching drum" (Bradley 2000a, 58). During his early sessions at Federal Studios, Buster recorded such ska tunes as "Little Honey," "Humpty Dumpty," "African Blood," and "Time Longer than Rope." The notable big hit among these was "Humpty Dumpty," by Monty Morris. Though this tune was actually recorded relatively late, at the end of 1960, Buster argues strongly that the records released before his productions were not ska, because they did not contain the important percussive element and did not depart significantly enough from the general R&B boogie that was still prevalent in those early years.

1. Notably, Chang and Chen (1998) write that Jah Jerry, the legendary Rastafari guitar player of the ska days, made sure to emphasize the afterbeat rather than the downbeat in the recording of the seminal "Oh Carolina" track.

This perspective unintentionally validates "Oh Carolina" as the truly seminal ska record (though Prince Buster may not have consciously realized this) in that the unique percussive rhythms that underlaid the track emphasized the ska feel provided by the piano and the guitar, more so than in "Easy Snappin'." In this respect, it may be argued that the Rastafari influence was present at a pivotal historical point in time: the dawn of ska music. In other words, Rastafari (and ultimately Rastafari music, that is, Nyahbinghi drumming) played a direct role in the birth of indigenous Jamaican popular music.

In response to those who might argue about "Oh Carolina" being placed squarely in the ska genre, what cannot be denied is that this song represented a more significant departure from the R&B material (both American and Jamaican) than any other record that preceded it, including Theophilus Beckford's "Easy Snappin'." With its strong African rhythms fused with Owen Gray's piano and Jah Jerry's guitar, this track was simply ahead of its time. It was not in any way trying to imitate the R&B boogie from New Orleans or any of the R&B material from any other part of the United States. It drew on the indigenous essence of the Jamaican Rastafari movement, fused with the innovative Jamaican musicianship of Owen Gray and Jah Jerry, and became the first record that would be a part of the legacy of indigenous Jamaican popular music (Chang and Chen 1998).

Whatever else is said about "Oh Carolina," it cannot be denied that it represents a significant notch in Jamaica's cultural history. It is probably the first instance of one of Jamaica's few surviving African-based art forms being unapologetically expressed through a mainstream medium. It also represents a bond between Rastafari and the Jamaican music industry that is still in place today, about which Lloyd Bradley (2000a, 61) so profoundly writes: "While Reggae gives Rasta access to the World Stage, Rasta's depth of spirituality means Reggae will always have something to say."

The Rastafari movement throughout its history in Jamaica had always been attractive to the Black working class and underclass (the "sufferahs"). That it was an integral part of the Jamaican popular music scene was arguably inevitable, because the core supporters of Jamaican popular music have always been the ghetto communities and the sufferahs. Though it was not until 1959 that this happened, despite the relatively large Rastafari communities residing in Kingston during the 1950s, indicates how marginalized Rastafari were at the time. They were considered to be the dregs of the society, the underclass's underclass, Jamaica's social outcasts, and as such were not readily engaged by the movers and shakers of Jamaica's music fraternity. When "Oh Carolina" proved to be a spectacular hit, Rastafari and Jamaican popular music became inextricably intertwined. Despite the strongest efforts of the top record producers and top players in the Jamaican recording industry to ignore Rastafari and its message, the philosophy and ethos of the movement diffused among the industry's key musicians and artists so that its sentiments were expressed lyrically, if not musically. In fact, the not-so-well-known proto-roots tune "Ghana Independence," sung by Laurel Aitken and recorded in 1957 to mark Ghana's independence, carried a distinct African percussive underlayer that was arguably inspired by both the drumming and the African consciousness of the Rastafari movement. The classic tune "Freedom," which was sung by Clancy Eccles and produced by Coxsone in late 1959, spoke of freedom from the shackles of colonialism and was clearly Rastafari inspired. There was "The Lion of Judah" by Delroy Wilson, recorded in 1963, as well as the smash ska hit of 1964, "Carry Go Bring Come" by the Rastafari group Justin Hinds and the Dominoes. We must mention also the classic ska tune "Beardman Ska" by the Skatalites. (Rastafari were known as beardmen in those days.) There was "The Whip" by the Ethiopians and "Another Moses" by the Mellowcats, which also featured the Rastafari drumming of Count Ossie (Bradley 2000a; Barrow and Dalton 2004).

Although the notable ska groups Justin Hinds and the Dominoes and the Ethiopians are widely considered to be Rastafari inspired, if not Rastafari, little has been said about the Rastafari orientation of Jamaica's most famous ska band, the Skatalites (especially of the centerman of the band, Don Drummond). This group was extremely central to the ska age, backing such singing stars as Delroy Wilson, the Maytals, Stranger Cole, and the Wailers. They also produced monumental instrumental hits of their own, such as "Guns of Navarone."

Unfortunately, the group had a relatively short life span, formally being established in June 1964 and then dispersing toward the end of 1965.

The Skatalites consisted loosely of Lloyd Knibbs on drums, Lloyd Brevett on double bass, Jackie Mittoo on piano, and Ernest Ranglin, Jerome "Jah Jerry" Hines and Harold McKenzie on guitar. On saxophones were Tommy McCook, Roland Alphonso, and Lester Sterling. On brass were Johnny "Dizzy" Moore and Oswald "Baba" Brooks (trumpet) and Don Drummond (trombone). The band also featured top quality singers such as Lord Tanamo, Tony DaCosta, and Jackie Opel (Barrow and Dalton 2004). With their brilliant musicianship, they not only recorded some of Jamaica's best ska tunes ever but also made a sterling contribution to the development of Jamaican jazz. The band strengthened the bond between Rastafari and Jamaican popular music by recording Rastafari-themed tracks such as "Beardman Ska" and "Addis Ababa" and backing and supporting notable Rastafari vocalists, such as Vernon Allen and Bongo Man, who otherwise probably would not have gotten a chance to record. Vernon Allen recorded the seminal Rastafari tunes "Far I Come" and "Babylon" in late 1964 with the Skatalites. Bongo Man recorded "Where Is Garvey" a few weeks later, which appeared on the flip side of the Skatalite hit tune, "Guns of Navarone," the best-selling ska record of all time.

As Jamaican music moved toward the rocksteady era, Peter Tosh of the Wailers recorded "Rasta Shook Them Up." This track was done to commemorate Haile Selassie's visit to Jamaica in 1966, and it marks the Wailers' transition to Rastafari. As the music became firmly entrenched in the rocksteady period, Bob Andy recorded "I've Got to Go Back Home," a track that is essentially about repatriation to Africa.

During the 1960s, Rastafari was always present in the flanks of Jamaican popular music, from the dawn of the ska era, to rocksteady, right through to the dawn of the reggae era, but not as visibly and overtly as during the 1970s. During the 1960s, Rastafari covertly moved within the music circles, fostered by the ghetto musicians who were all either of the faith or sympathetic to it. Many Rastafari lived in Back-a-Wall (until July 1966), which was an area of Kingston in which many of Jamaica's key musicians and session players used to hang out or reside themselves. The two groups intermingled organically, reasoning and sharing their struggles of ghetto life. Even Duke Reid of Treasure Isle Studio fame, who is well documented as disliking Rasta and all their accouterments (Bradley 2000a), ended up exhaustively utilizing the undeniable talents of Justin Hinds and the Dominoes. In contrast to Reid's studio, however, Coxsone's Studio One was a haven for Rastafari in those early oppressive days of the 1960s. A whole host of Rastafari musicians and artists such as the Skatalites, Toots and the Maytals, Count Ossie and his Mystic Revelation of Rastafari, and Vernon Allen recorded there.

The relative invisibility of Rastafari adherents during the 1960s, as compared to the 1970s, can also be attributed to the lack of popularity of the dreadlocks among Rastafari at the time. Dreadlocks became widely entrenched in the movement during the late 1960s to the early 1970s. By the late 1960s the recording studios were full of young artists sprouting dreadlocks (Chang and Chen 1998).

By the 1970s, Rastafari had effectively taken control of the reggae scene, transforming it lyrically, melodically, and instrumentally to the point that it became a medium of spiritual upliftment and Black consciousness. Many of Jamaica's top reggae artists were not only incorporating Rastafari themes into their songs but were openly and visibly embracing the faith (Bradley 2000a). Artists such as Alton Ellis, Bob Andy, Winston Rodney, Horace Andy, Johnny Clarke, and Jimmy Cliff notably adopted Rastafari in the early 1970s. Key Rastafari groups that epitomize the 1970s include the Mighty Diamonds, Culture, Third World, Inner Circle, the Royal Rasses, the Wailing Souls, the Meditations, the Congoes, the Itals, Sly and Robbie (who were in Peter Tosh's Word, Sound and Power band and Black Uhuru), and Bob Marley's reformulated Wailers group, complete with the I Threes (Reckord 1998). Across the Atlantic in England, two of the best-known reggae bands to date, the Rastafari bands Aswad and Steel Pulse, emerged in the 1970s.

Another key factor in the extensive domination and influence of Rastafari on the reggae scene in the 1970s was the emergence of the Twelve Tribes of Israel Mansion. (This mansion of Rastafari was founded by Vernon Carrington [Prophet Gad] in 1968.) The Twelve Tribes of Israel Mansion embraced reggae music wholeheartedly as an intrinsic part of the Rastafari life and committed themselves to a once-monthly ritualistic reggae dance. Rastafari players, singers, musicians, and artists were attracted to this mansion, which nurtured and actively encouraged budding musicians and singers in their artistry. In contrast to the other Rastafari mansions, this mansion became a virtual reggae factory, shaping and molding new reggae artists for the reggae industry. Notable Twelve Tribe Rastafari artists were Bob Marley, Dennis Brown, Freddie McGregor, Rita Marley, Judy Mowatt, Fred Locks, and the band Israel Vibration. The 1970s clearly marked the height of the Rastafari presence within the reggae music industry.

By the end of the 1970s, the soon-to-be most famous Jamaican of all time, Bob Marley, had truly arrived. He was extended a most honorable invitation by the president of the then newly independent Zimbabwe (Rhodesia) to be the headline act in the nation's independence celebrations. Marley accepted the invitation, which proved to be a defining point in the historical trajectory of the symbiotic relationship between Rastafari and reggae. Marley's widely publicized performance in Zimbabwe not only resulted in the increased performances of Rastafari reggae artists in Africa but also resulted in the firm establishment of a Rastafari consciousness among continental Africans, especially in West and South Africa. The evidence of this was in the emergence of home-grown African artists such as Alpha Blondy, from West Africa, and Lucky Dube, from South Africa, in the 1980s.

Ironically, however, in Jamaica, the birthplace of reggae, things took a turn for the worse as the 1980s progressed. Hard new drugs slowly and insidiously usurped the peaceful Rastafari musical era, changing the feel of what had been largely message-oriented music.[2] The 1990s, thankfully, saw a resurgence of Rastafari influence, this time under the guise of the Bobo Shanti Mansion, with such artists as Sizzla, Capleton, and Anthony B. Even in today's hip-hop hybrid dancehall culture, Rastafari is still a source of inspiration and influence, albeit to a much more limited extent than that which existed in the 1970s.

2. Kingston experienced a large influx of cocaine during the 1980s, contributing not only to an increase in violent crime but also a change in the kind of reggae music that was being produced.

A Focus on Sizzla Kalonji

A Leading Influence on a New Generation of Rastafari Youth

ALLAN BERNARD

We seek to explore the relationship between the dancehall and Rastafari by analyzing the music and deeds of dancehall's leading Rastafari chanter, Sizzla Kalonji. Dramatic changes have occurred in his music, and there has been a proliferation of interest in his lifestyle and actions. However, the questions we raise, the way we define Rastafari and the dancehall, and the information we seek are often seen as taboo and sensitive. Many scholars prefer to either not engage in such debates or to only interact with those who share views on these issues rather than with those who might challenge them.

This chapter proposes that we move away from this myopic approach if we are to better understand attempts at repositioning Rastafari in this dispensation and in the musical genius of Sizzla. This discourse does not attempt to justify the actions and deeds of the artist, but we use his music as a point of departure to better understand and appreciate the current trajectory of Rastafari, dancehall, and the global realities of popular culture.

Part of my intent in writing about Sizzla and Rastafari[1] is to develop a dialogue with colleagues (friends, academics, commentators, and Rastas)

1. This essay forms part of what was initially a love for and interest in Sizzla's music that became a study and research focus in 2002 at the Culture 2 Conference at University of

and those who are either fans or sympathizers of the artist, the space, or the movement. For the most part, these groups share diametrically opposing views for one reason or another. I adopted a dialectical format for the analysis in this chapter so that readers are aware of the varying views associated with Rastafari, dancehall culture, and Sizzla himself.

Dancehall's Cultural Renaissance

A sudden upsurge of interest in "the dancehall" has occurred in different spheres of academia in the past decade. Whether as an object of investigation or as something invoked to explain a particular behavior or interest, dancehall as an autonomous space[2] or an institution has been highlighted in an extraordinary outpouring of studies by scholars of diverse theoretical proclivities from all the major disciplines. The range of topics explored has

---

the West Indies (UWI), Mona. I presented a paper entitled "Love, Life and Revolution: Sizzla Kalonji Giving It to Dem." Although the paper was far from academic, it drew criticism and interest from academics and practitioners that took the form of guidance and encouragement and broadened my focus. I went from simply liking the artist and the music to exploring in more fundamental ways the artist's impact on the space called dancehall and vice versa. A further broadening of my focus came in 2003 at the Global Rastafari Reasoning in Jamaica, where I was invited to be a part of a panel captioned "Rastafari Upholding an Ancient Order in a Modern World." It was after this gathering of Rastafari that I recognized the continuities and varying tendencies that were either unresolved or treated with benign neglect in the Rastafari quest to reposition itself in the twenty-first century. They were confronted by Sizzla in his own path as the premier Rastafari chanter in the dancehall space. Subsequently, in 2005 at the Second Annual Graduate Students Conference at UWI, Mona, I gave a paper entitled "Rastafari Upholding an Ancient Order in a Modern World: A Study of Sizzla's Music," outlining some thoughts on Sizzla, Rasta, and dancehall as the most potent popular cultural space.

2. Dancehall as a distinct genre of Jamaican popular music took shape in the early 1980s. It was ushered in by the Youthman Promotion Movement (1983) and consolidated by innovations in computerized sounds that began in the 1980s. The space has evolved into what is now Jamaica's most potent popular cultural space, lending itself to various musical forms globally. However, dancehall is yet to take its place as the continuation of Jamaica's illustrious musical tradition—from ska to rocksteady to reggae—and is still viewed by many as a vulgarization of reggae music.

been wide and, for the most part, descriptive. Cultural studies, anthropology, sociology, and sympathetic disciplines in the field of humanities seem to be leading the charge in this area of scholarship. I believe that this chapter, though, may be the first serious ethnographic study of any dancehall artist. Dancehall culture and dancehall artists have been considered anecdotes to the more popular study of reggae history (Stanley-Niaah 2004). By the same token, Rastafari has been seen as an important antecedent to Jamaican popular music, and much has been done by way of structured studies to highlight and explore the work of major Rastafari reggae musicians. However, meaningful work on Rastafari in popular culture has yet to transcend the reggae barrier, and many view the sounds of Rastafari in dancehall with disdain and impugn its legitimacy. It is interesting to note that Rastafari suffered a similar fate in the early years of reggae music (Scott 1997).

Almost all the studies on dancehall were based on observations, case studies, and participant observations. This is true of my own study, which I called "the cultural Renaissance," and which was developed through self-analysis and participant observation studies. My initial observations were conducted during the crowded, mediocrity-prone fray of misogynistic, money-driven, and thug-centered dancehall music of the late 1980s to mid-1990s in the inner-city communities of urban Jamaica (Boyne 2002). The music needed a savior and found one in the unmistakably soothing and inspirational sounds of the Rastafari singer Garnet Silk. Garnet started a wave of transformation in the dancehall that was unprecedented for his time. While accredited for being the pioneer of this movement, Garnet was still unable to impact that youthful cadre of dancehall acts that was vital to its sustainability. This cultural renaissance found its greatest convert and messenger in a most unlikely source: a hardcore "badman" artist called Panhead.[3] Panhead was a young and upcoming artist who did not have a string of hits under his belt but was sharp and lyrical. Panhead's youthfulness and reputation as a serious artist enabled him to impart the message

3. Panhead's only two mainstream dancehall hits were "Respect to All Gunman" and "African Princess," the latter now a signature dancehall classic. These songs also reflected his transformation.

of culture and Rastafari to the youth better than any other artist could at the time. His own transformation served as a beacon that others followed; he not only talked the talk but also walked the walk. His untimely and tragic death marked the watershed moment of this transformation period in which many young dancehall artists took up the cultural and Rastafari banner. Capleton and Buju Banton stood out as the forerunners during this transformation period. This was also the context in which Sizzla emerged and the tradition that he came to embrace, a tradition characterized by a cultural explosion in dancehall music, informed and directed by Rastafari.

Love, Life, and Revolution: Sizzla Give It to Dem

Sizzla's entry into the dancehall saw him quickly extending hegemony over its cultural dimensions, surpassing others who were before him and who were heirs apparent in this regard. As a lyricist, Sizzla's music is tripartite: constantly loving the Black woman, always defending the ghetto youths, and giving Rastafari praise. Sizzla came to embody the aspirations, wishes, and desires of young people from the downtrodden majority who were alienated socially, economically, and politically. This demographic also represents the core participants in the dancehall space (Stolzoff 2000; Stewart 2002).

Of a mature and confident disposition, Sizzla is highly motivated and enthusiastic, with a strong sense of self and an adaptive orientation. Both his willingness to learn and his awareness of his own existential realities positioned him to add value to the dancehall space and meet the challenges associated with contemporary Jamaican realities.

Sizzla impressed audiences and critics alike with his high musical standards, prowess, and creativity as a young dancehall artist. From the outset, he announced himself not simply as a premier artist but as a student of Rastafari with a strong inquiring mind. He further differentiated himself from most of his peers by the consistency and developmental quality of his lyrics, which were underlined by critical thinking, clear analysis, and conceptual depth. In his high-performing dancehall act he demonstrates familiarity with a wide range of relevant political and social issues and a maturing Rastafari competence. He has an ability to distill complex material and arrive at sound practical positions in articulating and representing the voices of the poor and dispossessed. He is equally good at criticizing the current conditions within society, insightfully referencing his arguments to the context of modern-day realities. Altogether, he shows versatility and depth, even in his music's present developmental mode.

The clues to Sizzla's appeal may be found not only in the status derived from his musical achievements but in his personal conduct, his ability to connect through song with the plight and sensibilities of Jamaica's inner-city life, and his articulateness as a new voice of Rastafari. These gifts, when assessed closely, would, however, evolve into some of the most glaring contradictions in the artist, his music, and his appreciation of Rastafari. Any assessment of Sizzla must grapple with the overall complexities of dancehall culture and Rastafari for positive and meaningful dialogue, because he has come to represent both.

Commentators who engaged in the various debates on the trajectory of Sizzla's music and his representation of Rastafari have offered little by way of analysis and insight. Indeed, the puritan criticisms of Sizzla are seen as an indictment of Rastafari for participating in such a secular space (dancehall). Current work, however, increasingly views dancehall as an autonomous space that, although obviously influenced by the society surrounding it, also shapes social and political processes in a significant way. There is a recognized need, therefore, to improve conceptualizations of the structures and capabilities of the dancehall and to explain more adequately how the dancehall is utilized and reorganized. In addition, how dancehall affects communities through their interventions—or abstentions—and through its relationships with other key institutions within society needs to be explored. Rastafari, being one such institution, would find it necessary to participate in this space.

One must not forget that Sizzla entered the dancehall not as a Rastafari chanter but as a youth with a "consciousness" message. His debut album, *Burning Up,*[4] was first a social commentary rather than an attempt at prais-

4. On his debut album (1995) Sizzla shows he is one of the best new DJs on the scene. The riddims and delivery are pure dancehall, but the message is far from the slackness and

ing Jah. Further, it must be noted that Sizzla's influences prior to getting into the music business were not the Rastafari icons of the reggae genre but the hardcore dancehall sounds of Shabba Ranks and (pre-Rastafari) Buju Banton. Therefore, it was Rastafari's involvement in the dancehall space that was to give him the guidance to persevere and impact more meaningfully, as evidenced in his follow-up Rastafari-influenced albums of 1997, *Black Woman and Child* and *Praise Ye Jah.*[5]

Sizzla Kalonji: Da Real Thing

By 2002, despite his numerous albums[6] consciously influenced by Rastafari and his positive impact on the music (and its seemingly refreshing cultural and positive turn), Sizzla had yet to yield a number one song on any of the various dancehall or musical listings. Further, the *context* in which he now operated was altered significantly as the cultural consciousness paradigm emanating from a charged sociopolitical and socioeconomic atmosphere gave way to a more relaxed and carefree environment, wherein entertainment as opposed to social commentary was the order of the day (Gutzmore 2002).

This entertainment was characterized by the two most controversial themes in dancehall music, which are broadly defined as slackness and gun lyrics (Pereira 2002). Sizzla's music shifted to reflect these concomitant changes in the times and the space. His lyrics took on a pure entertainment outlook by utilizing language and themes that did not epitomize his earlier

---

gun lyrics of dancehall's early days. Sizzla uses the form to empower the content of songs like "Gun Ting Don't Pay" and "Nah Give In." This album is another indication of the return of the conscious lyrics in the dancehall.

5. Both *Black Woman and Child* and *Praise Ye Jah* signaled Sizzla's arrival as not only a force to be reckoned with in the dancehall, but as a legitimate Rastafari chanter leading the cultural renaissance in the music. The title tracks on both albums were to become dancehall classics.

6. These included but were not limited to: *Freedom Cry* (1998), *Good Ways* (1998), *Be I Strong* (1998), *Royal Son of Ethiopia* (1999), *Bobo Ashanti* (2000), *Words of Truth* (2000), *Black History* (2001), *Rastafari Teach I Everything* (2001), and *Taking Over* (2001).

Rastafari chants. Gun lyrics and girl lyrics came to occupy a significant portion of his musical catalogue. In many quarters he was referred to as the "slack Rasta DJ" or the "gunman Rasta DJ." His actions and deeds outside the dancehall space did not fare any better, and he remains under suspicion, from both the security forces and the wider society, for gun- and gang-related violence. This expectation was explained, in part, by the romanticism associated with dancehall in which elements of traditional identity (culture) are cast in positive terms and things new (entertainment) are seen in an overwhelmingly pejorative light.

Nonetheless, my current thinking about dancehall and dancehall culture has been altered significantly. Perhaps culture was not typical of consciousness, nor was entertainment the province of slackness. Yet, who could doubt that those who support consciousness were radically different from those who support slackness-dominated dancehall? Given the possibility that the dimensions of consciousness and slackness were more often normal and spawned from the experiences of people they represent, perhaps not everything thought about this genre requires change (Cooper 2000, 2004). It is against this background that I attempt to understand the evolution and growth of Sizzla and his music.

People had all but given up on Sizzla as the savior for dancehall until 2002, when his album *Da Real Thing* was released. The content was solid and the vibe was a return to the Sizzla of old: love for women, defending ghetto youth, and giving Rastafari praise. *Da Real Thing* gave Sizzla two number one hits, with eight of the thirteen tracks receiving airplay. Many began to rationalize his "uncharacteristic" songs and actions as a phase, welcoming him back as the leader of the cultural movement in dancehall once more. However, Sizzla did not see himself as "the" ray of hope, but maybe "a" ray of hope. He continued to reflect themes of slackness and gun lyrics in his songs, against the wishes of his proponents. He had, nonetheless, silenced many of his critics while continuing to push the boundaries of Rastafari by challenging traditionally accepted standards of morality in the movement and the dancehall.

He quickly followed up *Da Real Thing* with *Light of My World* (2003), *Rise to the Occasion* (2003), and *Jah Knows Best* (2004); all of which subscribed to his traditional thematic focus as a Rastafari chanter. However, as a hardcore dancehall entertainer, his arsenal of gun and girl lyrics simultaneously grew exponentially. In 2005, his *Soul Deep* album and his signing with Damon Dash Records signaled that he was willing to enter the world of musical hybridization (crossover). This move was controversial because many still believe that this was the quintessential sign of selling out, losing focus, and betraying one's roots. The fact that he was branded and accepted as a Rasta chanter made this criticism all the more vociferous.

Sizzla, Dancehall, and Rastafari

The subject matter of dancehall, like all other cultural spaces, is located in more than one dimension and owes its origin and development to an interaction with other institutions within the society. Yet, it has its own agenda as an autonomous space and a need to resist the fashions and trends of the moment and the pressures of power in order to look with detachment at its own objectives. This enduring concern of dancehall, as evidenced by the usual range of discussions offered, has two distinct aspects. One is broadly descriptive: slackness versus culture debate. The other is analytical: the question of dancehall's position in popular culture, the obligation of dancehall to its origins, dancehall as a political tool, and the future of dancehall as part of our culture of resistance.

If we are to define slackness as lewd and obscene lyrics, then many of Sizzla's songs certainly fall into that category. But for Sizzla, this is a mere reflection on intimacy and companionship.[7] However, this position is weak given the wholesale acceptance and legitimization of the definition by Rastafari at large. Such lyrical content was always viewed as condoning the immoral activities of Babylon, a system that Rastafari vowed to not be a part of.

A comparative approach to understanding Rastafari's position on lewd and obscene lyrics will bring into sharp focus the issue of time, space, and language. Bob Marley's "rub up on me belly like a guava jelly" and "push

7. Professor Carolyn Cooper revealed this position taken by Sizzla from an informal interview she conducted with him at Judgement Yard, August Town (2002).

hood a fire" could certainly be considered lewd and obscene. The same is also true for gun lyrics. Peter Tosh, in this regard, is seen as revolutionary but Sizzla is seen as promoting violence and glorifying badness. The difference is in the language and the context in which the language is viewed. More importantly, Bob Marley and Peter Tosh operated in a time when socially conscious and revolutionary music took precedence over all other material; hence, not much focus, and by extension criticism, was leveled at songs that fell outside of such purview. Today, the context is different; with the emphasis now on the entertainment value of the space, such content is not only in the forefront but under constant scrutiny.

From a systemic point of view, it is essential to note that Rastafari, by its own actions or deeds, has never placed itself on a pedestal as the flag bearer of righteousness and all things moral in the sight of God and man. In fact, Rastafari's ascendance to this illustrious position is due primarily to persons outside the movement and their yearning for a symbol of moral authority where church and state have often proven unworthy. Subsequently, an unwritten pact established Rastafari as the gatekeepers of righteousness. It is not difficult to see why, for Sizzla and Rastafari, they are more likely to be judged for their breaches of the pact than for their adherences.

On the flip side of that same token, it should not be assumed that persons outside the Rastafari movement see Rasta as without faults or larger than life. The above compromise was clearly symbolic but held in the highest esteem. The pact remained intact if it was not visibly violated, even if the invisible was in violation of expected standards and guidelines. Sizzla's meddling in the secular dancehall space heralds a breach of this existing pact and compromise between Rastafari and the wider society. He committed what is viewed as a cardinal sin in this regard: making visible the invisible (Stewart 2002).

Although Sizzla's actions might have burst the bubble of many non-Rastafari observers, they had a somewhat inverse effect on many Rastafari, particularly those youth who grew up in the 1980s and 1990s. Here again the space, time, and language would determine how one appreciates Rastafari. For these young warriors, Sizzla captured the essence of their reality and the influences under which they came. Sizzla's explicit and sexually charged lyrics portrayed, for the first time in popular culture, Rastafari as a sexual being, which served as a liberating force for many in the movement. Ironically, I overheard an elder Rastafari responding to the demonization of the controversial "Pump Up Her Pum Pum" who rhetorically asked, "How will the Black woman get the child if you do not pump up her pum pum?" The issue of sex and sexuality draws only silence from the Rastafari community, with the curious constantly engaging in a dialogue of the deaf.

Herein lies the dilemma that has not been squarely addressed by the Rastafari community. Does a significant generational gap now exist between the older Rastaman and woman and the Rastafari youth? Is there a significant difference between how the older Rastafari orient and carry themselves in comparison to the Rastafari youth?

Needless to say, Sizzla's popularity among the hardcore dancehall audience did not wane but was in fact significantly bolstered, as "Pump Up Her Pum Pum" quickly became a huge dancehall anthem for the girls and rudeboys alike. Is this something that we should be proud of? Well, obviously no, but for many Rastafari youth (and we should remember that Sizzla is primarily a voice for the youth), Sizzla has been a sexually liberating force, a voice that says it is ok to be both Rasta and sexual.

There are also epistemological and ontological questions to be addressed. How did Sizzla move from Rastafari chanter to hardcore dancehall entertainer? What compelled him to change his tune from "Black Woman and Child" to "Pump Up Her Pum Pum" or from "Praise Ye Jah" to "Big Long Guns"? The issue here is change and how we operationalize it. No one can question his genius as a musician or his commitment to Rastafari, and so it becomes difficult to say that he has changed and his music is no longer potent, a myth he has dispelled time and time again, in my opinion.

The better view is to see him as a Rastafari youth who participated in a cultural reality of his own making, and in doing so, he maintained a particular appreciation of Rastafari that suits such a reality. After all, this is a young man who led the Rastafari charge from the tender age of nineteen. Unlike his contemporaries, he did not undergo that exuberant youthful rite of passage. Others, however, have chosen only to recognize or ascribe to him those songs in his arsenal that they think are appropriate while denying the ones they consider anomalies. While this approach will work at the level of the personal, it holds little by way of sustainability. Sizzla is not singing from two sides of his mouth, and it is erroneous for anyone to say that about him to justify their own disgust with his choices. What these songs represent are different facets of the artist; to deny him this reality could be harmful for his fans and the Rastafari movement alike.

The older heads in the Rastafari movement need to take stock of the fact that Sizzla is speaking to the reality of the Rastafari youth and is genuinely connecting with them at a level to which they can relate. A bridge between the generations can be made, but only if efforts toward increased dialogue between InI are significantly increased.

Part 7 Political Dimensions of the Rastafari Movement

16

Reluctant Candidates?

Rastafarians and Partisan Politics in Jamaica and Elsewhere

ANITA M. WATERS

Virtually every scholar of Rastafari has noted the movement's deep distrust of "politricks" (Edmonds 2003, 49; West-Duran 2003, 122; Barrett 1977a; Chevannes 1994; Marshall 2006, 66; Kebede, Shriver, and Knottnerus 2000). Electoral politics are seen by Rastas, according to Ennis Edmonds, as "the art of deception, machination and manipulation" and "the unending scheme of the powerful to maintain their position of privilege and to keep the populace in its place" (2003, 49). In the 1960s and 1970s, the use of Rastafarian symbols by politicians was unexpected because Rastafarians professed publicly to be at least uninterested in and more often hostile to partisan politics. For some Rastas, engagement in "statical" matters only would make sense after repatriation to Ethiopia; whereas, in Jamaica they saw themselves as sojourning strangers in a strange land. Some Rastas explain their reluctance to vote by the fact that voters are forced to make the mark "X," which indicates something wrong or negative (Symonette 2007).

While politicians in the 1960s and 1970s could pepper their discourse with Rasta phrases, closer association with the movement would not have garnered support among the masses of voters. State suppression and popular disdain of Rastas is well documented in the case of Jamaica. This was certainly true in other parts of the Caribbean as well. An editorial in the *Trinidad Guardian* named Rastas as "the most unloved group of persons in our midst" and "a particular menace to society" (van Dijk 1998, 191–92). Antigua banned Rastas from immigrating to the island, blaming them for "acts of terrorism," and even suppressed information about Rastafari by forbidding Father Joseph Owens, a pioneering scholar of the movement, from lecturing there in 1978. Legislation outlawing Rastafari in Dominica included a virtual license to kill people exhibiting Rasta symbols and modes of dress (van Dijk 1998, 186).

Despite the fact that participation in electoral politics has not been part of what Charles Tilly (1995, 42) calls the "repertoire of contention" among Rastas, the political impact of the movement has been considerable. A. E. Gordon Buffonge argues that Rasta has posed the most consistent and persistent challenge to the Jamaican state, and it has had real political consequences (2001, 3). Jahlani Niaah argues that Rasta philosophy offers an "archive of resistance praxis" aimed toward "hegemonic dissolution" (2008, 124). Columnist Cedric Wilson (2005) argues that Rastafari was responsible for bringing issues to the fore that "created the mood, the rethinking of the socio-economic model of the 1960s and 70s."

The tenet of isolation from partisan politics needs to be reexamined for three reasons.

First, the movement's place in the larger civil society of Jamaica has changed in the past two decades or so. The movement has been "routinized," to use Ennis Edmonds' (2003) characterization. Rasta images have been appropriated by mainstream institutions of bourgeois government and capitalist economy.

Second, other seemingly definitive tenets of Rastafari are giving way to new formations. Rather than retreating from the mainstream economy as in the past,[1] there is evidence of Rasta's embrace of consumer culture, especially Internet technology (Marshall 2006, 64). Young working-class people in Jamaica today combine aspects of Rasta culture with "discourses regarding consumerism and individualism . . . associated with neoliberal capitalism" (Thomas 2004, 14).

1. Some Rasta groups are still characterized by withdrawal from the cash economy. Blackstone (2006) describes such a group in England.

Third, disunity and differentiation have always been endemic to the movement, so discontinuities in its forms of participation should be expected. Marshall writes that Rastafari has an "individualist orientation" that "resists institutions" creating "a degree of heterodoxy among Rastafarians" (Marshall 2006).

The disagreement between different factions is illustrated by their position on monarchy. In March 2008, when Prince Charles and his wife visited Jamaica, Rastas were on both sides of a political divide; while some participated in a drumming session with the prince, others picketed outside. In 2002, when Queen Elizabeth visited, some Rastafarians demonstrated against her presence. Brother Leroy Lindsay of the Imperial Ethiopian World Federation wrote to the *Gleaner* that Rastas should not protest the queen but instead should appeal to her to help in the restoration of the Ethiopian monarchy (Lindsay 2002).

Successes in Caribbean Elections

Early successes of Rastafarians occurred outside of Jamaica. The first to enjoy success in the electoral arena was Enerva Trotman in Guyana, a "dreadlocked Rastafarian of ten years' standing" who won a seat in 1986 for the ruling People's National Congress (van Dijk 1998, 192). In 2002, Trinidad elected a Rastafarian, Fitzgerald Hinds, to parliament as a member of the ruling People's National Movement. One of his first acts as an MP was the official welcome to Crown Prince Zerah Yacob Asfa Wossen, the grandson of Haile Selassie, who visited Port of Spain in November 2002. In 2007, the *Bahama Journal* noted whole communities of Rastafarians were registering to vote for the first time during the week before the general elections in February of that year (Symonette 2007). There seemed to be unanimity among Rasta leaders in the Bahamas that the time had come to influence the electoral process, not only by voting but by seeking Rastafarian parliamentary candidates in the near future.

Another success is Terrence Nelson, an elected local senator from St. Croix in the US Virgin Islands, with whom I spoke at the end of 2008. He said he did not originally have the ambition to go into politics, but after his college education in North Carolina he returned to St. Croix to teach.

He became a member of the American Federation of Teachers, and then a shop steward. "I noticed certain dysfunctions in government, breakdowns in government operations. People were seeking relief through me as their shop steward. People made demands on me and I saw that the problems with government stemmed from lack of proper accounting, not from a lack of funding." He felt that as an elected official, "I could give people assistance on a broader scale." In 2004, he ran in a contest in which the seven candidates with the most votes are elected. He was the fourth. In 2006, he was the candidate with the most votes. He has enjoyed continued success and is now in his fourth term as senator. Senator Nelson expressed surprise that no Rasta is in political leadership in Jamaica. Interestingly, he attributes his own success in St. Croix to the more liberal politics of the United States, especially the antidiscrimination laws.

He felt resistance as a Rasta from some of his political colleagues, but believes that they are becoming more accepting. "But now people realize that I'm a statesman, I'm educated; they feel a sense of trust. They know that Rastas follow righteous principles." The Rasta community also expressed disagreement with his running for office. When criticized, he asks "Why have other people making decisions for you? I tell them look at Haile Selassie—he was the king of a nation."

Senator Nelson said that people from all over the world go to Jamaica to learn about Rasta culture. His view of Rasta is inclusive: "Rasta is not only black, it's humanity, close to nation, communion, I love God's spirit in all people." It is compatible with Christianity, in Senator Nelson's view, because it grew out of the Ethiopian Coptic tradition, which he said is the oldest form of Christianity. He has a sense that as a Rastafarian, he is representing people in the Virgin Islands who were previously without a voice in government, and he said just this in his inaugural speech after he was sworn in.

Rastafari and Jamaican Electoral Politics

In Jamaica, the earliest example of deviation from the hard and fast rule that Rastas do not get involved in partisan politics was of course Ras Sam Brown, who ran for the Western Kingston seat in Jamaica's parliament in 1962. He won few votes but drew attention to the movement and articulated a manifesto of "Twenty-One Points" (Barrett 1977a, 148). He built a Rastafarian-based political party in the community of Back-a-Wall, which motivated the Jamaica Labour Party (JLP) government to destroy that neighborhood in 1966, effectively crippling Ras Sam Brown's political future (Moyston 2001). While he was clearly in the vanguard of cultural politics, he never had widespread voter support. One Rasta said this about him:

> He was a real original. He ran as an independent. People didn't want to have anything to do with him. I saw him on his campaign. He wore a dashiki; he was into a Pan-African thing, and that was the first time I ever saw a dashiki. I didn't know what it was called. Usually when a candidate was campaigning, everybody rushes up to shake their hand, even people from the other side. But nobody was much interested in Sam Brown. He lost badly, but he wrote some beautiful poetry. (qtd. in Waters 1999 [1985], 49)

The first Rastafarian legislator in Jamaica was not elected but instead appointed to the senate as an independent in 1984 after the People's National Party (PNP) boycotted the 1983 elections. Barbara Blake-Hannah, daughter of a well-known activist and journalist, was one of those who had been inspired by, and then disillusioned about, Michael Manley's leadership. She served one term in the senate and worked for the JLP government in the Office of the Minister of Culture.

The 1990s saw more concerted effort into electoral politics with the participation of the Imperial Ethiopian World Federation, which was founded in Jamaica in 1983 by Ascento Foxe.[2] In the early 1990s, it began lobbying efforts for constitutional changes and launched a political party in 1997 (IEWFPP 2008). It ran five candidates in the 1997 general election, seven in 2002, and eleven in 2007, though only three of its candidates are in the results section of the *Gleaner*'s election site ("Jamaica Local Government Elections" 2007), and each of these three received zero votes.

2. This group coexists with the Ethiopian World Federation that was founded in Harlem in 1937, when Emperor Selassie was seeking international support in the struggle against Italian aggression.

The IEWFPP manifesto (in 2002) called for "a variety of social programs to benefit Rastafarians and low-income 'grass-roots' Jamaicans: low cost housing, affordable medical care, and better education." However, its organization seems mostly to be based in Brooklyn, New York, in a storefront church. I was unable to contact members of this group. Its Web site seems to have been recently updated, but the contact phone numbers were all out of service and e-mails evoked no response. The Web site includes an organizational chart with responsibilities and incumbents' names, a calendar of holidays like Selassie's birthday and coronation days, detailed dress codes, codes of conduct for sex-segregated temple worship, and a long and detailed appeal for donations.

The emergence on the scene of this group evidently inspired others. Columnists in the *Observer* began to talk about "a re-emergence of the element of Rastafari in party politics," or to ponder what a Rasta political party would look like. In one column Barbara Blake-Hannah (2002) said given Rasta culture's influence, "First time visitors to Jamaica are surprised to see no Rastas in national positions of power . . . not even in the tourism industry." Marcus Garvey's party, the People's Political Party, has reportedly been revived by some Rasta brethren, but had not put candidates forward (Barnett 2006, 891) until the most recent elections in December 2011, when the Marcus Garvey People's Political Party (MGPPP) fielded candidates in ten constituencies, who received between 20 and 76 votes each out of thousands of votes cast.

Ras Astor Black is one Rasta who is a perennial independent candidate in Jamaican politics. He first entered electoral politics as a third-party candidate in March 2001 in a by-election, under the auspices of his own political party, the Jamaica Alliance Movement (JAM), and received 44 votes. The following year, he ran in the general elections, winning 35 votes compared to over 9,000 for the JLP and almost 7,000 for the PNP candidates. In April 2005, he contested a West Kingston constituency, a long-time JLP garrison district held from 1962 onward by Eddie Seaga, and then being sought by JLP leader Bruce Golding. Golding won the election with 8,000 votes compared to Black's 8 votes. He ran in 2007 for his home seat in Trelawny, winning 64 votes compared to the PNP's 10,000 and the JLP's

9,000. Most recently, he contested the seat for Trelawney North, a district in which he resides, but again garnered only 57 votes; the successful PNP candidate had more than 10,000.

When asked his reasons for entering electoral politics, Ras Astor Black related a history of some of his development efforts in the north coast area. Having lived for more than a decade in the United States, he returned and began to try to develop projects in the media and tourism sectors. He felt his efforts were constantly being thwarted by the Jamaican government and by the two political parties that control it. As he told the *Observer*:

> Doing things for Rastafari development is taking too long. I don't know if it is because they want to hold down Rastafari, but I want to get projects going and I can't get them going in Jamaica because of bureaucracy. That is why I want a voice. (*Observer* 2005)

He believed that one lawyer in particular was standing in the way of a project he was developing in partnership with some US-based owners of a property. This lawyer was being groomed by the PNP to be a member of parliament. Being able to run against that particular individual was one factor that pushed him toward electoral politics. "As long as he runs, he will have me in front of him. He will never represent the people of Jamaica because he is not a good person."

Ras Astor tells, with relish, a story about that particular nomination day. The lawyer in question turned in his nominating papers on the steps of the Montego Bay courthouse and released a dove from a box he had been carrying. According to the *Gleaner*, "Instead of rising gracefully into the sky, the poor creature flew straight into a nearby breadfruit tree and then collided with electrical wires" (Plunkett 2002). In Black's words: "The dove flew north, then flew south, then drop at his feet. [They] asked me what I think. I say 'Judgment.'"

This candidate faced opposition from within the Rasta community, but he believes Rastas are becoming more accepting of his and others' candidacies. He has encouraged Rastafarians to register to vote for the practical reason of obtaining tax registration numbers (TRNs) as well as to enable them to participate in elections. He said in 2003 that Rastas were definitely registering to vote. "Every Rastafari in Jamaica realize that without political power, nothing is happening."

Some of the issues that Ras Astor Black has raised over his campaigns include squatters' rights, Internet access for schools, and better wages for workers in the hospitality industry.

The *Gleaner* and *Observer* have often pointed out Ras Astor Black's lack of success at the polls as well as his paucity of supporters at public events. In one article, he was said to be the only candidate without supporters, and he entered the race for West Kingston without even the required witness (Henry 2005). One columnist, Cedric Wilson, said despite the impracticality of some of the policies he advocated, the candidate exhibited "remarkable tenacity" in his "indomitable belief that the life of the ordinary Jamaican can be far better" (Wilson 2005). Because the seat that Black was contesting once included the neighborhood called Back-a-Wall, Wilson went on to say that Black "journeyed from his home . . . to run as a candidate in West Kingston, the very birthplace of the Rastafari faith, it was a symbolic trip. And in doing what many would never dare to even contemplate, he epitomises the soul of Jamaica."

Conclusion

Why have Rastas enjoyed greater electoral success outside Jamaica than inside? One possible reason is the structural constraints of the parliamentary system. Appealing to a philosophy that claims universal truths is not what moves the Jamaican electorate. Instead, members of parliament must be able to serve their unique and diverse constituencies. Another structural constraint is the pattern of two-party rule that the British institutionalized before granting independence. In Jamaica, Rasta candidates have been third-party candidates, whereas in Trinidad, Guyana, and St. Croix, Rastas have run as members of regular parties. Furthermore, Rastas are not united among themselves. The three points of Rasta involvement in Jamaican politics that I examined here (Imperial Ethiopian World Federation, People's Political Party, and the Jamaica Alliance Movement) do not act in concert with each other.

There are strong indications that Rasta participation in electoral politics is on the rise. The actual number of Rastafarian candidates rose to a high of eleven in 2011. Even more notably, the first dreadlocked member of Parliament was elected. Damion Crawford, the UWI lecturer and former PNP Youth Organization president, was elected to represent East Rural St. Andrew. Although he is an avowed Christian and does not identify publicly with the ideology or practice of Rastafari, the PNP touted him as the "first Rastafarian" to be elected MP (L. Douglas 2011). The new PNP government led by Prime Minister Portia Simpson has appointed Crawford Minister of State for Tourism and Entertainment, a testimony to his expertise as a lecturer in tourism management at the University of the West Indies as well as his political popularity.

To return to Charles Tilly's concept of a "repertoire of contention" (Tilly 1995, 42), adding electoral politics to Rastafari's repertoire of contention widens the possibility for further influence in the future, not only regionally, but also in Jamaica. More than that, it may mean a broadening and deepening of democratic participation for both the Rasta community and others on the margins of community engagement.

17

Rodney and Rastafari

Cultural Identity in 1960s Jamaica

CADENCE WYNTER

After more than four hundred years of colonial rule, the British Caribbean colony of Jamaica gained constitutional independence on August 6, 1962, although the state built up under the colonial government remained. It was perhaps to be expected that Britain's culture and value system reigned supreme in Jamaica, because Britain had ruled for more than three hundred of those years. On the eve of independence, the British system continued, supported and maintained by small mixed race and "White" middle and upper classes that dominated the majority African-descended working class. Independence presented Jamaica with the opportunity "to repudiate the British cultural image and reappraise the historic African connection" (Lewis 1968, 196). As it turned out, the opportunity was lost. Foreign capital, mostly from the United States, had moved into Jamaica between 1945 and the late 1950s with the express purpose of modernizing and developing the country. As a result, "The West Indian middle class minus any economic power [were] still politically paralyzed before their former masters, who [were] still masters" (Singham and Singham, 1973, 271). Continued foreign domination resulted in internalized and institutionalized dependency throughout the society, obliging the ruling elite to rely upon their foreign backers as they struggled to maintain a facade of legitimacy and control of the country. Thus, racial oppression and class exploitation in Jamaica stemmed from the same source, and the grip of capitalism continued to oppress and exploit African-descended people.

Simultaneously, the growing Black and mixed race bourgeoisie became polarized from Black and poor Jamaicans. The impoverishment in Jamaica that historically had a racial component continued after constitutional independence was achieved, reinforced by the class and color system that oppressed the country's Black population.

Among the many negative effects of colonial rule and foreign penetration was the further complication around the issues of identity. Like many newly independent Caribbean countries, "Jamaica bought into a hybrid, creolization model that valorized assimilation away from a historical antecedent of slavery and Africa" and continued to promote "mimicry of European cultural values and aesthetics" (Nettleford 1979, 34). Rather than severing the long-standing cultural ties with Britain (and more recent ties with North America), the government of Jamaica sought to strengthen adherence to cultures and values that were not representative of the majority population. The Rastafari, who were a marginalized people in early twentieth-century Jamaica, struggled to establish Black consciousness and Black racial and cultural identity.

Born in the hills of Jamaica in the early 1930s, Rastafari challenged capitalism and colonialism, both of which branded African-descended people as inferior. Rastafari set about wiping out "the inherited inferiority complex and facelessness of the Negro in a white world" (Lewis 1968, 176), questioning the fundamental basis of colonial society. They recognized the recently crowned emperor of Ethiopia, Ras Tafari Haile Selassie, as their divine ruler rather than the colonial Jamaican government. Rastafari also questioned the fundamental basis of Jamaican society—which they called Babylon—and believed it to be characterized by a hostile, corrupt, hypocritical, and biased Eurocentric environment (Savishinsky 1994, 19–21). Rastafari prioritized the teaching of history and culture about Africa, from which the majority of the Jamaican population descended, rejecting the idealized dominant European aesthetic. Skillfully combining religious discourse with biblical themes of suffering and redemption and invoking the rallying call "Is fi wi time now," Rastafari sought salvation not in Jamaica, but in repatriation:

> Shall we refuse God's offer for repatriation back home to Africa and a life of everlasting peace and freedom, with Him under our own vine and

> fig tree, and go back into slavery, under these wicked unrighteous and oppressive rulers of Jamaica? (Gray 1991, 50)

British colonial officials first claimed that the pronouncements of Rastafari were nothing more than the ranting of a lunatic fringe that would disappear as quickly as it had appeared. Belatedly, the colonial authorities realized that Rastafari was not a temporary messianic movement but a philosophy with an intellectual purpose and a commitment to advance Jamaica's African-descended population. Rastafari vehemently rejected Jamaican society and its multiple iniquities; drawing strength from their African heritage, they sought a better life in the Promised Land. Directed to the African-descended people who disproportionately numbered among the poor and marginalized segment of society, Rastafari rhetoric was at odds with the British colonial regime.

By the early 1960s, Rastafari had been publicly denounced, derided, and subjected to constant harassment, brutal raids, and repeated arrests by the colonial authorities. Yet their numbers, largely drawn from but not limited to poor and marginalized Black Jamaicans of African descent, had grown. Foremost a religious faith, though outside the Jamaican mainstream, Rastafari philosophy was framed in religious terms with an uncompromising racial assertiveness (Campbell 1987, 1980). Believing that they, like the majority population of Jamaica, were displaced Africans held in captivity, Rastafari promoted their African identity and heritage. A deeply ingrained cultural alienation among the African-descended Jamaican population had resulted in all things African being routinely despised and devalued, which was no less insidious than their widespread material poverty (Erskine 2005, 145). Rooted among Jamaicans who lived in abject poverty and were often excluded from the larger society, Rastafari urged their fellow sufferers to eschew dependency and take responsibility for their liberation, which could only come through self-sufficiency. Not unlike the teachings of Marcus Garvey in the early years of the twentieth century, Rastafari teachings vigorously advocated self-sufficiency through self-awareness and provided an alternative source of meaning and identity to lives that were frequently mired in hopelessness, alienation, and despair.

Many Jamaicans preferred all things foreign and endeavored to acquire and adopt anything foreign, particularly from Europe and North America, a preference that symbolized the negation of everything Caribbean and Black (Erskine 2005, 146). Conversely, Rastafari unapologetically and consistently rejected activities, behaviors, and material goods that obliged them to attain standards set by the British regime. They urged African-descended Jamaican people to look to Africa for their spiritual and economic needs; teaching by example, Rastafari advocated for and assisted in the recovery of their most socially potent selves (Gray 1991, 83). They vehemently rejected the dominant European ideology and its racism that was long embedded in Jamaican society. Rastafari's anticolonial and anti-imperialistic Black consciousness attracted the attention of some Jamaicans but repelled those who viewed them with suspicion and fear, which was only to be expected. Fear was a common response and feature in the evolution of cultural manifestations and expressions among African-descended people in the Americas, because African-descended cultures had been "characterized by repression and marginalization and made to appear inferior to the culture of the rulers even in the eyes of the people giving birth to it" (McComie 1995, 389).

Rastafari gave voice to the experience and situation of Jamaica's African-descended Black masses, and having broken the silence, they refused to be silenced and to coexist with the oppressive government. Although they shunned politics and political institutions as signifiers of Babylon's corrupt and corrupting system that contaminated those who participated in it, Rastafari sought to empower and liberate marginalized Black people in Jamaica. In doing so, they carved out a space for dissidence among poor people in Jamaica's masses (Gray 1991, 74). Efforts to promote African identity were generally ignored by Jamaicans who aspired to join the upper levels of society, the members of which resolutely supported the country's Anglophile orientation and viewed poor Jamaicans as a potentially rebellious element that had to be contained. As in the days of slavery—when none could truly claim to be free while the majority remained enslaved—a constitutionally independent Jamaica could not prosper when so many of its citizens were unable to secure even the basic necessities of life. Thus, the problems that had long confronted Jamaica remained unsolved because "so much of what is taken to be rational and the bearer of truth is rooted in domination and subjugation, the relationship of forces—in a word, power" (Nettleford 1995, 46).

Steadfastly refusing or perhaps unable to confront Jamaica's problems, government officials began to use state rhetoric (in short, nationalism) to provide an ideological façade about society, namely, that all sectors were the same. Those who opposed this formulation were branded as traitors to the "national" interest and charged with importing sinister foreign ideologies deemed unsuitable for the Jamaican people (Bradley 2000b, 205). For example, in May 1967, the Undesirable Publications Law was revised to include all English-language publications from Moscow as well as those from all international organizations financed by the USSR, Peking, and Cuba. Orders were issued in July 1968 to ban all publications authored and co-authored by Malcolm X, Stokely Carmichael, and Elijah Mohammad of the Nation of Islam.

Earlier that year, in January 1968, Walter Rodney, who described himself as "a Guyanese, a black man, and an African," was invited to teach African history at the University of the West Indies (UWI), Mona, campus in Jamaica. However, a few months later, on October 15, 1968, he was declared persona non grata and prevented from reentering Jamaica after attending a Black writer's conference in Canada. In writing the exclusion order, Roy McNeil, the minister for home affairs, declared, "I have never come across a man who offers a greater threat to the security of this land than Walter Rodney" (Bradley 2000b, 196).

On October 16, 1968, the day after Rodney was banned, frustrated UWI students and some professors took to the campus streets in protest, while members of the Black masses took to the streets of Kingston. The two groups were confronted by riot police, who fired tear gas at them, charged at them, and beat them. A contingent of the more militant protestors attacked the commercial district in Kingston, where they damaged government buildings, looted businesses, and set fire to public buses. The protest was quickly contained by the police, but the next day headlines in the *Daily Gleaner,* the leading newspaper and a bastion of conservatism, blared "Campus Row Brings Out Vandals." Gangs of youth were reported to have rampaged through the central area of Kingston shouting "Black Power," though later reports claimed that "the pattern of destructive campaign shows evidence of planning beyond the capacity of hoodlums" (*Daily Gleaner* 1968, 8).

The following day, October 18, Prime Minister Shearer addressed Parliament and informed members of the House that

> the main agitators included non-Jamaicans and Jamaicans inside and outside the University campus, some identifying themselves as Rastafarians, some being known criminals and potential hoodlums . . . All of this has been organized under the guise of a Black Power Movement . . . Dr. Rodney had not specifically limited the Black Power Movement's animosity and talk of rebellion against whites alone but against mulattoes and all brown-skinned persons as well. (*Daily Gleaner,* 1968)

Prime Minister Shearer assured the public that the government had acted just in time in order to "save the nation" after evidence had come to light confirming that Walter Rodney had a "Castro plot," which had first brought him under suspicion. Surveillance reports, Shearer claimed, confirmed that as a result of Rodney's secret activities in areas of Jamaica, he presented "a grave security risk." As far as the government of Jamaica was concerned, Walter Rodney was a "communist" who had engaged in "subversive activities" that posed serious threats to the people of Jamaica. Thus, four days after the student-led protest evolved into a riot led by poor urban Black Jamaicans, military units and police units remained stationed outside the exits and entrances to Mona campus. Aircraft conducted overhead patrols, campus gates remained locked, classes were cancelled, and students who lived on campus were not allowed to leave the university in groups. What had Walter Rodney been engaged in that posed such a serious threat to Jamaica's security and required such Draconian measures to be adopted?

Within a few weeks of his arrival in Jamaica in January 1968, Walter Rodney started giving free public lectures at Mona campus and encouraged the attendance of poor urban dwellers, which included Rastafari, youth, and unemployed workers. Rodney also moved beyond the university to a variety of spaces where he sought to educate, work with, and, importantly, learn from the masses. In his many speeches, Rodney clarified the ways in which contemporary African history related to the plight of marginalized people and their communities in Jamaica and the liberation of African-descended people across the Caribbean and around the world. Explaining the links between these seemingly unrelated struggles, Rodney elucidated the ways in which they were in fact parts of the same global liberation movement of Black people. Rodney contended that the key to mental and political liberation, as well as the acquisition of a new sense of dignity and self-respect, could be found in discovering and reconnecting poor Black people in Jamaica with their African heritage. Calling attention to the need for change among this sector of the Jamaican population, he urged that change "begin with a revaluation of ourselves as blacks and with a redefinition of the world from our standpoint" (Rodney 1975, 33).

While emphasizing the importance of Black cultural values and aesthetics, Rodney commended Rastafari for having "completely and inexorably broken with Jamaican society and its values" (Rodney 1975, 13). He acknowledged that "in our epoch, the Rastafari have represented the leading force of this expression of Black consciousness. They have rejected this philistine white West Indian society" (Erskine 2005, 88). Rodney applauded the role of Rastafari as a leading force of Black consciousness (or, in other words, Black Power) in Jamaica and the wider Caribbean. Some scholars have suggested that Rodney's definition of Black was based on the concept of power rather than pigmentation: Black = non-White = powerless (Chevannes 1977, 249). Rodney defined Black Power as "a doctrine about black people, for black people, preached by black people." He suggests that the reality of "skin color" being the "binding factor" is not the way things ought to be (Rodney 1975, 16). Admitting the limitations of such a stance, he made clear that he was nonetheless obliged to recognize the reality of the contemporary world. Rodney noted that Rastafari had brought the racial question in Jamaica out in the open and, in doing so, had exposed "the white power which is our enemy." He defined White power as power "which is exercised over black peoples, irrespective of whether the particular country belonged originally to whites or blacks" (Rodney 1975, 18).

Placing Black Power in its global context, Rodney highlighted the correlation between color and power in the contemporary world and pointed out the ways in which the international division of labor paralleled the racial division of the world and enabled Europeans to dominate Black and other Third World peoples. These divisions also permitted the domination of capital over labor as well as the domination of Whites over Blacks politically, economically, militarily, and culturally. The ultimate result of such divisions was that

> everywhere the black masses suffer from poverty. . . . There is nothing with which poverty coincides so absolutely as with the color black. . . . That association of wealth with whites and poverty with blacks is not accidental. (Rodney 1975, 19)

In the context of the Caribbean, Rodney asserted, Black Power necessitated breaking with imperialism, which is historically White and racist. He argued that the Black masses in the Caribbean needed to assume power, because "a black man ruling a dependent State within the imperialist system has no power" (Rodney 1975, 18). If a country such as Jamaica was to progress in a way that valued its cultural identity, then national identity had to be rooted in Africa. In its own way, Rastafari had initiated this process in Jamaica, speaking on behalf of a significant part of the population too frequently dismissed as "the powerless." In fact, the Black masses were the force of Black Power and needed to assume their power and reconstruct society in the image of the African-descended majority.

Black Power did not aim to replace White racism with "Black supremacy," but where Black people constitute the majority population, as in Jamaica, they should exercise control commensurate with their numbers. Rodney repeatedly explained that Black Power did not mean only Black people assuming power, because he was well aware that other ethnic minorities had long resided in the Caribbean. Acknowledging the right of all individuals to enjoy basic human rights, he stated, however, that any ethnic minorities residing in the Caribbean would not continue to enjoy "privileges to exploit African people" due to elimination of "the subordination and exploitation of the black masses by whites and their brown and black lackeys" (Rodney 1975, 16). This philosophy and its goals placed Walter Rodney at odds with the government and ruling classes in Jamaica and beyond. He challenged state power at a time when the Jamaican government was seeking to consolidate power in the face of challenges from local and international movements and contending ideologies, not least of which was the Castro administration in neighboring Cuba. As far as the Shearer administration and its allies were concerned, the government's actions were justified and wholly in the interest of preserving law and order against what was perceived to be the threat of Black Power. The idea of racial harmony in Jamaica and the new national motto "Out of Many, One People" were now exposed for what they were: myths.

Rodney denounced the Black and Brown petites bourgeoisie that had assumed power in the newly independent country for having willingly become the lackeys of British and North American imperialists. Those who had joined the ranks of the dominant and privileged classes, even before independence, had not altered the racial characteristics of the class structure and had no interest in doing so. Rather than redressing class exploitation and social inequalities in Jamaican society, the new ruling elite had in fact contributed to their increase by upholding the values and interests of the White power structure. The vast majority of Jamaicans had thereby been left to languish in poverty.

The consciousness of Rastafari, though different from Black Power, nonetheless complemented the Caribbean Black Power ideology advocated by Walter Rodney in the late 1960s. While Rastafari promoted pride in African culture, exposing Jamaica's disdain for its African heritage, Walter Rodney explained the correlation between the liberation of colonized Black minds exposed to African consciousness and the connection between African history and liberation. In its formative years, Rastafari had been despised as being a community for Jamaican social outcasts. On the eve of independence, though, the movement had not only survived but had substantially increased its number of adherents; for the most part, these adherents did not include members of the middle class. Walter Rodney's active leadership among sectors of Jamaica's masses and his ongoing critique of oppression, traditional and new, would see the way opened for the appearance of many middle-class youths among Rastafari in Jamaica. The message of Rastafari contributed to the education of all Jamaicans by presenting vivid images of life for poor Jamaicans. The gap between Rastafari and the Black Power movement, literally and figuratively, was bridged by intellectuals such as Walter Rodney. Rodney and Rastafari, each in their own way, contributed to a heightened, if only temporary, race consciousness among the Jamaican population in the early years after constitutional independence was attained. Rastafari sought to instill pride in African heritage, not unlike predecessors such as Paul Bogle, who called for the Black masses to remember their race and "cleave to the black," as well as Marcus Garvey and Black Nationalism. Walter Rodney would later abandon the cultural nationalist perspective in favor of a democratic Marxist perspective that explained race in terms of class and allowed the proposal of a more inclusive political agenda. Before his untimely death, he moved away from identification primarily in racial terms. In an effort to create a movement of national unity, he argued that a focus on race hindered the formation of alliances between the broad sectors of the working class and sectors of the racially diverse middle class (Dupuy 1996, 110–11). Nonetheless, if culture constructed from the lived experiences and realities of a people serves as the principal means of building a cohesive national identity, then "this notion of creativity, which lives in the 'belly bottom' of the nation's children, is what has brought Jamaica international acclaim and it is what will continue to forge a Caribbean cultural identity imbued with the history of struggle, survival, and resistance" (Hume 2000, 3).

Conclusion

MICHAEL BARNETT

The wide-ranging assortment of essays presented in this volume stand as a testament to the significant evolution that the Rastafari movement has undergone, from its inception in Jamaica in the early 1930s to the present dawn of a new African millennium, more than eighty years after its birth.

Apart from the Rastafari movement's somewhat increased participation in politics, termed "politricks" by many in the movement, there are other indications of modifications in what were once entrenched perspectives by the movement. Attitudes toward death are changing, and Rastafari women are beginning to be allowed to participate in rituals that were once restricted to males.

So far as the Rastafari movement in Jamaica is concerned we see that a distinct modification of old attitudes has taken place. For one thing, even though the desire for repatriation to Africa is still as strong as ever among Rastafari adherents, many Jamaican Rastafarians have integrated to a greater extent into the wider Jamaican society than was the case in the early years of the movement. This is partly because there has been greater acceptance of Rastafari adherents by the wider society as well as a lessening of the discrimination that used to be blatantly leveled at them. Rastafari has bridged class lines in Jamaica and may no longer be regarded as a movement consisting only of lower-class and impoverished Jamaicans. Rather than disassociating themselves completely from civic life in Jamaica, some Rastafari have gone as far as contesting national and localized parish elections. In fact, as we enter the new millennium (at the time of this writing), a revamped and revitalized version of Marcus Garvey's People's Political Party, spearheaded by the Rastafari attorney Ras Miguel Lorne and composed of a predominantly Rastafari membership, has entered the Jamaican political landscape, adding to the Rastafari political presence of Ras Astor Black and Ascente Foxe's IEWF (Imperial Ethiopian World Federation) Party. The recently relaunched Marcus Garvey People's Political Party made national headlines when it fielded a Rastafari candidate, Devon Evans, against the former JLP incumbent, Shahine Robinson, for the North East St. Ann seat in Parliament. These were a group of Rastafari that were striving to embed and to inculcate the Rastafari worldview into every sinew of the Jamaican society (that is, to Rastacize Jamaica), in the same vein and tradition that the Rastafari political trailblazer Ras Sam Brown had attempted to do in the 1962 Jamaican National Elections.

Significantly, we now have many more Rastafari adherents who are themselves extensively engaged in Rastafari studies and actively writing on the movement. There are now numerous insider perspectives that make up (what some might consider to be) the cacophony of voices on Rastafari that continue to reverberate both inside and outside the academy. This is a welcome development and a much-needed complement to the numerous outsider perspectives that once dominated the field. This anthology stands as a testament to this new emerging dynamic; several of the contributors to this volume are Rastafari practitioners as opposed to being simply Rastafari sympathizers.

I perceive the new millennium to be one that can bring much promise and many possibilities for the movement, amid an undeniable atmosphere of uncertainty and rapid change. In the year 2010 alone, the Rastafari and wider Caribbean intellectual academy lost two great stalwart researchers and thinkers. Professor Rex Nettleford transitioned suddenly and unexpectedly in February, and then even more surprisingly, Professor Barry Chevannes, whom I considered to be in many ways Professor Nettleford's academic successor, transitioned in early November. The contributions that both these Jamaicans made to the Jamaican Rastafari movement (if not the wider global Rastafari community) cannot be denied. Professor Nettleford played a significant role in opening up the hallowed gates of the University of the West Indies to the Rastafari community (as did Professor

Chevannes), allowing brethren and sistren to partake and benefit from the resources of the university. Numerous Rastafari conferences were able to convene at the university, such as the famous International Rastafari conference of 1983 and its sequel, the Global Reasoning Conference of 2003, as a result of Professor Nettleford's open and clear support. He endorsed (financially and otherwise) the recent Rastafari Studies Conference that was convened at the university in the summer of 2010 to commemorate the fifty years since the publication of the now famous University of the West Indies Rastafari Report and to honor Sir Roy Augier and himself (who were both original authors of the report bar one). Sadly, Professor Nettleford sojourned to the ancestors a few months before the conference took place.

Professor Chevannes, fondly known as a plainclothes Rasta by many in the movement, largely because of open advocacy and support for the movement, was instrumental in the establishment of a Rastafari-oriented Folk Philosophy Fellowship at the University of the West Indies, of which there were three notable beneficiaries: Mutabaruka, Robin (Bongo Jerry) Small, and Mortimo Planno. He was also instrumental in the planning and convening of the aforementioned milestone conference for the Mona campus of the University of the West Indies in 2010.

In his foreword to this anthology, Professor Nettleford notes the immeasurable contribution that the Rastafari movement has made to Jamaican music. He also notes that it is the appropriation of the movement's vision, ideology, and religion by talented popular musical artists and dub poets that has not only fostered its global reach to the far corners of the planet but has also contributed in continuing to increase its popularity. In this regard, the chapters in the Rastafari and reggae section have focused on the musical dimension of the movement, from the origins of traditional Rastafari music (Nyahbinghi drumming) to its incursion into the dancehall space. Of particular note in this new African millennium is the continued and growing presence of young Rastafari artists in the dancehall and reggae arena, ever since the much acclaimed Rastafari reggae and dancehall resurgence of the 1990s. In addition to Capleton, Sizzla Kalonji, and Anthony B (who all rose to prominence in the 1990s), we now have artists such as Fantan Mojah, Natural Black, Warrior King, Richie Spice, Chuck Fender, I-Wayne, Luton Fyah, Gyptian, I-Octane, Khago, Tarrus Riley, and

Queen Ifrica, just to name a few. These artists have a distinct appeal to the new generation of Rastafari youth as well as to the younger dancehall fans in general. Their brand of roots music has a distinctly different feel than that of the golden age of roots reggae music (the 1970s), when artists such as Jacob Miller, Bob Marley, Peter Tosh, Bunny Wailer, Fred Locks, Dennis Brown, and Burning Spear ruled the airwaves.

Of interest is that many of the Rastafari artists of the 1970s were members of the Twelve Tribes of Israel Mansion, whereas many of the Rastafari artists of today profess to be from the Bobo Shanti Mansion. In an article published in the renowned and highly acclaimed Rastafari publication, *Rootz, Reggae and Kulcha* (the brainchild of I. Jabulani Tafari and published by Rootz Foundation, of which Priest Douglas Smith is the president), John Homiak argues that the popularization of the Bobo Shanti Mansion through notable reggae artists, such as Sizzla and Capleton, should be seen as a twenty-first-century manifestation of a deep-rooted cyclical process within the movement itself; a process that periodically strives to renew the message of Rastafari for new and upcoming generations. In Homiak's opinion it is the young generation of urban Black males in particular (particularly in Jamaica but also in the Anglophone Caribbean, the United States, Canada, and England) who have adopted the Bobo style of dress, with the tightly wrapped head turban and other conventions such as the salute. According to him, the "Dread" energy of the Marley era has become exhausted, and by the mid-1980s the wearing of dreadlocks in and of itself had began to lose its semantic vibrancy as a symbol of resistance and militancy. The Bobo Shanti personification of Rastafari represents a new, fresh vitality, with its strong Black Nationalistic fervor and its relatively isolated, uncompromising positioning in Jamaica.

I must say that I concur with the essence of some of Homiak's assertions here, as it is undeniable that up until the 1990s the Bobo Shanti Mansion, which still has its headquarters at Bull Bay in Jamaica, was undoubtedly the most secluded, isolated, and relatively unknown mansion of Rastafari. In this regard to many Rastafari youth it represented a well of untainted, untouched, and uncommercialized Rastafari energy and livity.

Ironically, this popularized Bobo Shanti trend among the reggae fraternity is a glaring contradiction, at least to the discerning Rastafari scholar.

The Bobo Shanti order (known formally as the EABIC, the Ethiopia Africa Black International Congress) has been traditionally known as perhaps the most priestly and livitical order in the Rastafari confraternity. As such, the constant lyrical purging by "fiyah" by turban-wearing artists such as Capleton (popularly known as the Fiyah-man) and Sizzla Kalonji of all things deemed immoral and Babylonian clearly contradicts the austerity, the humility, and the dignified discipline of the Bobo Shanti encampment at Bobo Hill in Bull Bay.

It is in fact the Nyahbinghi House that is and has traditionally been the Fiyah House (arguably following in the tradition of the notable elder Bongo Wato and his Youth Black Faith Movement). The real contradiction lies in the fact that many of the priests at Bobo Hill have gone on record with their disapproval, disavowment, and total rejection of reggae music, which they claim is not conducive to their priestly livity. This has inevitably led to something of a generation gap in the Bobo Shanti Mansion, in terms of its orientation to the wider society. How this will pan out, with regard to the political goals and objectives of this mansion, only time will tell.

The political and cultural activism of the movement still continues, but is (at the time of writing) notably being facilitated by a relatively small proportion of Rastafari adherents who have made up their minds not to wait on divine intervention to alleviate the problems or the conditions of the global African family. In the United States, for instance, the Rootz Foundation was created, based in South Florida and headed up by Priest Douglas Smith and I. Jabulani Tafari. In Washington, D.C., is the IDOR (Universal Development of Rastafari), which is headed up by such Rastafari brethren as Ras Wayne and Ras Kwasi. The women in the Rastafari movement are now truly coming into their own, with the formation of the Empress of Zion chapters in such various places as South Africa, Canada, Atlanta, and Jamaica. This organization was masterminded by Queen Mother Moses. And the relatively new culture shaping Rastafari organization TAFARI (The Association for Africans Reclaiming Identity) was founded in South Florida but is now primarily based in Jamaica. It is also noteworthy that Ras IvI has now become the de facto coordinator and organizer for the Nyahbinghi Mansion in Jamaica. So the movement is clearly in a process of dynamic evolution.

Ultimately, it is hoped that this volume will serve to raise pivotal and important questions about the future of the movement as it traverses what in my mind I consider to be a crossroads, both literally and figuratively. As I mentioned in the introduction, the movement can either move toward further fragmentation and dilution of its potential potency or toward greater unification, in which case it will be able to achieve many of its key goals and objectives, not least among them being a more humane and just world.

References

Index

References

Abu-Lughod, Lila. 1986. *Veiled Sentiments: Honor and Poetry in a Bedouin Society*. Berkeley: Univ. of California Press.

Alim, Samy. H. 2003. "We Are the Streets: African American Language and the Strategic Construction of a Street Conscious Identity." In *Black Linguistics: Language Society, and Politics in Africa and the Americas,* edited by Sinfree Makoni, G. Geneva Smitherman, Aretha F. Ball, and Arthur K. Spears, 40–59. Foreword by Ngugi Wa Thiong'o. London: Routledge.

Allen, Douglas. 1997. *Culture and Self: Philosophical and Religious Perspectives, East and West*. Boulder, CO: Westview Press.

Alleyne, M. 1989. *Roots of Jamaica Culture*. London: Pluto Press.

Asante, Molefi K. 1990. *Kemet, Afrocentricity and Knowledge*. Trenton, NJ: Africa World Press.

———. 1991. "The Afrocentric Idea in Education." *Journal of Negro Education* 60(2): 170–80.

———. 1998. *The Afrocentric Idea*. Rev. and expanded. Philadelphia: Temple Univ. Press.

———. 1999. *The Painful Demise of Eurocentrism: An Afrocentric Response to Critics*. Trenton, NJ: Africa World Press.

———. 2003. *Afrocentricity: The Theory of Social Change*. Chicago: African American Images.

Asher, George, and David Naulls. 1987. *Maori Land*. Wellington: New Zealand Planning Council.

Bamikole, Lawrence. 2007. "Creolization and the Search for Identity in Caribbean Philosophy." *Caribbean Quarterly* 53(3): 70–82.

Bankie, B. F. 2003. "Mortimo 'Bro Cummie' Planno: The Pan African Nationalist I Know." Unpublished paper made available by author.

Barnett, Michael A. 2000. "Rastafarianism and the Nation of Islam as Institutions for Group–Identity Formation among Blacks in the United States: A Case

Study Comparing Their Approaches." PhD diss, Florida International Univ., Miami.

———. 2002. "Rastafari Dialectism: The Epistemological Individualism and Collectivism of Rastafari." *Caribbean Quarterly* 48(4): 54–61.

———. 2003. "Intra-Racial Encounters in Defining African Identity in the Americas: A Comparative Analysis of Black Leadership and Social Movements." *Ideaz* 2(1).

———. 2005. "The Many Faces of Rasta: Doctrinal Diversity within the Rastafarian Movement." *Caribbean Quarterly* 51(2): 67–78.

———. 2006. "Differences and Similarities between the Rastafari Movement and the Nation of Islam." *Journal of Black Studies* 36(6, July): 873–93.

Barnett, Paul. 2007. *The Roots of Reggae Music.* Radio show broadcast on Nov. 18. Cambridge, UK: 209 Radio.

Barrett, Leonard E. Sr. 1977a. *The Rastafarians: Sounds of Cultural Dissonance.* Boston: Beacon Press.

———. 1977b. *The Rastafarians: The Dreadlocks of Jamaica.* Kingston: Sangster Books.

———. 1988. *The Rastafarians: Sounds of Cultural Dissonance.* Boston: Beacon Press.

———. 1997. *The Rastafarians: Sounds of Cultural Dissonance.* Boston: Beacon Press.

Barrow, Steve, and Peter Dalton. 2004. *The Rough Guide to Reggae.* London: Penguin Books.

Beckwith, Martha Warren. 1929. *Black Roadways: A Study of Jamaican Folk Life.* Chapel Hill: Univ. of North Carolina Press.

Bedasse, Monique. 2006. "Rasta Evolution: The Twelve Tribes of Israel in Transition." In *Diamond Jubilee Commemorative Edition of Perspectives on Rastafari,* ed. 2, edited by Michael Barnett, 42–60. Miami: Tafari Communications.

Belai, Bathseba H. 2007. *Enabling Diaspora Engagement in Africa: Resources, Mechanisms and Gaps. Case Study: Ethiopia.* Ottawa: Association for Higher Education and Development. http://www.aheadonline.org/enablingdiasporaengagementmay2007.pdf.

Bellah, Robert N. 1992. *The Broken Covenant: American Civil Religion in Time of Trial.* Chicago: Univ. of Chicago Press.

Bengali, Shashank. 2008. "Ethiopian Children Go Hungry as Government Response Faulted." *McClatchy Newspapers,* May 30. http://www.mcclatchydc.com/117/story/39021.html.

Bergman, Billy. 1985. *Hot Sauces: Latin and Caribbean Pop*. New York: Quill.

Bewaji, Ayotunde. 2003. *Beauty and Culture: Perspectives in Black Aesthetics*. Ibadan, Nigeria: Spectrum Books Limited.

Bilby, Kenneth M., and K. B. Fu-Kiau. 1983. "Kumina: A Kongo Based Tradition in the New World." *Cahiers Du Cedaf* 8(4).

Binney, Judith. 1995. *Redemption Songs: A Life of Te Kooti Arikirangi Te Turuki*. Auckland: Auckland Univ. Press.

Bjeren, Gunilla. 1985. *Migration to Shashemene: Ethnicity, Gender and Occupation in Urban Ethiopia*. Stockholm: Nordic Africa Institute.

Blackstone, Lee Robert. 2006. "A New Kind of English: Cultural Variance, Citizenship and DiY Politics amongst the Exodus Collective in England." *Social Forces* 84(2, Dec.): 803ff.

Blake-Hannah, Barbara M. 1997. *Rastafari: The New Creation*. New York: Masquel Books.

———. 2002. "Rastafari May One Day Lead the Nation." *Jamaica Observer*, Aug. 10.

Boedeker, Edgar C. 2001. "Individual and Community in Early Heidegger: Situating das Man, the Man-self, and Self-ownership in Dasein's Ontological Structure." *Inquiry: An Interdisciplinary Journal of Philosophy* 44(1): 63–99.

Bonacci, Giulia. 2007. "Pionniers et Heritiers: Histoire du Retour des Caraibes a L'Ethiopie, 19e et 20e Siecles." PhD diss., Ecole des Hautes Etudes en Sciences Sociales, Paris.

Bosmajian, Haig. 1992. "The Language of Sexism." In *Race, Class and Gender in the United States: An Integrated Study*, edited by Paula S. Rothenberg, 341–47. New York: St. Martins Press.

Boyce Davies, C., and B. M'Bow. 2007. "Towards African Diaspora Citizenship: Politicizing an Existing Global Geography." In *Black Geographies and the Politics of Place*, edited by Katherine McKittrick and Clyde Adrian Woods, 14–45. Cambridge, MA: South End Press.

Boyne, Ian. 2002a. "How Dancehall Holds Us Back." *Sunday Gleaner*, Dec. 29.

———. 2002b. "How Dancehall Promotes Violence." *Sunday Gleaner*, Dec. 22.

Bradley, Lloyd. 2000a. *Bass Culture: When Reggae Was King*. London: Penguin Books.

———. 2000b. *This Is Reggae Music: The Story of Jamaica's Music*. Harmondsworth: Penguin Books.

Brathwaite, Edward Kamau. 1973. *The Arrivants: A New World Trilogy*. New York: Oxford Univ. Press.

———. 1978. "Kumina: The Spirit of African Survival in Jamaica." *Jamaica Journal* 42.

Brown-Spencer, Elaine. 2006. "Spiritual Politics: Politicizing the Black Church Tradition in Anti-colonial Praxis." In *Anti-colonialism and Education,* edited by George J. S. Dei and Arlo Kempf, 107–26. Rotterdam: Sense Publishers.

Buffonge, A. E. Gordon. 2001. "Culture and Political Opportunity: Rastafarian Links to the Jamaican Poor." *Research in Social Movements, Conflict and Change* 23:3–35.

Burkett, Randall K. 1978. *Garveyism as a Religious Movement.* Metuchen, NJ: Scarecrow Press.

Burks, Mary Fair. 1993. "Trailblazers: Women in Montgomery Bus Boycott." In *Women in the Civil Rights Movement: Trailblazers and Torchbearers, 1941–1965,* edited by Vicki L. Crawford, Jacqueline Anne Rouse, and Barbara Woods, 71–83. Bloomington: Indiana Univ. Press.

Butler, Judith. 1999. *Gender Trouble: Feminism and the Subversion of Identity.* London: Routledge.

Butler, Kim D. 1998. "*Ginga Baiana:* The Politics of Race, Class, Culture, and Power in Salvador, Bahia." In *Afro-Brazilian Culture and Politics: Bahia, 1790s to 1990s,* edited by Hendrik Kraay, 158–76. Armonk, NY: M. E. Sharpe.

Campbell, Horace. 1980. "Rastafari: Culture of Resistance." *Race and Class: A Journal for Black and Third World Liberation* 22:1–23.

———. 1987. *Rasta and Resistance from Marcus Garvey to Walter Rodney.* Trenton, NJ: Africa World Press.

———. 2007. *Rasta and Resistance from Marcus Garvey to Walter Rodney.* Hertfordshire, UK: Hansib Publishing.

Cassidy, F. G. and R. B. Le Page. 1984. *Dictionary of Jamaican English.* 2nd ed. Cambridge, UK: Cambridge Univ. Press.

Chang, Kevin O'Brien, and Wayne Chen. 1998. *Reggae Routes: The Story of Jamaican Music.* Kingston: Ian Randle.

Chevannes, Barry. 1977. "The Literature of Rastafari." *Social and Economic Studies* 26:239–62.

———. 1979. "The Social Origins of Rastafari." Kingston: Institute of Social and Economic Research, Univ. of the West Indies.

———. 1994. *Rastafari: Roots and Ideology.* Syracuse: Syracuse Univ. Press.

———. 1995. "New Approaches to Rastafari." In *Rastafari and Other African-Caribbean Worldviews,* edited by Barry Chevannes. London: McMillan.

———. 1998a. "New Approaches to Rastafari." In *Rastafari and Other African-Caribbean Worldviews,* edited by Barry Chevannes. New Brunswick, NJ: Rutgers Univ. Press.

———.1998b. "The Origin of the Dreadlocks." In *Rastafari and Other African-Caribbean Worldviews,* edited by Barry Chevannes. New Brunswick, NJ: Rutgers Univ. Press.

———. 1998c. "The Phallus and the Outcast: The Symbolism of the Dreadlocks in Jamaica." In *Rastafari and Other African Caribbean Worldviews,* edited by Barry Chevannes. New Brunswick, NJ: Rutgers Univ. Press.

———.1998d. "RastafarI and the Exorcism of the Ideology of Racism and Classism in Jamaica." In *Chanting Down Babylon: The Rastafari Reader,* edited by Nathaniel S. Murrell, William D. Spencer Adrian A. McFarlane, 55–71. Philadelphia: Temple Univ. Press.

———.1999. "Between the Living and the Dead: The Apotheosis of Rastafari Hero." In *Religion, Diaspora, and Cultural Identity.* edited by J. Pulis, 337–56. Amsterdam: Gordon and Breach.

———. 2006. *Betwixt and Between: Explorations in an African-Caribbean Mindscape.* Kingston: Ian Randle Publishers.

———. 2010. Closing Ceremony Speech. Given at the Rastafari-Studies Conference, Mona Campus, Jamaica Univ. of the West Indies. DVD. Rastafari Studies Unit Archive.

Christensen, Jeanne. 2003. "The Philosophy of Reasoning: The Rastafari of Jamaica." PhD diss., Univ. of Colorado, Boulder.

Cohen, Roger. "Beyond America's Original Sin." *New York Times,* March 20, 2008. http://www.nytimes.com/2008/03/20/opinion/20cohen.html.

Cooper, Carolyn. 2000. *Noises in the Blood: Orality, Gender and the "Vulgar" Body of Jamaican Popular Culture.* Durham: Duke Univ. Press.

———. 2004. *Sound Clash: Jamaican Dancehall Culture at Large.* London: Palgrave Macmillan.

Daily Gleaner. 1968. "Campus Row Brings Out Vandals." Oct. 17, 8.

Daily Gleaner. 1968. Oct. 18, 1.

Daily Gleaner. 1972. "Selassie as God? Zambian Says Planno Is 'Talking through His Halo.'" June 29, 1.

Davis, S., and P. Simon. 1992. *Reggae Bloodlines: In Search of the Music and Culture of Jamaica.* New York: Da Capo Press.

Dawes, Kwame 1999. *Natural Mysticism: Towards a New Reggae Aesthetic in Caribbean Writing.* Leeds, UK: Peepal Tree Press.

Dear, John. 1994. *The God of Peace: Toward a Theology of Nonviolence*. Maryknoll, NY: Orbis.

DeCosmo, Janet L. 1994. "The Concept of 'Surplus Populations' and Its Relationship to Rastafari." *In Depth: A Journal for Values and Public Policy* 4(1): 69.

Dei, George J. S. 1994. "Afrocentricity: A Cornerstone of Pedagogy." *Anthropology and Education Quarterly* 25(1): 3–28.

———. 1996. *Anti-racism Education: Theory and Practice*. Halifax, NS: Fernwood.

Dei, George J. S., Marcia I. James, Luke L. Karumancerhy, Sonia James-Wilson, and Jasmin Zine. 2000. *Removing the Margins: The Challenges and Possibilities of Inclusive Schooling*. Toronto: Canadian Scholars Press.

Derrida, Jacques. 2001. *Writing and Difference,* ed. 2. Translated by Alan Bass. New York: Routledge.

Desmangles, Leslie G., S. D. Glazier, and J. M. Murphy. 2003. "Religion in the Caribbean." In *Understanding the Contemporary Caribbean,* edited by Richard S. Hillman and Thomas J. D'Agostino, 263–304. Kingston: Ian Randle.

Diop, Cheikh Anta. 1978. *The Cultural Unity of Black Africa: The Domains of Patriarchy and of Matriarchy in Classical Antiquity*. Chicago, IL: Third World Press.

do Nascimento, Abdias. 1989. *Brazil: Mixture or Massacre? Essays in the Genocide of a Black People*. Dover, MA: Majority Press.

Douglas, Luke. 2011. "PNP Says Crawford Will Be First Rasta MP." *Jamaica Observer,* Nov. 2.

Douglas, Mary. 1970. *Natural Symbols: Explorations in Cosmology*. New York: Pantheon Books.

Durie, Mason H. 1998. *Te Mana, Te Kawanatanga: The Politics of Maori Self-Determination*. Auckland: Oxford Univ. Press.

Dovlo, Elom. 2002. "Rastafari, African Hebrews and Black Muslims: Return 'Home' Movements in Ghana." *Exchange* 31(1): 2–22.

Dupuy, A. 1996. "Race and Class in the Postcolonial Caribbean: The Views of Walter Rodney." *Latin American Perspective* 23:107–29.

Eaton, Kathleen. 2008. *The Adventures of Ali Thunda*. Bloomington, IN: Trafford Publishing.

Edmonds, Ennis. 2003. *Rastafari: From Outcasts to Culture Bearers*. New York: Oxford Univ. Press.

Elsmore, B. 1989. *Mana From Heaven, A Century of Maori Prophets in New Zealand*. Tauranga: Tauranga Moana Press.

———.2000. *Like Them That Dream: The Maori and the Old Testament.* Auckland: Reed Books.

Erskine, Noel Leo. 1981. *Decolonizing Theology: A Caribbean Perspective.* Maryknoll, NY: Orbis Books.

———. 2005. *From Garvey to Marley: Rastafari Theology.* Gainesville: Univ. of Florida Press.

———. 2007. *From Garvey to Marley: Rastafari Theology.* Gainesville: Univ. of Florida Press.

Ethiopian Government. 1995. The Constitution of the Federal Democratic Republic of Ethiopia. Addis Ababa.

Ethiopian World Federation (EWF). 2008. "History of the EWF." http://www.ethiopianworldfederation.com/history.html.

Faristzaddi, Millard. 1987. *Itations of Jamaica and I Rastafari.* Vol. 1. Miami: Judah Anbesa.

Forsythe, Dennis. 1983. *Rastafari for the Healing of the Nation.* Kingston: Zaika Publications.

Foucault, Michel. 1980. *Power/Knowledge: Selected Interviews and Other Writings 1972–1977,* edited by Colin Gordon. New York: Pantheon.

French, J. and H. Ford-Smith. 1986. "Women, Work and Organizations in Jamaica, 1900–1944." Report. The Hague: Institute of Social Studies.

Freire, Paulo. 2003. *Pedagogy of the Oppressed.* New York: Continuum International.

Garvey, Amy Jacques. 1986. *The Philosophy and Opinions of Marcus Garvey.* Dover, MA: Majority Press. E-book published in 2009, http://www.jpanafrican.com/ebooks/eBook%20Phil%20and%20Opinions.pdf.

Government of Jamaica. 1961. *Mission to Africa Report.* Kingston: Government of Jamaica Printery.

Gray, Obika. 1991. *Radicalism and Social Change in Jamaica, 1960–1972.* Knoxville: Univ. of Tennessee Press.

Gutzmore, Cecil. 2002. "Incline Thine Ear: Roots, Reality and Culture in Jamaican Dancehall DJ Music." Bob Marley Lecture. Library of the Spoken Word/Radio Education Unit, Univ. of the West Indies, Mona, Jamaica.

Hall, Douglas. 1988. *In Miserable Slavery: Thomas Thistlewood in Jamaica, 1750–86.* Warwick Univ. Caribbean Studies. London: Macmillan Books.

Hallen, Barry. 2002. *A Short History of African Philosophy.* Bloomington: Indiana Univ. Press.

Hameso, Seyoum, and Tilahun Ayanou Nebo. 2000. "Ethiopia: A New Start?" *Sidama Concern* 5:3. http://www.sidamaconcern.com/books/ethiopia_a_new_start.htm.

Hanigan, James P. 1986. *As I Have Loved You: The Challenge of Christian Ethics.* Mahwah, NJ: Paulist Press.

Hawkeswood, W. G. 1983. "I'n'I Ras Tafari: Identity and the Rasta Movement in Auckland New Zealand." Master's thesis, Univ. of Auckland.

Henry, Balford. 2005. "4 Candidates for West Kingston Poll." *Jamaica Observer,* March 24.

Henry, Paget. 1997. "Rastafarianism and the Reality of Dread." In *Existence in Black,* edited by Lewis Gordon, 157–64. New York: Routledge.

———. 2000. *Caliban's Reason: Introducing Afro-Caribbean Philosophy.* New York: Routledge.

Hill, Jack. 2003. "Black Religious Ethics and Higher Education: Rastafarian Identity as a Resource for Inclusiveness." *Journal of Beliefs and Values* 24(1): 3–13.

Hill, Robert A. 1981. "Dread History: Leonard P. Howell and Millenarian Visions in Early Rastafari Religions in Jamaica." Epoche 9.

———. 1983. "Leonard P. Howell and Millenarian Visions in Early Rastafari." *Jamaica Journal* 16(1): 24–39.

Himes, Michael J., and Kenneth R. Himes. 1993. *Fullness of Faith: The Public Significance of Theology.* Mahwah, NJ: Paulist Press.

Homiak, John P. 1985. "The 'Ancients of Days' Seated Black: Eldership, Oral Tradition and Ritual in Rastafari Culture." PhD diss., Brandeis Univ., Waltham, MA.

———. 1987. "The Mystic Revelation of Rasta Far-eye: Visionary Communication in a Prophetic Movement." In *Dreaming: Anthropological and Psychological Interpretations,* edited by Barbara Tedlock, 220–45. Cambridge, UK: Cambridge Univ. Press.

———. 1998. "Dub History: Soundings on Rastafari Livity and Language." In *Rastafari and Other African-Caribbean Worldviews,* edited by Barry Chevannes. New Brunswick, NJ: Rutgers Univ. Press.

———. 1999. "Movements of Jah People: From Sound Scapes to Mediascape." In *Religion, Diaspora and Cultural Identity: A Reader in the Anglophone Caribbean,* edited by John Pullis, 87–123. Amsterdam: Gordon and Breach.

———. 2009. "The Boboshanti: International Routes Return Reggae to Its Levitical Roots." *Rootz, Reggae and Kulcha* 10(1): 22–23.

hooks bell. 1981. *Ain't I a Woman: Black Women and Feminism.* Boston: South End Press.

———. 1989. *Talking Back: Thinking Feminist, Thinking Black.* Boston: Sheba Feminist Publishers.

Hope, Donna. 2001. *Inna Di Dancehall Dis/place: Socio-Cultural Politics of Identity in Jamaica.* Masters thesis, Univ. of the West Indies, Mona.

Howell, Leonard Percival [G. G. Maragh]. 1997. *The Promised Key.* Kingston: Headstart Printing and Publishing. Originally published around 1935.

Hume, Yanique. 2000. "Rex Nettleford." In *Postcolonial Studies at Emory,* online publication developed by Deepika Bahri. Atlanta: Emory Univ. http://www.english.emory.edu/Bahri?Nettle.html.

Ibrahim, Awad El Karim. M. 2003. "Wassup, Homeboy. Joining the African Diaspora: Black English as a Symbolic Site of Identification and Language Learning." In *Black Linguistics: Language Society, and Politics in Africa and the Americas,* edited by Sinfree Makoni, G. Geneva Smitherman, Aretha F. Ball, and Arthur K. Spears, 169–85. Foreword by Ngugi Wa Thiong'o. London: Routledge.

Imperial Ethiopian World Federation Political Party (IEWFPP). 2008. http://www.himchurch.org.

Isaacs, Harold. 1964. "A Name to Go By." In *The New World of Negro Americans,* 62–71. New York: The Viking Press.

Ishmahil (producer, director). 2002. Interview with Filmore Alvaranga. In *Roaring Lion: The Rise of Rastafari.* London: RiceNPeas Films. http://www.ricenpeas.com.

Isis Productions. 1999. *Classic Albums: Bob Marley and the Wailers. Catch a Fire.* VHS.

JAHUG: Jah Rastafari Nyahbinghi Order Theocracy Reign, vol. 5: Alpha and Omega. Edited by Carl Gayle. Repatriation Productions, 1980; reprinted June 1992.

Jalata, Asafa. 2008. "Struggling for Social Justice in the Capitalist World System: The Cases of African Americans, Oromos, and Southern and Western Sudanese." *Social Identities* 14(3): 363–88.

Jamaica Local Government Elections. 2007. http://jamaica-elections.com/local/2007/index.php.

Jones, Lisa. 1994. Africa™. In *Bulletproof Diva: Tales of Race, Sex and Hair,* 298–302. New York: Doubleday.

Kebede, Alem Seghed, T. Shriver, and J. D. Knottnerus. 2000. "Social Movement Endurance Collective: Identity and the Rastafari." *Sociological Inquiry* 70(3): 313–37.

Kiros, Teodros. 2001. *Explorations in African Thought*. New York: Routledge.

Kitzinger, Sheila. 1969. "Protest and Mysticism: The Rastafari Cult of Jamaica." *Journal for the Scientific Study of Religion* 8(2): 240–62.

Kraay, Hendrik. 1998. Introduction to *Afro-Brazilian Culture and Politics: Bahia, 1790s to 1990s,* edited by Hendrik Kraay, 3–29. Armonk, NY: M. E. Sharpe.

Lake, Obiagele. 1985. *A Feasibility Study on the Prevalence and Cultural Determinants of Breast Feeding Among Jamaican Rastafarians*. Ithaca, NY: Cornell Univ.

———. 1998. "The Dekinking of African Hair: Style or Stigma." Unpublished paper.

———. 2003. *Blue Veins and Kinky Hair: Naming and Color Consciousness in African America*. Westport, CT: Praeger.

Landman-Bogues, J. 1976. "Rastafarian Food Habits." *Cajanus* 9(4): 228–33.

Leary, Joy deGruy. 2005. *Post Traumatic Slave Syndrome: America's Legacy of Enduring Injury and Healing*. Milwaukie, OR: Uptone Press. http://www.joydegruy.com/ptss/index.html.

Lee, Helen. 2003. *The First Rasta: Leonard Howell and the Rise of Rastafarianism*. Chicago: Lawrence Hill Books.

Leib, Elliot. 1983. "Churchical Chants of the Nyahbingi." Notes to Heartbeat Records album no. HB 20. Cambridge, MA: Heartbeat Records.

———. 1984. "The Kongo Presence in Early Rastafari Culture in Jamaica." Paper presented at the 1984 African Studies Association Meeting, Los Angeles.

Lewis, Gordon K. 1968. *The Growth of the Modern West Indies*. New York: Monthly Review Press.

Lewis, Linden. 1991. "The Groundings of Walter Rodney." *Race and Class* 33(1): 71–82.

Lewis, Rupert. 1998. *Walter Rodney's Intellectual and Political Thought*. Kingston: Univ. of the West Indies Press; Detroit: Wayne State Univ. Press.

Levine, Hal, and Manuka Henare. 1994. "Mana Motuhake: Maori Self Determination." *Pacific Viewpoint* 35(2): 193–210.

Lindsay, Leroy. 2002. Letter to editor. *Daily Gleaner,* March 16.

Lorde, Audre. 1986. "Is Your Hair Still Political?" *Essence,* Sept., 40.

Lynch, Michael P. 1997. "Three Models of Conceptual Scheme." *Inquiry* 40(4): 407–26.

Macleod, Arlene. 1991. *Accommodating Protest: Working Women, the New Veiling, and Change in Cairo*. New York: Columbia Univ. Press.

Madubute, Haki R. 1979. *From Plan to Planet, Life Studies: The Need for African Minds and Institutions*. Chicago: Third World Press.

Mansingh, Ajai, and Laxmi Mansingh. 1985. "Hindu Influences on Rastafarianism." *Caribbean Quarterly Monograph,* 96–115.

Marley, Rita. 1979. "Looking at Rita Marley." *Sunday Gleaner Magazine,* Aug. 5.

Marshall, Wayne. 2006. "Bling-Bling for Rastafari: How Jamaicans Deal with Hip-Hop." *Social and Economic Studies* 55(1–2): 49–74.

Matunga, Hirini. 1994. "*Waahi Tapu:* Maori Sacred Sites." In *Sacred Sites, Sacred Places,* edited by David L. Carmichael, Jane Hubert, Brian Reeves, and Audhild Schanche, 217–26. London: Routledge.

Mazama, Ama. 2001. "The Afrocentric Paradigm: Contours and Definitions." *Journal of Black Studies* 31(4): 387–405.

McBrien, Richard P. 1994. *Catholicism: New Edition*. New York: Harper Collins.

McComie, Val T. 1995. "The Continuing Crisis of Identity in the Americas." In *African Presence in the Americas,* edited by Carlos Moore, T. R. Sanders, and S. Moore, 383–91. Trenton, NJ: Africa World Press.

McDonald, Stephen G. n.d. "Rastafari Cultural Transition and Psychosocial Identity." Unpublished manuscript.

McLeod, Rosemary. 1988. "The Williams' of Ruatoria: Living on the Edge." *North and South,* Oct., 64–79.

McPherson, E. S. P. 1996. "Account for the Spread of the Rastafari Religion throughout the World." In *The Culture-History and Universal Spread of Rastafari: Two Essays,* edited by E. S. P. McPherson. Bronx: Ethiopian National Front.

Metge J. 1995. *New Growth From Old: The Whanau in the Modern World*. Wellington: Victoria Univ. Press.

Mies, M. 1986. *Patriarchy and Accumulation on a World Scale*. London: Zed Books.

Miller, Toby. 2001. "Introducing . . . Cultural Citizenship." *Social Text* 69(19): 1–5.

Minda, Ababu. 2004. "Rastafari in 'The Promised Land': A Change of Identity." *Africa Insight* 34(4): 31–39.

Mita Merata. 1998. *The Dread*. Documentary film for TV3. Auckland, New Zealand.

Mitchell, Tony. 1994. "He Waiata no Aotearoa: Maori and Polynesian Music in New Zealand." In *North Meets South: Popular Music in Aotearoa/New*

Zealand, edited by Philip Hayward, Tony Mitchell, and Roy Shuker. Sydney: Perfect Beat Publications.

Mohammed, Patricia. 1988. "Sistren Workshop: An Analysis of the Method." In *Gender in Caribbean Development,* edited by Patricia Mohammed and Catherine Shepherd, 348–52. Women and Development Project. Mona: Univ. of the West Indies.

Moore, Joseph G. 1953. "Religion of Jamaican Negroes: A Study of Afro-Jamaican Acculturation." PhD diss., Northwestern Univ., Evanston, IL.

———. 1979. "Music and Dance as Expressions of Religious Worship in Jamaica." In *The Performing Arts,* edited by J. Blacking and J. W. Kealiinojomoku. The Hague: Mouton.

Morris, Mervyn. 2005. *Mutabaruka: The Next Poems/The First Poems.* Kingston: Paul Issa Publications.

Moyer, Eileen. 2005. "Street-Corner Justice in the Name of Jah: Imperatives for Peace among Dar es Salaam Street Youth." *Africa Today* 51(3, Spring): 31–58.

Moyston, L. 2001. "Rastafari and Politics." *Jamaica Observer,* Aug. 21.

Muchunu, Noloyiso. 2006. "Dreadlock Boys 'Turned Away from School.'" *The Mercury,* Jan. 20.

Nagashima, Yoshiko S. 1984. *Rastafarian Music in Contemporary Jamaica.* Tokyo: Institute for the Study of Language and Cultures of Asia and Africa, Tokyo Univ. of Foreign Studies.

Nettleford, Rex. 1970. *African Redemption: The Rastafari and the Wider Society 1959–1969.* Monograph. West Indies Special Collection. UWI Library.

———. 1973. "National Identity and Attitudes to Race in Jamaica." In *Consequences of Class and Colour: West Indian Perspectives,* edited by D. Lowenthal and L. Comitas, 35–56. New York: Anchor Books.

———. 1979. *Caribbean Cultural Identity: The Case of Jamaica.* Los Angeles: Univ. of California Press.

———. 1985. *Dance Jamaica: Cultural Definition and Artistic Discovery.* New York: Grove Press.

———. 1995. "The Aesthetics of Negritude: A Metaphor for Liberation." In *African Presence in the Americas,* edited by Carlos Moore, T. R. Sauders, and S. Moore, 33–54. New Jersey: Africa World Press.

Niaah, Jalani. 2003. "Poverty (Lab) Oratory: Rastafari and Cultural Studies." *Cultural Studies* 17(6): 823–42.

———. 2005. "Absent Father(s), Garvey's Scattered Children and the Back to Africa Movement." In *Negotiating Modernity, Africa's Ambivalent Experience,* edited by Elisio Salvado Macamo. CODESRIA Africa in the New Millennium series. London: Zed.

———. 2008. "Grafting a New History: Rastafari Memory Gems Articulating a 'Hermeneutics of Babylon.'" In *Africa and Its Diasporas: History, Memory and Literary Manifestations*, edited by Naana Opoku-Agyemang, Paul E. Lovejoy, and David V. Trotman, 123–46. Trenton, NJ: Africa World Press.

Niaah, Jalani, and Sonja Stanley-Niaah. 2006. "'Ace' of the Dancehall Space: A Preliminary Look at U Roy's Version and Subversion in Sound." *Social and Economic Studies* 55(1–2): 167–89.

Nicholas, Tracy. 1979. *Rastafari. A Way of Life*. New York: Anchor Books.

Nussbaum, M. C. 2000. *Women and Human Development: The Capabilities Approach*. Cambridge, UK: Cambridge Univ. Press.

Observer. 2005. "Ras Astor Black to Run in West Kingston By-election." Jan. 22.

Okere, Theophilus. 1983. "African Philosophy: A Historico-Hermeneutical Investigation of the Conditions of Its Possibility." Lanham: Univ. Press of America.

Owens, Joseph. 1976. *Dread: The Rastafarians of Jamaica*. Kingston: Sangster Books.

Patel, Hitendra. 2002. *Children of Zion*. DVD produced for master's in creative and performing arts in film and television, Univ. of Auckland, New Zealand.

Patterson, Orlando. 1971. *The Children of Sisyphus*. Kingston: Bolivar Press.

Pereira, Joseph. 1994. "Gun Talk and Girls Talk: The DJ clash." *Caribbean Studies* 27(3–4): 208–23.

———. 2002. "Kwako's Shut: Dancehall and Decency in Jamaican Society." Paper presented at Second Conference on Caribbean Culture, Univ. of the West Indies, Mona.

Peters, Melanie. 2004. "Rastafarian Circumcised Against His Will." *Sunday Tribune*, July 4. http://www.iol.co.za/index.php?set_id=1&click_id=139&art_id=vn20040704124240917C136839.

Planno, Mortimo. 1979. "The Truth About the Rastafari Movement as told by Brother Cummie." Interview by Tam Fiofori. *Spear: Nigeria's National Magazine*.

———. 1996. *The Earth Most Strangest Man: The Rastafarian*. Foreword by Lambros Comitas. New York: Research Institute for the Study of Man.

———. n.d. Private Papers of Mortimo Planno at the Rastafari Archive Project, Univ. of the West Indies, Mona.

Plunkett, Nagra. 2002. "Peace Dove Takes a Dive." *Daily Gleaner*, Oct. 1.

Pollard, Velma. 1994. "Dread Talk." *The Language of Rastafari*. Kingston: Canoe Press.

Post, Ken. 1978. *Arise, Ye Starvelings: The Jamaican Labour Rebellion of 1938 and Its Afermath.* The Hague: Martinus Nijhoff.

Rawls, John. 1993. *Political Liberalism.* New York: Columbia Univ. Press.

Reckord, Verena. 1977. "Rastafari Music: An Introductory Study." *Jamaica Journal* 11(1–2).

———. 1998. "From Burra Drums to Reggae Ridims: The Evolution of Rasta Music." In *Chanting Down Babylon: The Rastafari Reader,* edited by Nathaniel S. Murrell, William D. Spencer, Adrian A. McFarlane. Philadelphia: Temple Univ. Press.

Roberts, John Storm. 1972. *Black Music of Two Worlds.* New York: Praeger.

Rodney, Walter. 1975. *The Groundings with My Brothers.* London: Bogle-L'Ouverture.

———. 1990. *The Groundings with My Brothers.* London: Bogle-L'Ouverture.

———. 1981. *How Europe Underdeveloped Africa.* 2nd ed. Washington DC: Howard Univ. Press.

Rowe, M. 1980. "The Woman in Rastafari." *Caribbean Quarterly* 26(4).

———. 1998. "Gender and Family Relations in RastafarI: A Personal Perspective." In *Chanting Down Babylon: The Rastafari Reader,* edited by Nathaniel S. Murrell, William D. Spencer, Adrian A. McFarlane, 72–88. Philadelphia: Temple Univ. Press.

———. 2008. "The Woman in Rastafari." Revised and updated by Rex Nettleford and Veronica Salter. *Caribbean Quarterly and Caribbean Studies Initiative* (Kingston), 219–29.

Roy-Campbell, Zalani. M. 2003. "Promoting African Languages as Conveyors of Knowledge in Educational Institutions." In *Black Linguistics: Language Society, and Politics in Africa and the Americas,* edited by Sinfree Makoni, G. Geneva Smitherman, Aretha F. Ball, and Arthur K. Spears, 83–102. Foreword by Ngugi Wa Thiong'o. London: Routledge.

Rushing, Andrea Benton. 1988. "Hair Raising." *Feminist Studies* 14(2): 325–35.

Russell, Bertrand. 1972. *The History of Western Philosophy.* London: Simon and Schuster.

Russell, K., M. Wilson, R. Hall. 1992. *The Color Complex: The Politics of Skin Color Among African Americans.* New York: Harcourt-Brace-Jovanovich.

Ryle, Gilbert. 1949. *The Concept of Mind.* London: Hutchinson Books.

Ryman, Cheryl. 1980. "The Jamaican Heritage in Dance: Developing a Traditional Typology." *Jamaica Journal* 44.

———. 1984. "Kumina: Stability and Change." *ACIJ Research Review* 1.

Said, Edward. W. 2003. *Orientalism*. London: Penguin Books.

Sankeralli, Burton. 1995. "The Rastafari." In *At the Cross Roads: African Caribbean Religion and Christianity*, ed. Burton Sankeralli, 126–33. Trinidad and Tobago: Caribbean Conference of Churches.

Savishinsky, Neil J. 1993. "Rastafari in the Promised Land: The Spread of a Jamaican Socio-Religious Movement and Its Music and Culture Among the Youth of Ghana and Senegambia," 342. PhD thesis, Columbia Univ., New York.

———. 1994. "Rastafari in the Promised Land: The Spread of a Jamaican Socio-Religious Movement Among the Youth of West Africa." *African Studies Review* 37:19–50.

Sackeyfio, Christina N. T. 2006. "Hip-hop Cultural Identities: A Review of the Literature and Its Pedagogical Implications for the Schooling of African-Canadian Youth." Master's diss., Ontario Institute for Studies in Education, Univ. of Toronto.

Schuler, Monica. 1979. "Myalism and the African Religious Tradition in Jamaica." In *Africa and the Caribbean: The Legacies of a Link*, edited by Margaret E. Crahan and Franklin Knight. Baltimore: Johns Hopkins Univ. Press.

———. 1980. "Alas, Alas, Kongo: A Social History of Indentured Immigration into Jamaica, 1841–1865." Baltimore: John Hopkins Univ. Press.

Scott, David. 1997. "'Wi a di Govament': An Interview with Anthony B." *Small Axe* 2(Sept.): 79–101.

Semaj, Leahcim T. 1980. "Models for a Black Psychology of Liberation." Background for the presentation "The Transformation of Black Identity." Given at the 13th Annual Convention of the Association of Black Psychologists, Cherry Hill, New Jersey, Aug. 13–17.

———. 2000. "Rastafari: From Religion to Social Theory." *Caribbean Quarterly: Rastafari Monograph*, 23–33.

Serunjogi, Titus. 2006. "Bob Marley: The Legend Still Lives." *New Vision* (Kampala).

Serequeberhan, Tsenay. 1991. *African Philosophy: The Essential Readings*. Minnesota: Paragon House.

Sewell, T. 1990. *Garvey's Children: The Legacy of Marcus Garvey*. London: Macmillan Publishers.

Sharp, A. 1997. *Justice and the Maori: The Philosophy and Practice of Maori Claims in New Zealand Since the 1970s*. Auckland: Oxford Univ. Press.

Shaw, William. 2007. *Migration in Africa: A Review of the Economic Literature on International Migration in 10 Countries.* Washington: World Bank Development Prospects Group.

Simpson, George Eaton. 1954. "Jamaican Cult Music." Notes to Ethnic Folkways Library album no. FE 4461. New York: Folkways Records.

———. 1955. "The Ras Tafari Movement in Jamaica: A Study in Race and Class Conflict." *Social Forces* 34:2.

———. 1985. "Religion and Justice: Some Reflections on the Ras Tafari Movement." *Phylon* 46(4): 286–91.

Singham, A. W., and N. L. Singham. 1973. "Cultural Domination and Political Subordination: Notes Towards a Theory of the Caribbean Political System." *Comparative Studies in Society and History* 15: 258–88.

Sister Ilaloo. 1981. "Rastawoman as Equal." *Yard Roots* 1(1): 5–7.

Smith, John K., and Joseph Blasé. 1991. "From Empiricism to Hermeneutics: Educational Leadership as a Practical and Moral Activity." *Journal of Educational Administration* 29(1): 6–21.

Smith, M. G., Rex Nettleford, and Roy Augier. 1960. *The Rastafari Movement in Kingston, Jamaica.* Mona, Jamaica: Institute of Social and Economic Research, Univ. College of the West Indies.

Sofola, J. A. 1978. *African Culture and the African Personality.* Ibadan, Nigeria: African Resources Publishers.

Solomon, Patrick, and Howard Palmer. 2004. "Schooling in Babylon, Babylon in School: When Racial Profiling and Zero Tolerance Converge." *Canadian Journal of Educational Administration and Policy* 33.

Spoonley, Paul. 1988. *Racism and Ethnicity.* Auckland: Oxford Univ. Press.

Stanley-Niaah, Sonjah. 2004. "Kingston's Dancehall: A Story of Space and Celebration." *Space and Culture* 7(1): 102–18.

———. 2007. "Mapping Black Atlantic Geographies: From Slave Ship to Ghetto." In *Black Geographies and the Politics of Place,* edited by Katherine McKittrick and Clyde Adrian Woods, 14–45. Cambridge, MA. South End Press.

Steady, Filomina. 1981. "The Black Woman Cross Culturally: An Overview." In *The Black Woman Cross-Culturally,* edited by Filomina Steady. Cambridge, MA: Schenkman Books.

Stevenson, Nick. 2003. "Cultural Citizenship in the 'Cultural' Society: A Cosmopolitan Approach." *Citizenship* 7(3): 331–48.

Stewart, David, and H. Gene Blocker. 2001. *Fundamentals of Philosophy.* New Jersey: Prentice Hall.

Stewart, Kingsley. 2002. "So Wha, Mi Nuh Fi Live To?" Interpreting Violence in Jamaica through the Dancehall Culture." Ideaz 1(1).

Stolzoff, Norman. 2000. *Wake the Town and Tell the People: Dancehall Culture in Jamaica*. Durham: Duke Univ. Press.

Symonette, Bianca. 2007. "Rastas Break Tradition." *Bahama Journal*, Feb. 15.

Tafari, I. Jabulani. 1996. *A Rastafari View of Marcus Mosiah Garvey, Patriarch, Prophet, Philosopher*. Jamaica: Great Company.

Tafari-Ama, Imani M. 1989. "A Historical Analysis of Grassroots Resistance in Jamaica: A Case Study of Gender Relations in RastafarI." Unpublished thesis. The Hague, Netherlands.

———. 1998. "Rastawoman as Rebel: Case Studies in Jamaica." In *Chanting Down Babylon: The Rastafari Reader*, edited by Nathaniel S. Murrell, William D. Spencer, and Adrian A. McFarlane, 89–106. Philadelphia: Temple Univ. Press.

———. 2006. *Blood, Bullets and Bodies: Sexual Politics Below Jamaica's Poverty Line*. Kingston: Multimedia Communications.

Tarei, Wi. 1992. "A Church Called Ringatu." In *Tihei Mauriora: Aspects of Maoritanga*, edited by Michael King, 138–43. Auckland: Reed Books.

Thibodeaux, Normand. 2005. "Africa Luring Back Many Expatriates." *Boston Globe*, March 6.

Thomas, Bert J. 1992. "Caribbean Black Power: From Slogan to Practical Politics." *Journal of Black Studies* 22:392–410.

Thomas, Deborah A. 2004. *Modern Blackness: Nationalism, Globalization, and the Politics of Culture in Jamaica*. Durham: Duke Univ. Press.

Tilly, Charles. 1995. *Popular Contention in Great Britain, 1758–1834*. Cambridge, MA: Harvard Univ. Press.

Turner, Harold. 1991. "Rastafari and the New Zealand Maori." In *South Pacific Journal of Mission Studies* 1(4).

Turner, J. H., R. Singleton Jr., and D. Musick. 1984. *Oppression: A Socio-History of Black-White Relations in America*. Chicago: Nelson-Hall.

van Dijk, Frank J. 1993. *Jahmaica: Rastafari and Jamaican Society, 1930–1990*. Utrecht: ISOR.

———. 1998. "Chanting Down Babylon Outernational: The Rise of Rastafari in Europe, the Caribbean, and the Pacific." In *Chanting Down Babylon: The Rastafari Reader*, edited by Nathaniel S. Murrell, William D. Spencer, and Adrian A. McFarlane, 178–98. Philadelphia: Temple Univ. Press.

Vibe. 2006. "Bob Marley: 'The Real Revolutionary.'" *Vibe*, May, 116.

Voeks, Robert A. 1997. *Sacred Leaves of Candomblé: African Magic, Medicine, and Religion in Brazil.* Austin: Univ. of Texas Press.

Wafer, Jim. 1991. *The Taste of Blood: Spirit Possession in Brazilian Condomblé.* Philadelphia: Univ. Pennsylvania Press.

Wallace, Anthony F. C. 1956. "Revitalization Movements." *American Anthropologist* 58(2): April.

Walker, R. J. 1990. *Ka Whawhai Tonu Matou: Struggle Without End.* Auckland: Penguin Books.

Warner-Lewis, Maureen. 1977. "The Nkuyu: Spirit Messengers of the Kumina." *Savacou* 13.

Waters, Anita. 1999 [1985]. *Race, Class and Political Symbols: Rastafari and Reggae in Jamaican Politics.* New Brunswick: Transaction Press.

Watson, Llewellyn. 1973. "Social Structures and Social Movements: The Black Muslims and the Rastafarians in Jamaica." *British Journal of Sociology* 24(2): 188–98.

Weber, Max. 1947. *The Theory of Social and Economic Organization.* Translated by A. M. Henderson and Talcott Parsons. Glencoe, IL: Free Press.

West-Duran, Alan. 2003. "Jamaica." In *African Caribbeans: A Reference Guide,* edited by Alan West-Duran, 113ff. Westport, CT: Greenwood Press.

White, Garth. 1980. "Reggae: A Musical Weapon." *Caribe* (Dec.).

———. 1984. "The Development of Jamaican Popular Music: Part 2. The Urbanization of the Folk—The Merger of the Traditional and Popular in Jamaican Music." *ACIJ Research Review* 1.

White, Shane, and Graham White. 1995. "Slave Hair and African American Culture in the Eighteenth and Nineteenth Centuries." *Journal of Southern History* 41(1, Feb.): 6–26.

Wint, Eleanor, in consultation with members of the Nyahbinghi Order. 1998. "Who Is Haile Selassie? His Imperial Majesty in Rasta Voices." In *Chanting Down Bablyon: The Rastafari Reader,* edited by Nathaniel S. Murrell, William D. Spencer, and Adrian A. McFarlane, 159–65. Philadelphia: Temple Univ. Press.

Willey, David. 2008. "Fewer Confessions, New Sins." BBC online, March 10. http://news.bbc.co.uk/1/hi/world/europe/7287071.stm.

Williams, Ishon. 2000. "The Seven Principles of Rastafari." *Caribbean Quarterly Rastafari Monograph,* 16–22.

Wilson, Cedric. 2005. *Daily Gleaner.* Column. April 15.

Wittgenstein, Ludwig. 1969. *On Certainty.* New York: Harper Touchbooks.

———. 1988. *Philosophical Investigations*. Translated by G. E. M. Anscombe. Oxford: Basil Blackwell.

Yawney, Carole D. 1978. "Lions in Babylon: The Rastafarians of Jamaica as a Visionary Movement." PhD diss., Department of Anthropology, McGill Univ.

———. 1980. "I-Threes Soaring Hearts." *Reggae News*, Spring issue.

———. 2001. "Exodus: Rastafari, Repatriation, and the African Renaissance." In *A United States of Africa*, edited by Eddy Maloka, 133–85. African Century Publications Series no. 4. Pretoria: Africa Institute of South Africa.

Index

Italic page numbers indicate tables.

www.ingramcontent.com/pod-product-compliance
Lightning Source LLC
LaVergne TN
LVHW050922080826
845145LV00001B/168